MW01106892

Vicious Circuits

Post 45 Kate Marshall and Loren Glass, Editors
Post•45 Group, Editorial Committee

Vicious Circuits

Korea's IMF Cinema and the End of the American Century

Joseph Jonghyun Jeon

Stanford University Press

Stanford, California

STANFORD UNIVERSITY PRESS

Stanford, California

An early version of Chapter 1 appeared as "Memories of Memories: Historicity, Nostalgia, and Archive in Bong Joon-ho's *Memories of Murder*," *Cinema Journal* 51, no. 1 (2011): 75–95. Copyright © 2011 by the University of Texas Press. All rights reserved.

An early version of a part of Chapter 2 appeared as "Residual Selves: Trauma and Forgetting in Park Chan-wook's *Oldboy*," *positions* 17, no. 3 (2009): 713–40.

A version of Chapter 5 was published as "Neoliberal Forms: CGI, Algorithm, and US Hegemony in Korea's IMF Cinema," *Representations* 126, no. 1 (2014): 85–111.

Printed in the United States of America on acid-free, archival-quality paper

Library of Congress Cataloging-in-Publication Data
Names: Jeon, Joseph Jonghyun, 1971- author.
Title: Vicious circuits : Korea's IMF cinema and the end of the American century / Joseph Jonghyun Jeon.
Other titles: Post 45.
Description: Stanford, California : Stanford University Press, 2019. | Series: Post 45 | Includes bibliographical references and index.
Identifiers: LCCN 2018022960 | ISBN 9781503606692 (cloth : alk. paper) | ISBN 9781503608450 (pbk. : alk. paper) | ISBN 9781503608467 (e-book)
Subjects: LCSH: Economics in motion pictures. | Motion pictures—Korea (South)—History. | Motion picture industry—Korea (South)—History. | Korea (South)—Civilization—American influences.
Classification: LCC PN1995.9.E27 J46 2019 | DDC 791.43/6553—dc23 LC record available at https://lccn.loc.gov/2018022960

Typeset by Kevin Barrett Kane in 10/15 Minion Pro

Cover design by Angela Moody

Cover photograph from MacArthur Memorial and Archives

for Youngmin

Contents

Acknowledgments

This is a book about a crisis that creates conditions under which further crises become inevitable. Such malevolent inertia has come to define the contemporary moment in even wider vistas than are explored in this study. In times like these our care networks become ever more crucial, so I am particularly grateful to all those that provided guidance, interlocution, and camaraderie as I worked through this project. I thank my colleagues at the University of California–Irvine, Pomona College, and the Claremont Colleges, especially Aimee Bahng, Kevin Dettmar, Chris Fan, Richard Godden, Sharon Goto, Oren Izenberg, Kyung Hyun Kim, Jordan Kirk, Aaron Kunin, Jerry Lee, Jim Lee, Julia Lee, Jonathan Lethem, Warren Liu, Ted Martin, Annie McClanahan, Radha Radhakrishnan, Colleen Rosenfeld, Jim Steintrager, Michael Szalay, Mayumi Takada, Kyla Tompkins, and Kathy Yep.

I am also grateful to the many people who read and offered feedback for parts of this book, exchanged work, and otherwise helped to shape this project, including Lauren Berlant, Chris Berry, Sara Blair, Dan Blanton, Sarah Brouillette, Jason Oliver Chang, John Cheng, Ke-young Chu, Seo-young Chu, Joshua Clover, J. D. Connor, Zara Dinnen, Florence Dore, Jamie Doucette, Sarah Evans, Gloria Fisk, Mark Goble, Yogita Goyal, Sean Grattan, Dan Grausam, Matt Hart, Andrew Hoberek, Hsuan Hsu, Tung-Hui Hu, Aaron Jaffe, Mark Jerng, Susan Kang, Jinah Kim, Se Young Kim, Sonja Kim, Yoonkyung Lee, Yoon Sun Lee, Michael LeMahieu, Andrew Leong, Colleen Lye, Eunha Na, Viet Nguyen, Justus Nieland, Peter Paik, Crystal Parikh, Albert Park, Hyungji Park, Josephine Park, Ignacio Sánchez Prado, Kent Puckett, Anthony Reed, Margaret Rhee, Haerin Shin, Min Hyoung Song, Leif Sorensen, Erin Suzuki, Amy Tang, Chris Taylor, Charles Tung, Keith Wagner, Benjamin Widiss, Cindy Wu, Ji-Yeon Yuh, and Nan Za. I would also like to thank my students at Pomona College, where I taught this material, especially James Doernberg, Henry Jenkins, and Timothy Reynolds.

This work was supported by the Academy of Korean Studies Grant (AKS-2012-R00). I was also fortunate to receive a Fulbright Research Fellowship in Seoul for 2016–17. Special thanks go to Moonim Baek, who sponsored me at Yonsei University during that year, and to Director Jai Ok Shim and her staff at the Fulbright Korean-American Educational Commission, who were all incredibly gracious. I also received a Hirsch Research Initiation Grant in 2014 at Pomona College, for which I am grateful. I am thankful to have been given the opportunity to lecture on various parts of this study, and I thank the audiences at those institutions and especially the people that invited me: Robert Ku at SUNY Binghamton, Jennifer Fay at Vanderbilt, Kevin Smith at UC Davis, Hyun Seon Park at Yonsei, and Stephen Angle at Wesleyan.

I thank Kate Marshall and Loren Glass, the editors of the P•45 series, for championing this book. Emily-Jane Cohen, Faith Wilson Stein, and Jessica Ling have been incredibly supportive during the process. My anonymous reviewers performed extraordinarily attentive readings, which helped improve the manuscript tremendously. I am also grateful to my copy editor Joe Abbott for his careful treatment of my work.

My family has been my primary source of support over the years. Christina Cha remains my kid sister, despite the fact that she aged out of that category long ago. My father, Sang Joong Jeon, has always been a model of principle and decorum, and my mother, Chung Ja Jeon, is my model for courage. I thank Jun-Seok Choe and Soon-Nyu Choe for all of the great food and good cheer on our summer trips to their home in Korea. To my daughter, Isobel, thank you for all the happiness you bring me every day. I really love being your dad. Try not to grow up too fast. Finally, this book is dedicated to Youngmin Choe, who has read each iteration of each part of this project as it moved clumsily from a series of conference papers to articles to chapters. But more than the enormous amount of feedback and dialogue without which this book would just not exist, thank you for all your love and care. Our life together, our family, is the best thing I have going.

A Note on Romanization

Because of the increasing prominence of Koreans in Western public discourse and the range of spellings that we increasingly encounter, Korean proper nouns, including names, will be romanized according to the way in which they are generally presented to English-speaking audiences, either by self-representation, film subtitles, or common usage. All other Korean words, including film titles, will be romanized according to the McCune-Reischauer system.

Vicious Circuits

INTRODUCTION
Revenge Circulates. Empires End.

Revenge circulates. This is the simple lesson of Park Chan-wook's *Sympathy for Mr. Vengeance* (*Poksunŭn Naŭi Kŏt*, 2002), the first film in Park's revenge trilogy. A fitting mantra for globalization, "an eye for an eye leaves the whole world blind" because, as centuries of revenge tragedy have demonstrated, the desire to get even produces a chain of debt for which the line of creditors grows long. Indeed, it is the disparity between the desire for equivalence and the inevitability of cascading debt that propels the ensuing dynamics, so it is no surprise that the trilogy's subsequent films—*Oldboy* (*Oldŭboi*, 2003) and *Sympathy for Lady Vengeance* (*Ch'injŏlhan Kŭmja-ssi*, 2005)—are not sequels but, instead, depictions of revenge cycling through entirely different casts of characters. The logic of these subsequent films thus extends that of *Sympathy for Mr. Vengeance*, in which the principals end up killing each other in justifiable acts of retribution: revenge circulates endlessly; we might even say viciously.

Aware of his role in larger systems of retribution, Dong-jin (Song Kang-ho) is surprisingly vexed when facing the man responsible for his daughter's death. Although filled with rage, he is also sympathetic, having learned that Ryu (Shin Ha-kyun) had not intended to kill Yu-sun (Han Bo-bae) and that the kidnapping was part of a botched plan to save Ryu's sister, who was in desperate need of a kidney transplant. Deaf and unable to speak, Ryu had been unaware of Yu-sun's difficulty in the water while he was solemnly burying his sister, who had committed suicide on discovering that Ryu had lost his job. Dragging him into the same river where his daughter had accidentally drowned, Dong-jin now faces Ryu, looking deep into his eyes not in anger but in search of empathy. "I know you are a good guy," he says with uncertain resolve, "but you know why I have to kill you, you understand?"[1] In a moment in which one might spew invective, Dong-jin instead seeks affirmation as the pair sit chest deep in frigid waters (fig. 1). As Ryu reaches for mercy, Dong-jin, finally finding his resolve, drowns him in the same waters where Yu-sun perished.

FIGURE 1. Dong-jin's sympathy for his daughter's kidnapper in *Sympathy for Mr. Vengeance* (Studio Box, 2002).

Dong-jin's unexpected moment of sympathy for Ryu reflects the fact that they occupy analogous and not just adversarial positions in the film's vengeance economy, though enmity ultimately takes precedence over affiliation. Indeed, it remains unclear just who the subject of vengeance is. Prior to returning home, where Dong-jin was lying in wait, it was Ryu who had actually been at Dong-jin's house to avenge the killing of his girlfriend, Yeong-mi (Bae Doona), whom Dong-jin had killed for her role in the kidnapping. Ryu had already meted out revenge on the organ harvesters who had stolen his money and kidney after falsely promising to deliver a matching one for his sister. By the end of the film, both characters owe and are owed vengeance as the plot accretes layers. In this entropic escalation the film dispels any naive belief that the revenge plot moves toward equilibrium; efforts to seek payback invariably overshoot, implicating strangers into expanding asymmetric networks. The books never get balanced.

Released in 2002, fewer than five years after the beginning of the so-called IMF (International Monetary Fund) Crisis in the Republic of Korea (ROK, or South Korea) late in 1997,[2] *Sympathy for Mr. Vengeance* was emblematic of the cinema that followed in the wake of the most significant economic crisis in the history of the nation. I begin *Vicious Circuits* with the simple observation that a dominant trait of this cinema is its preoccupation with economic phenomena. The suddenness and severity of the crisis left many to wonder what had happened to an economy that had recently earned far more salutary language—like "Miracle on the Han" and "Asian Tiger." Thus, in the opening shot of Lone Kang's *Looking for Bruce Lee* (*Isoryongŭl ch'ajarat!*, 2002), the protagonist, Han, emerges from around a corner, looks directly at the camera, and addresses the viewer, asking in English, "What happened?"[3] It is a common question in the post–IMF Crisis period that expresses in dismay the sense that Korean modernity—its so-called compressed modernity—happened too fast. It is a question, for example, that both *Memories of Murder* (*Sarinŭi Ch'uŏk*, 2003) and *Oldboy* implicitly ask about the postauthoritarian period extending from the late 1980s to the early 2000s, a period represented in those films as if it had been missed entirely.

Han's question is well worth asking. What happened: to Korean cinema, to Korea, to the global political economic system? To answer such questions, we will turn to what I will call *Korea's IMF Cinema* as a way to periodize not simply the nation's arrival as a global economic actor—as is typical of scholarship under the rubric of *Hallyu* (or the Korean Wave)—but, more specifically, its compelled political and economic restructuring following the 1997–98 crisis, after which both the social reorganization of Korea and the global systemic dynamics driv- ing it come into clearer focus. For a number of reasons this quintessentially corporate art form—made as much in the boardroom as in the studio—became an ideal site for thinking through the postcrisis political economy because it represented changes in Korean economic history from postwar authoritarian developmentalism through market liberalization in the 1990s, particularly as the boardroom itself became a more anxious location. The Korean film industry had always been the object of an explicit government focus and historically an extension of its industrial policy. As a result, Korean films reflected the industry's orientation toward quasi-industrial production and trade protectionism in the 1960s and, in the 1990s, toward the ongoing negotiations with US governmental and Hollywood interests regarding open markets.

But, crucially, Korea's IMF Cinema did not just depict the economy at this moment of transition; it also was this economy's material embodiment. In addi- tion to representing economic phenomena, it was an important sector in which the same pressures and changes that affected the economy at large were operative. More than the fact of its corporate genesis, Korea's IMF Cinema has a privileged relationship to crisis itself. Having recently eclipsed the Korean film industry in revenue, television K-dramas and K-pop music may indeed speak better to contemporary political economy. Indeed, their lower production costs, quicker turnaround times, and distribution advantages seem to arise from the most current demands and infrastructures of contemporary global popular-culture consumption. But because film occupies a place *in between* older industrial de- velopmentalism and newer ventures involving technology, logistics, and finance, it better marks the transitional character of the past few decades, as the Korean economy belatedly faced the same postindustrial struggles that beset Western economies in the 1970s. So although the "K-pop idol factory" may be "the most elaborate hit-making operation on Earth," as John Seabrook opined in 2015,[4] that factory is somewhat more metaphorical than it is for the Korean film industry, in which the logic of the studio hewed more closely to that of the more traditional sites of manufacturing that had formed the basis for the nation's postwar economic ascent. Indeed, even as the Korean film industry embraced Western financial practices and new methods of speculative investment, there remained an industrial logic at the core of government policies, a stubborn developmental atavism within an emergent market-based orientation that mimicked authoritarian industrialism. Korea's IMF Cinema is far more vexed about the contemporary moment than is K-pop.

Reflecting this condition, Korea's IMF Cinema is filled with second-order representations of economic phenomena that, beyond simply documenting crisis effects in a social realist mode, attempt a systematic diagnosis of how such an economy emerges as a matter of processes, incentives, and imbalances and how this economy comes to reproduce itself according to Western models. Committed to rendering aesthetically the abstractions that are often the substance of economic discourse, these second-order representations of economic processes are often fantastical projections; nevertheless, they are reflexively bound to the real economy, invariably indexing (sometimes despite themselves) the changing stakes of the hegemonic world system at this moment of global transition.

To this end the films examined herein often emphasize self-reflexively the material elements of filmmaking, in the manner of what is often referred to in film criticism as *apparatus*. Though not without its problems—most significantly its ambivalence toward labor in its account of production—*apparatus* remains a useful materialist term because it connects film aesthetics, the medium's mode of production, and its attachment to hegemonic ideological formations. Deployed here less as an extension of psychoanalysis than as a precursor to late capitalist logistical infrastructures, *apparatus* also attends pointedly to those moments in contemporary filmic art (post-test-screening editing, algorithmic script development, transnational market-friendly casting, etc.) in which categories of aesthetics, production, and hegemony overlap increasingly as profit pressures come to circumscribe creative practices. Fully realized in the last chapter of the book as *protocol*, *apparatus* links art, business, and ideology in a way that centers the material relations that animate a work of art. Accordingly, in Korea's IMF Cinema, the filmic apparatus in this broad sense becomes mobilized as a means to think about the economic apparatus. The question of how a film works becomes a way to think about how economies work.

In locating the revenge dynamic both in concrete social relations between characters and in the more abstract register of circulation, *Sympathy for Mr. Vengeance* taps into a long history of cultural production that understands revenge in economic terms. Reflective perhaps of early mercantile economies, English Renaissance revenge dramas used the dynamics of payback to think through logics of exchange.[5] Revenge in American modernist fiction, as in William Faulkner's *The Sound and the Fury* (1929), might be regarded as a way to process the insurmountable debt burdens of the past in the long wake of chattel slavery.[6] What might be more distinctive about the present case is its scale, as befitting a now thoroughly globalized frame less bounded by the limits of family, kingdom, and nation. Something is rotten not just in the state of Denmark but in the world system at large. Revenge escalates quickly from relations between specific individuals, outward toward the more systemic relationships within a crisis economy, which in turn become more far-reaching and more intense. *Sympathy for Mr. Vengeance* is thus particularly self-conscious about the way in which characters are abstract embodiments of social positions, as well as the way in which conflicting interests within the film's vengeance economy implicate actors that initially seemed remote from their lives. It is happenstance, for example, that leads Ryu and Yeong-mi to kidnap Dong-jin's daughter instead of the daughter of Ryu's former employer as they had originally planned, yet the class chasm dividing company owner from terminated employee determines their relationship in the film. In personal terms Dong-jin and Ryu are only tangentially linked (Dong-jin is a friend of Ryu's boss), but their relationship is intimate in an economy in which the interests of company owners and workers become predictably conflicted under increasingly fraught conditions. A mark of its expanding scale, revenge here is more structural than personal. Dong-jin has to kill Ryu despite his reservations, and his plea for Ryu's understanding indexes a strong presumption of what the situation (and not his own desire) demands. Indeed, the imperative that Dong-jin expresses might be said to mark the precise point at which private logics become socially determined.

Appropriately then, the origin of the revenge plot in the film is not individual greed or lust but corporate downsizing. After Ryu loses his job, Ryu and Yeong-mi reconnoiter Ryu's former employer, who has a young daughter whom they are thinking about kidnapping. Hiding in their car at a distance in a ritzy neighborhood where business owners live, they witness a recently fired employee of Dong-jin's stand in front of a car occupied by Ryu's old boss and Dong-jin, along with their daughters. After begging unsuccessfully for his old job, the former worker mutilates himself before the two men and their two daughters with a box cutter, performing the tragedy of his own disposability before the men who hold power. We discover later that the same man has committed suicide along with his entire family (a phenomenon that became chillingly familiar after the IMF Crisis). It is at this moment that Ryu realizes that he cannot kidnap his own boss's daughter, leading the couple to target Dong-jin instead. This, then, becomes a choice to extract revenge not from the person he perceives to be directly responsible for his misfortune but from the kind of person who might be.

The tragedy of job loss has determined Ryu's existence after losing his job at the factory, where he operated heavy machinery. Much of the film's opening twenty minutes takes pains to depict Ryu's difficult labor, including an extended banal sequence in which we watch him work, take an entire scheduled break, and then return to work again, a managerial buzzer coldly signaling the beginning and end of the rest period. At the end of the shift we follow Ryu and his fellow laborers as they stagger, exhausted from their dim workstations, out into the sunlight, which hurts their eyes. In such minimally cut scenes, which seem to harken routine surveillance more than documentary exposé, labor time becomes nearly synonymous with the film's running time; and the point of beginning the film here is to link the human drama that unfolds in the plot to this fundamentally industrial mise-en-scène. Through such scenes, the film offers the abstract reason for vengeance (the worker's alienation from the mode of production and then his callous dismissal when the labor becomes no longer necessary) before its diegetic occasion (a kidnapping gone wrong). Revenge follows from such systemic relations under deindustrializing forces rather than from breaches of moral decorum and thus come to seem a rational decision rather than a flight of passion.

The film locates this revenge/crisis economy in history specifically by moving away from the scene of industrial labor in its first act to the brutal postindustrial nightmare of black-market organ harvesting, when Ryu is cruelly duped into giving away his kidney along with all of his money and left in an abandoned building. The structural presentation of revenge in the film points to the broader systemic logic of a slowing economy, in which any gain must necessarily be one of forced extraction. Capital accumulation comes increasingly at someone else's expense in a zero-sum game. You have to kidnap someone's child to pay for your sister's transplant; you have to fire an employee to protect your profits. Predatory organ harvesting becomes a fitting allegory for accumulation in which the point is to claim larger pieces of a shrinking pie. Revenge becomes the quintessential gesture of such a milieu—the only available action, and one that is understood as defensive even when it is aggressive. The Nietzschean pleasure in revenge as repayment for debts incurred here modulates into the taking of profits.[7] Understood less as payback, revenge under crisis conditions becomes a primary mode of accumulation, in which profits must be protected against stagnation at someone else's expense. Revenge thus becomes an engine of decline. As with Dong-jin's quandary at the river with Ryu's life in his hands, sympathy becomes an inherent by-product of an economy threatening stagnation, which puts everyone under varying degrees of analogous pressures. In depicting the circulation of revenge in the context of declining profitability in an increasingly postindustrial regime, *Sympathy for Mr. Vengeance* encapsulates succinctly the political economy in the Republic of Korea at the millennium.

But you know why I have to kill you, you understand?

At the End of the American Century

Empires end. In contrast to revenge's endless circulation, the teleology of empire is certain. From Rome to Great Britain, the end may be protracted and seem impossible, but history demonstrates its inevitability. In *The Long Twentieth Century* Giovanni Arrighi offers a theory for this characteristic in the overlapping rise and fall of capitalist hegemonies, beginning with Genoa at the height of Italian city-states from the fifteenth to the early seventeenth century, continuing in the Dutch cycle from the late sixteenth century through the eighteenth century, moving then to the British Empire from the middle of the eighteenth century to the beginning of the twentieth century, and ending with the most recent global hegemony, that of the United States, which began in the late nineteenth century and ended sometime in the early twenty-first.[8] In this *longue durée* Arrighi argues that these hegemonic systems rose and fell following Marx's general formula for capitalist investment, MCM′, in which the liquidity of money capital (M), seeking a profit, is invested into commodity capital (C), before converting back to money capital with a now expanded liquidity (M′).[9] Accordingly, the four hegemonic empires discussed in the study accord with a pattern of virtuous and then vicious cycles, in which a phase of material expansion, reliant on a rapid increase of commodity production, is followed by a phase of financial expansion in which the money form is imagined to be set free of the commodity form, or MM′, Marx's shorthand for what is ultimately a fictitious mode of accumulation.[10] At a certain point in these hegemonic cycles the pressure to maintain profits requires that capitalists move their investments in trade and production toward financial modes of accumulation and speculation.

Decline, in Arrighi's schema, is marked temporally by the *signal crisis* (the beginning of the end) and the *terminal crisis* (the end of the end).[11] Occurring around 1970 for the United States, the *signal crisis* inheres in the hegemonic empire's turn to financialization. For Robert Brenner the pivot is around 1973, the beginning of what he terms the *long downturn* of the US economy after the postwar boom, triggered primarily by a fall in manufacturing profitability that caused a protracted decline in the general economy.[12] This crisis produced, in turn, a cycle in which there is decreasing incentive for investment in production, which in turn accelerates the growing disparity between industrial and financial sector profitability.[13] As Joshua Clover has clarified, after the signal crisis "no real recovery of accumulation is possible, but only more and less desperate strategies of deferral."[14] In a later study, Arrighi dates this terminal crisis as occurring sometime during the US war in Iraq, which began in 2003, though he acknowledges the persistence of US military power thereafter.[15] As various bubble periods from 1973 to 2008 demonstrated, the intervening period between signal and terminus, as in the case of the Reagan-era 1980s, can initially look like a *belle époque* because financial accumulation appears robust while eliding the larger downward trends.[16] Also obscured are the considerable costs of such a turn, not the least of which in the United States was a massive buildup of personal and governmental debt along with an equally dramatic increase of inequality among the general populace.

The interstitial period between signal and terminal crises in the United States is indeed an important context for the IMF Crisis in the Republic of Korea. On December 3, 1997, the IMF announced its approval of a $57 billion bailout package, the largest in its history, aimed at stabilizing the Korean economy after a credit crisis that had erupted earlier in the year, causing a precipitous devaluation of the *wŏn* (the national currency). Although they were certainly overleveraged compared to typical Western firms, some economists have argued that they were not by Korean historical standards, which operated according to the so-called Asian high-debt model, a model that employed different strategies for managing risk.[17] The more specific problem was the preponderance of specifically short-term debt, which would typically roll over but did not under crisis conditions that emerged in part because panicked investors refused to grant customary extensions. These dire circumstances, along with the harsh terms of the bailout itself, had a profound effect on the national economy, which had enjoyed a long run of robust growth since the 1960s.

Most immediately, massive and sudden unemployment transformed the national outlook. In the immediate aftermath, three hundred thousand workers lost their jobs every month, in large part to meet IMF demands for government and corporate restructuring.[18] Many came to believe that the terms of the bailout were worse than the original crisis. In a bit of graveyard humor, Koreans joked that IMF stood for *I'm fired*, and, more somberly, coined the phrase *IMF suicide* to describe the dramatic increase of self-inflicted deaths after the crisis. Before the crisis, suicide rates had been average for economically developed countries; after it, these rates spiked to the highest in the world and have remained high to the present.[19]

Vicious Circuits locates the Korean IMF Crisis in the milieu of the end of the American century, understood via Arrighi as the end of the US cycle of hegemonic accumulation. Initially coined in 1941 by Henry Luce in a famous *Life* magazine editorial that urged US participation in World War II,[20] *the American Century* was a rallying cry for a new global order, just as its recursion, *the Project for a New American Century* under the George W. Bush administration, was an attempt to retain this order at the moment of its dissolution.[21] Although it may seem to be located at the margins of an empire that did not necessarily regard itself as such, at least not in the historical colonial form,[22] the IMF Crisis in Korea elucidated the limit point of what was a relatively long and profitable (if checkered) partnership, as economic priorities began to diverge. The Korean economy had sputtered in 1989 before returning to steady growth through the early 1990s. In this climate, emboldened *chaebŏl* (the large Korean conglomerates that played a crucial role in Korean economic development),[23] finally freed from authoritarian management, began to clamor for less state control in favor of Western-style liberal markets.[24] At the time, as well, Korea's trade surplus with the United States became a larger concern for the United States, which began to apply pressure for more reciprocity.[25] Particularly with the failure of the American war in Vietnam, South Korea became an even more crucial Cold War ally,[26] an example that Western-style democracy and capitalism could thrive in Asia and a bulwark against rising Asian communism, even though these features depended on dictators and large amounts of US financial aid to prove the point.[27]

There are good reasons to resist thinking of the IMF Crisis as Korea's signal crisis. Although it certainly realized subimperial ambitions, the ROK never threatened global hegemony as Japan did,[28] and the quality of Korean capital accumulation cycles differs. Furthermore, with its history of colonial occupation and then Cold War conflict, profitability pressures were always balanced against security concerns. This ingrained military protectionism inevitably affected economic policy, mitigating somewhat the preoccupation with short-term profits that drives the turn in the signal crisis toward finance. Despite these differences, however, it remains clarifying to adopt the general form of Arrighi's transitional crisis and to regard Korea's IMF Crisis as the definitive point in Korean economic history in which the virtuous cycle turns vicious.

The signal crisis of the US empire in the early 1970s came as a response to declining industrial productivity as increasing costs and diminishing profits compelled American manufacturers to move operations abroad, and it gave rise to a series of fixes that would fuel speculative bubbles in finance, technology, and real estate, all of which would burst with escalating degrees of severity. Similarly (though later) in Korea, policy makers faced the end of favorable developmental conditions in the 1990s, as labor costs rose and competition increased from rapidly industrializing neighbors in the region, particularly in China and Southeast Asia. In this context policy makers decided to move gradually away from a once highly orchestrated industrial policy toward a more market-based orientation. While the IMF bailout package is often correctly heralded as a key moment in this transition, these changes were already under way by the early 1990s under the Kim Young-sam administration,[29] which made what it dubbed *segyehwa* (literally *globalization*) explicit state policy, culminating with the changes that the ROK was forced to make as a price of admission to the OECD (Organization for Economic Co-operation and Development) in 1996.

When the crisis struck in 1997, economists armed with phrases like *crony capitalism* and *moral hazard* blamed the historic cooperation of the Korean *chaebŏl* and the authoritarian state, which had managed a carefully coordinated strategy until the late 1980s designed to limit competition within Korea and to maximize leverage.[30] American economist Paul Krugman, for example, blamed a nepotistic system of financial excess that had created an irrational environment encouraging risky lending.[31] Critics also targeted state intervention and protectionism in economic planning, which they claimed prevented the natural ability of markets to achieve equilibriums, as part of justifications for market liberalization.[32] A number of economists have pushed back against these pervasive critiques of protectionist stances and state-managed capital flows. Ha-Joon Chang, for example, has insisted that it was in fact the turn *away* from developmental industrial policy begun in the early 1990s that, in fact, caused the crisis.[33]

On one point, however, there was no disagreement. The structural adjustments demanded by the IMF as a condition of the bailout package radically reshaped the Korean economy, even with such changes already under way since the early 1990s, according to the script that has become familiar globally since 1973: trade liberalization, labor flexibility, and financialization oriented toward global firms. Although the ROK was often praised for its rapid recovery,[34] long-term trends indicate that the crisis may have precipitated something like Robert Brenner's *long downturn*.[35] Although economists have disagreed about the extent to which this restructuring accomplished the financialization of the Korean economy, the signature characteristic of Arrighi's signal crisis,[36] some synthesis of their opposing positions is possible—namely, that although IMF restructuring changed the policy orientation of the Korean economy, the real economy itself has not, at least not yet, completely followed suit.[37] The IMF forced changes on the Korean economy that did not necessarily match its fundamental features, proceeding instead by a familiar playbook already implemented under similar conditions all around the world, particularly in Latin America. The Korean economy was and remains export-oriented with a remaining (though diminished) industrial base, such that a fuller recourse to financialization would not make sense.

Economic repair, however, was a secondary goal. Under the thinly veiled guidance of US Treasury Secretary Robert Rubin, a longtime executive at Goldman Sachs, and Deputy Secretary (and eventual Rubin successor) Lawrence Summers, the IMF had worked to make Korean assets available to Western capital after years of protectionist shielding, and it was primarily Washington Consensus pressure that provided the impetus for such a dramatic restructuring.[38] Stanley Fischer, the IMF's first deputy managing director during the crisis, later stated that the "IMF had displayed no interest in what had actually caused the crisis" and instead "was exclusively focused on how the crisis could be used as leverage."[39] The IMF's own internal audit also admitted that the structural adjustments had been ill-advised and that the IMF had been ideologically blind to other options.[40] Shin and Chang note the phenomenon of "IMF Mission Creep" since the 1980s, in which the organization's original purpose, to "deal only with current account balance of payments problems," gave way to an interventionist agenda aimed at full liberalization of product and capital markets.[41] As Shin and Chang put it (in the language of Genesis), IMF restructuring remolded "the Korean economy *in the image of* the (idealized) Anglo-American system, in the name of keeping up with the 'global standards.'"[42]

This remolding was not mere narcissism. Though not without benefits, the IMF bailout was also an exercise of hegemonic power, with structural adjustments supplementing military might, confirming Paul Virilio's observation that market conquest and military supremacy have become increasingly overlapping phenomena.[43] Furthermore, this expression of hegemonic reach came at a time when actual hegemony, in Arrighi's definition, had already ended. No longer able to provide the "motor force of a general expansion,"[44] the United States instead sought to build a self-reproducing hegemonic system at a point when it could no longer hold up its end of the bargain. But more than just creating favorable conditions for Western capital, there was an all-out fire sale of state and corporate assets to Western agents. General Motors was allowed to purchase Daewoo Motors and its $10.7 billion of assets for the tidy sum of $400 million, with the Korean government throwing in provisions to minimize downside risk.[45] In addition, this became a period in which foreign ownership in Korean firms spiked.[46] Writing in 1998 about the Asian financial crisis in general, economists Robert Wade and Frank Veneroso stated, "The combination of massive devaluations, IMF-pushed financial liberalization, and IMF-facilitated recovery may even precipitate the biggest peacetime transfer of assets from domestic to foreign owners in the past fifty years anywhere in the world."[47] In such vulture capitalism, what is lost in these transfers of state and corporate asset to Western firms is measured not just in the capital value of those assets but in the future profits of these potentially productive industries.

The broader context for the IMF structural adjustment program in Korea is the historical transformation of the hegemonic American economic system from an introverted, but robust, domestic market at midcentury into an extroverted one that extended its reach and organizing logics by century's end, creating an interdependent system with strategic advantages to compensate for its vanishing strength. Symptomatic of the signal crisis of US hegemony, the emergence of this world system is what David Harvey calls a *spatial fix*: "Foreign trade (and the export of capital) can certainly increase the rate of profit in a variety of ways.

But . . . it merely ends up exacerbating those processes that gave rise to the falling rate of profit in the first place. What looks like a solution turns into its opposite in the long run."[48] Korea's IMF Crisis was a peripheral effect of a larger project of compensating for the declining industrial profits in the United States' long downturn, the construction of a belated imperial network premised on asymmetrical exchange rather than extracting colonial tribute. The much-heralded Korean Wave (or *Hallyu*) in this emergent global order might thus amount to only a counter-ripple in what is actually a sea change.

To attend to this great moment of global transition, I employ a transnational Americanist disciplinary orientation that crosses over into Asian studies. In this respect it builds on Laura Hyun Yi Kang's attempt to "de-Asianize" the crisis and to recontextualize it within the history of Western late capitalism.[49] For Kang, *Asianization* is an ideological process through which the profound imbrication of the world system is repressed in order to understand economic phenomena according to simplistic models that correspond, not coincidentally, to historical patterns of racialization, while obscuring the key role that US financial and military agents have played in the construction of a world order in which financial crises have become commonplace and open to manipulation by holders of mass capital.

My focus on the Republic of Korea thus offers a peripheral but critical perspective on the operations of late US empire as well as on the contradictions that ultimately corrode it. It is a particularly ideal vista from which to view the end of the American century, that is, the transition between a US-centered world economy to one that, according to many commentators will be dominated by Asia. In this transitional moment in the global world order, Korea is doubly peripheral. On the one hand, the ROK has been historically committed to its close alliance with the United States (though not without internal dissent). Along with offering a relatively unprotected and robust market for American goods and services, Korea continues to serve as a strategic military location for a significant US troop presence, ranging from between about thirty thousand to forty-five thousand since 1973. On the other hand, China has become much more central to Korea's future economic prospects, having flip-flopped with the United States since the 1990s as the largest export markets for Korean goods. In 1995 the United States constituted 20 percent of Korea's total exports while China made up only 7.5 percent. After equalizing in 2003, the numbers fully reversed by 2014 when the United States represented only 12 percent to China's 24 percent.[50] Although the

ROK remains dependent on the US for security, the economic consequences of such a dependence have become increasingly clear, for example, the sanctions that China swiftly took against Korean products to demonstrate its displeasure over the Park Geun-hye administration's decision in 2016 to deploy the US missile defense system known as THAAD (or Terminal High Altitude Area Defense). Continuing a Cold War legacy, the Korean peninsula abides as a site of negotiation, a de facto border, between these competitors for global hegemony and, as such, reflects broader changes in political economy at the crossroads of Western and Asian capitalisms. Indeed, the DMZ is similar to the former Berlin Wall, functioning as a kind of Cold War border between the United States and an adversary with whom it did not otherwise share a physical border; one important difference, however, is that economic interdependence between the US and China serves as a crucial backdrop for any developing antagonism.

The dynamics initiated by the crisis abide in the present, despite periods of apparent growth. The turn to the new economies, real estate bubbles, and "fourth industrial revolution" evangelism notwithstanding, economic growth since the crisis has been predictably accompanied by ballooning household debt, growing inequality, and a continual erosion of the industrial base. IMF restructuring remolded the Korean economy in the American image and pulled it into a tighter symbiosis with US corporate interests. While it is certainly true that such a transition is inevitable—accumulation in its expansionary phase is followed by contraction in Arrighi so inevitably that we may regard them as part of a single process—IMF restructuring accelerated and made it certain. Martin Hart-Landsberg argued a decade ago, in an account that still pertains, "Korea is now trapped in a self-reinforcing downward spiral," being more dependent on foreign investments and export, and "foreign firms and *chaebol* exporters are in an excellent position to demand further concessions that . . . will only reinforce the same dependency."[51] Around the same time, Shin and Chang similarly described the nation as trapped in a "vicious circle," with rapidly increasing foreign debt making currency depreciation difficult and leading to decreased export earnings, which in turn raises the need for more foreign borrowing.[52]

Epitomized by massive contrivances like global containerization and algorithmic derivatives trading in transnational dark pools, which can seem either like acts of incredible ingenuity or incredible desperation depending on one's perspective, this new world order is largely propelled by *spatiotemporal fixes*—the temporal deferrals and geographical expansions through which firms seek new profits in capital and product markets[53]—and is characterized by what Joshua Clover terms "the circulatory shift."[54] Inherent in this shift are intense logistical refinements in networks of distribution and exchange that meanwhile cover over the fact that little new production results. In the United States (with predictable recursions in the ROK) the technology and subprime mortgage bubbles were accompanied by messianic language. The new economy was purported to have surpassed Fordist limitations, creating value through expansive circulatory networks only possible at the massive scales afforded by new technologies. The conceit was that value might be produced outside of production by maximizing the speed and efficiency of circulation and was in turn mirrored in political theory, most famously in Michael Hardt and Antonio Negri's *Empire* (2000), which, published at the height of a US technology bubble, found subversive possibility in the late capitalist expansion of its sphere of circulation and immaterial modes of production. "Through circulation the common human species is composed, a multicolored Orpheus of infinite power; through circulation the human community is constituted."[55]

A clear lesson of the political economy of the last two decades culminating in the Global Financial Crisis of 2008, however, is the limit point of such circulatory enthusiasm. We have learned that many new-economy businesses either focused on extracting rent from technologies of networked circulation itself or were corrosive to existing sectors in the name of efficiency—in the first tech boom to brick-and-mortar retail (e.g., Amazon) and more recently to service sectors (e.g., Uber). Messianic language notwithstanding—Marx was adamant that circulation creates no new value[56]—busts have followed each boom. As demonstrated by the global shipping crisis and the 2016 bankruptcy of Hanjin, formerly Korea's largest firm in that sector, circulation cannot proceed independently of production.

If the IMF Crisis is indeed the swerve that pulls Korea into the economic orbit of the United States, this orbit is a vicious circuit.

Korea's IMF Cinema

Less than two years after the initial bailout in 1997, on February 13, 1999, as the IMF was negotiating similar deals in Brazil and Indonesia, director Kang Je-gyu's production company, in conjunction with Samsung Entertainment, released *Shiri* (*Swiri*), a blockbuster film that went on to beat the Korean box office records previously set by the 20th Century Fox/Paramount coproduction *Titanic* in 1997. Incurring less than $3 million in costs and grossing $26.5 million,[57] *Shiri* set off a new boom in Korean filmmaking that culminated, one might say, with the Grand Prix award at the 2004 Cannes Film Festival for Park Chan-wook's *Oldboy*.

The backstory has become familiar: Kim purportedly viewed a report in 1994 that the export revenue alone of the Universal Pictures smash hit *Jurassic Park* (1993) had matched the foreign sales of Hyundai cars that year.[58] Acting quickly, Kim's government passed a series of measures designed to claim market share in global culture industries, perhaps most significantly the reclassification of the motion picture industry from "service" to "semimanufacturing," with the intention of encouraging more corporate investment by firms that would now enjoy the same kind of tax benefits that manufacturing companies did.[59] These changes, along with the end of formal censorship in 1996 by rule of the Korean Constitutional Court,[60] had a profound and immediate effect. Some large *chaebŏl*, like Samsung and Daewoo, interested in vertical integration strategies that would complement their positions in the growing home-entertainment market, had already entered the industry by the early 1990s, and the changes in the mid-1990s encouraged an expansion of these efforts, though they would soon leave it in the aftermath of the IMF Crisis.[61] In addition, new venture capital flowed into the industry by smaller entrepreneurial films, like Ilshin Investment and Mahan Film Venture Capital, with innovative financing strategies, like the forming of mutual funds to spread and diversify risk.[62] All this new capital also meant stepping up managerial efficiency: standardizing production, introducing accounting transparency, and building robust, integrated distribution networks, most prominently in the form of the cinema multiplexes that were beginning to sprout up throughout Korea.[63] We might think of this period beginning in the mid-1990s as the moment when Korean motion picture companies, which had been around since the era of Japanese colonialism and had flowered during the 1960s, began to behave like multinational corporations.

But if the industry was becoming increasingly modeled on Western corporate practices, there was something also insistently atavistic about the transition that remained true to Asian developmentalism. Not developmentalism in the classic sense, these film industry arrangements represented more of something like a *zombie developmentalism*, which remains undead in postmillennial Korean economic discourse in sectors beyond the culture industry. The 1995 Motion Picture Promotion Law under the Kim Young-sam administration, which provided tax breaks for production companies, was also aimed at redressing the lack of physical infrastructure in the industry.[64] Indeed, the law's reclassification of film as a kind of manufacturing product, and no longer a service, speaks to this transitional logic. So even as the industry moved to adopt Western financial practices, a stubborn developmentalism abided within an emergent market-based orientation that mimicked authoritarian industrial policies. On the one hand, new policy opened up an arena for speculative investment, first drawing large Korean firms and then other smaller entrepreneurs interested in the kind of large returns earned by *Shiri*. In this respect film behaved like a new economy product, the object of speculation whose value was determined by circulation. On the other hand, the new cultural policy mimicked authoritarian industrial policy of old. Accordingly, cinema, with its perceived prestige (as validated by international film festivals), seemed to imbue the cultural sector with a value that the ensuing wave of pop music and television dramas lacked.[65]

In its semi-industrial sensibility the vision of the film industry under the Kim Young-sam administration was reminiscent of film policy under the authoritarian Park Chung-hee regime. Though notoriously invested in constructing a machinery for propaganda, Park had also viewed film policy as a mirror of his industrial policies, forcing consolidation and vertical integration designed to streamline production and to eliminate weaker performing firms with the ultimate aim of increasing capacity. After taking power in May of 1961 by military coup, Park established the Ministry of Public Information within a month and passed the Motion Picture Law within a year in order to manage the industry. According to Brian Yecies and Aegyung Shim, Park was able to realize his vision of film as a complementary element of his broader industrial program: "Almost overnight, a 'studio system' resembling a factory assembly line had been born."[66] The result in the 1960s was what many critics regard as a golden age for Korean cinema, in which filmmakers were able to produce interesting films both because of and despite a state-sponsored machinery that managed production.

But with Hollywood profits eroding under the pressures of home video and new media, the pressures for liberalization in the Korean film market became more intense in the 1990s when the United States—led by the Motion Picture Export Association of America (MPEAA), which worked with the US State Department to open foreign markets for American movies[67]—ramped up the pressure to eliminate the quota system. Since 1966 under Park Chung-hee, the screen quota system had protected domestic film production by mandating that Korean movie theaters screen domestic films for a minimum number of days in order to secure the right to show the more profitable foreign films. After a brief period from 1970 to 1973 with relaxed quotas bowing to US influence, the quota was ramped up significantly in 1973 in an attempt to save a bankrupt domestic industry.[68] Then, in 1987, after years of pressure from Hollywood interest groups, American motion picture companies were granted the right to distribute directly to the Korean market without the use of intermediaries, undercutting the revenue that domestic distributors had enjoyed in the quota system.[69] Finally, in 2006 in the lead-up to US-ROK discussions about a controversial new bilateral free-trade agreement, which famously led to the explosive beef protests in 2008, the quota was further slashed, this time in half, which caused a sharp decline in the domestic industry in 2007. The efforts to curb such quotas were an extension of the general pressure the United States had applied to the ROK to open its markets during the Uruguay Round negotiations (1986–94), the multilateral trade discussions that eventually led to the formation of the World Trade Organization in 1994.[70] In this context Kim's conflicted policy represented a divided sensibility. Committed as he had to be to market liberalization, he maintained a desire to reproduce in the realm of culture the kind of industrial production that had been the engine of economic growth in the ROK and was now beginning to decline. The result in the 1990s, variously periodized as New Korean Cinema or the South Korean Film Renaissance, was a boom of a different sort in which the limiting factor was not state sponsorship but the film industry's desire for profits.[71]

In offering *Korea's IMF Cinema* as a periodizing term dealing narrowly with the decade after the IMF Crisis and before the global financial crisis (1997–2007) and even more specifically with the height of that period, 2000–2006, before the industry bubble burst in 2007,[72] *Vicious Circuits* asserts a dominant through-line within the broader categories above, one that implicates questions of cinematic production with broader trends in global political economy. So although it may encompass a relatively brief period of film production, Korea's IMF Cinema crucially marks the prehistory of the present and articulates the terms in which contemporary life in late capitalism becomes intelligible. I will focus, therefore, on a range of exemplary films that address the significant economic preoccupations of the period, which are also the opening swerves of the vicious circulation that comes to define the present. As a periodizing term, then, Korea's IMF Cinema has two crucial functions. The first is indexical: it marks the transitional moment in economic regimes begun under the Kim Young-sam administration and fully realized in the restructuring imposed by the IMF bailout package, as it became necessary, owing to internal and external pressures, to shift toward a program of free trade and liberal capital markets. The second is material: the film industry of the period was itself an economic response to the declining productivity of the industrial sector,[73] an attempt to compensate for slowing growth in production in a sector that became formally regarded, somewhat ambiguously, as "semimanufacturing." The story of Korea's IMF Cinema mirrors that of the Korean political economy during and since this transitional moment between virtuous and vicious cycles because both were restructured under identical pressures.

From Method to Mechanism

I begin with an examination of Bong Joon-ho's *Memories of Murder* and its forceful articulation of the profound historical anxiety that characterized the post-IMF period in Korea, an articulation that allows, in turn, for a reflection on critical method in general as it pertains to this history. In fictionalizing the infamously unsolved Hwaseong serial murders in the Korean countryside that occurred between 1986 and 1991, *Memories of Murder* employs and then jettisons detective genre conventions as a way of testing and then dismissing hermeneutic methods for making sense of the newly disorienting present. The film's interest is thus methodological, using the failure of investigation as a way to draw attention away from hermeneutic dead ends in favor of a materialist orientation in which the film apparatus is understood to be the concrete product of a political economy that invariably indexes the conditions that determine it. Its historiographic method moves us, then, from serial to system, away from recursive killings that no one can explain toward an understanding that makes sense of larger schemas.

After this opening methodological chapter, I move on to consider the abrupt social reorganization that the IMF Crisis prompted in Korea, particularly with respect to questions of employment and labor. To this end the second chapter examines the figure of the salaryman in the second entry in Park Chan-wook's revenge trilogy, *Oldboy*, and its extension in post-IMF gangster films, what I will term *kkangp'ae* films. One of the most visible figures in the immediate aftermath of the IMF Crisis, the despondent salaryman, having lost his job, becomes in these films a launch point for a critical effort to think abstractly about exploitation in the credit relationship in a period when national debt gave rise to consumer debt. We also learn through these films, however, that the salaryman is a reification that disavows systemic understandings of debt in favor of individual understandings that are consistently rendered intelligible as personal rather than structural pathologies. So although these films intuit the transformative changes accelerated by the IMF Crisis, they remain constrained by the reification that both accesses and limits their view.

Chapters 3 and 4 explore the effects of the crisis on the demographic that the salaryman reification often functioned to elide: youth and women, two segments of the population for whom the problem of unemployment was least addressed by policy makers. In both of these chapters economic realities become visible despite ideological fantasies designed to mitigate them. Chapter 3 investigates the phenomenon of Korean punk rock as represented in Lone Kang's independent film *Looking for Bruce Lee*. Less a misanthropic youth and more a new kind of worker, the *segyehwa* punk becomes an ideal figure for a new labor logic in the globalized Korean marketplace that privileges human capital over the forms of security implicit in the false promises of lifetime employment that were once proffered by Korea's *chaebŏl*. Although these figures understand their relationship to the world already in globalized terms, they also disavow its material realities. The fantasy of human capital, however, can only partially elide the reality of a collapsing youth job market. Under the rubric of what I will call *subsistence faming*, this fantasy, despite itself, reveals itself to be a survival strategy amid bleak alternatives.

Addressing what is perhaps the most underexamined aspect of IMF Crisis discourse, Chapter 4 centers on the depiction of gendered labor in Jeong Jae-eun's *Take Care of My Cat* (*Koyangirŭl Put'akhae*, 2001). The film's five protagonists, all young women seeking to enter the workforce, seem to actively participate in the logics that make their own labor obsolete, specifically in handheld cellular and digital technologies. The chapter focuses specifically on the representation of technological remediation that abounds in the film and is epitomized by a trope in which text messages between the young women appear on various diegetic surfaces, like windows or buildings. Such intermedial representations, in this case of digital handheld devices within the context of film, become a way to think about the problem of integrating the young women in the film, recent high school graduates, into a changing economy, which is powerfully manifested in the film's mise-en-scène as the infrastructural buildup occurring around these young women in their hometown of Incheon. The disparity between the growing technology and infrastructure in the film, on the one hand, and the limited prospects of the women, on the other, suggests that despite their fantasies of remediation, a more likely fate is obsolescence.

The final two chapters move from a focus on films that foreground post-IMF social reorganization to those that seem to engage directly with the systemic mechanisms of late US hegemony, the underlying material infrastructures and protocols that facilitate and govern the new economic order in the Republic of Korea, especially those that compel the social effects. Chapter 5 traces the overlapping recursive logics of CGI (computer-generated imagery) cinema, US military technology, and contemporary finance as presented explicitly in the blockbuster monster films *The Host* (*Koemul*, 2006) and *D-War* (*Tiwŏ*, 2007) and obliquely in the independent diasporic film *HERs* (*Hŏsŭ*, 2007). Each of these films indexes self-reflexively the algorithmic and mathematical procedures that link contemporary filmmaking to military and financial technologies. As a result, the surprising interplay of what might initially seem like three discrete realms of production reveals a deeper systemic logic that has driven the attempt to reproduce US power past its expiration date.

The final chapter investigates an increasingly clichéd trope in contemporary action cinema in the age of digital production, the *wire shot*, a first-person point-of-view shot of imagined wire traversal. These reifications index while disavowing the material history of the massive physical network of subterranean and undersea cables, first built by the US military, that might serve as a figure for a desire in late US hegemony to reproduce itself at the moment of decline, in a similar manner that the All Red Line system of telegraph cables in the late nineteenth century figured the late British Empire's desire for managerial efficiency at the moment that this was increasingly becoming a problem. Focusing on a trio of films by the Korean production company Tube Entertainment, all of which flopped at the box office, this chapter examines the way in which post-IMF Korean culture encodes the protocols of US financialization as the culmination of a long history of imbrication among transportation infrastructures, communications networks, and capital circulation. The films reveal the desire of these protocols to reproduce themselves in an autogenous fashion but also the final impossibility of this systemic reproduction.

Finally, the coda briefly explores the afterlife of Korea's IMF Cinema in more contemporary productions. Although I have periodized more narrowly, ending around 2008 with the bursting of the film industry bubble, the issues and tropes that this cinematic moment put into circulation remain prevalent in contemporary Korean cinema because the era of vicious circulation has not subsided. Specifically, the coda will look at Bong Joon-ho's second foray into Hollywood coproduction in his 2017 film *Okja* in relation to the failure of the Trans-Pacific Partnership trade agreement (TPP) that same year. Made in conjunction with Brad Pitt's Plan B Entertainment and released simultaneously in theaters and on the US-based streaming service Netflix, *Okja* is a transnational production explicitly about global commodity distribution that reflects on its own status in the global marketplace at the moment that marketplace seems about to close. Its choice of topic (global pork distribution) points to the conspicuous absence in the film: China, which constitutes one-half of the global pork market. *Okja* is thus a post-TPP film that thinks about what a world system would look like without US hegemony to center it.

Cinema at the End of Empire

The year *Sympathy for Mr. Vengeance* was released (2002) was a high-water mark for anti-American sentiment in the Republic of Korea, despite that nation's avowed allegiance to US interests. There had been a series of anti-American flare-ups since the Korean War, most often having to do with behavior by the US military, most visibly for its role in the suppression of the Gwangju Uprising in 1980[74] and in the mistreatment of women by servicemen.[75] Flare-ups notwithstanding, there was a period of diminished tension in the early to mid-1990s. By 2003, US troop levels in Korea had reached their highest levels since the late 1980s,[76] and the ROK was one of the few nations to supply troops in significant numbers for the US war in Iraq. In 2002, however, two US servicemen, driving an armored vehicle on their way back to their base after a training exercise, struck and killed two Korean schoolgirls.[77] The servicemen's acquittal in a US military court in December of 2002 triggered a series of large-scale, angry protests, as well as a general tense atmosphere.[78] Although there was considerable anger about the incident itself, the explosion of anti-American sentiment late in 2002 and into 2003 can be traced in part to the IMF Crisis and the widely held perception that the IMF bailout had been a thinly veiled imperial action.[79]

In *Sympathy for Mr. Vengeance*, anti-American sentiment is focalized in Ryu's girlfriend, Yeong-mi, played by the now transnational Korean actor Bae Doona. At one point we see Yeong-mi on the street passing out homemade political fliers to passersby, repeating slogans denouncing *chaebŏl* power, neoliberalism, and the US military. Linking the period's tension arising from American military presence to economic phenomena, the fullest realization of Yeong-mi's anti-American politics is her affiliation with the secret organization the Revolutionary

Anarchist Alliance (RAA), which remains something of a joke for all but the last few moments of the film. Idealistic and seemingly naive, Yeong-mi's politics function largely as comic relief throughout a brutal film in which it is badly needed. Even when a bound Yeong-mi, weary from torture, warns him about the RAA, an unimpressed Dong-jin covers her up with a blanket, dismissing her warning as desperate nonsense.

But in the final moments of the film, when the RAA appears as *deus ex machina*, there is nothing comical about it. We see the men together in a single shot, wordless and intensely smoking cigarettes, as they confirm Dong-jin's identity (fig. 2). Then they kill him without fanfare, attaching to his chest with a knife one of the kind of political death-sentence judgments that we had earlier seen Young-mi editing on her computer. Baffled, Dong-jin is left to wonder what happened, helplessly peering down at the document on his chest for some sort of explanation. We can hear his incoherent ramblings interspersed with dying gasps for air for a disconcertingly long time as the screen fades to black and the final credits role. Although this last vengeance killing certainly has a personal element as retribution for the murder of Yeong-mi, the killing at the hands of this austere gang of four, and the accompanying emphatic political gesture, shifts the context toward Dong-jin's crimes as a capitalist and away from his moral failings.

The circulation of revenge in the film, more ideological than personal, now seems to have extended beyond the film's diegesis, meted out in this case by men who we once thought to be the product of a childish fantasy, appearing from the distant horizon as if from outside of the film. An incidental detail within the

FIGURE 2. The RAA standing in front of their Korando in *Sympathy for Mr. Vengeance* (Studio Box, 2002).

mise-en-scène helps clarify their otherwise befuddling appearance in the story. Despite occupying vastly different social locations, both the RAA and Dong-jin drive Ssangyong automobiles. In the tight shot of the RAA members assembled in front of their jeep, we see from the insignia on the side of the jeep's hood that the RAA drives a Korando. First built by Ha dong-hwa Motors for the US military in 1964 for use in Asia (including during the US war in Vietnam), these jeeps were eventually rebranded and sold to the Korean domestic market as Korando, which is an abbreviation of the nationalist slogan, "Korea Can Do." A legacy of US military presence dressed up in Korean nationalism, the jeep became popular as the automotive industry grew to meet the demands of an emerging domestic market, protected by the same sort of measures that had shielded the local motion picture industry from foreign competition during the same period.[80] Eventually, in the 1980s, the company was acquired by the large conglomerate Ssangyong, and the model driven by the RAA in the film, the Korando K9, was manufactured until 1996.

Dong-jin, in contrast, drives a Ssangyong Rexton SUV, circa 2001. It is the car against which we see him slumped and dying at the end of the film as the Korando backs away. In 1997, the first year in Korean history in which export auto sales surpassed domestic sales and the year the Asian Financial Crisis began,[81] Ssangyong Motors was acquired by Daewoo Motors, only to be put into receivership in 2000 before Daewoo Motors was sold to General Motors. It was eventually purchased by the Shanghai Automotive Industry Corporation (SAIC) in 2004 but was again put in receivership when the Chinese company filed for bankruptcy in 2009.[82] It was then sold by the government to the Indian corporation Mahindra and Mahindra in 2011.[83] Built on a Mercedes platform for the emerging global SUV market, the Rexton was developed under the Daewoo umbrella for the short period during which it owned Ssangyong, just before the company's subsequent history as a transnational asset.

The two Ssangyong automobiles, the first made around 1996 and the second around 2001, bracket a transitional moment in Korean economic history that encompasses both cars and movies. With roots in US-ROK cooperation, the Korando signals the peaceful coexistence of parallel Cold War interests. In contrast, the post–IMF Crisis Rexton, with its vaguely British name, German girding, and orientation toward a newly prioritized export market, was produced by an automobile firm that by 2011 had changed hands five times within the space of thirteen years, as Korean heavy industries began to face overcapacity in the face of stiffening global competition.

Unsurprisingly, throughout this tumultuous period—for both the nation and Ssangyong Motors—the big losers were not the firms who were protected by bankruptcy courts and government bailouts but the company's workers. Facing mass layoffs and frustrated with fighting the moving target of ownership through this chain of mergers and acquisitions, 976 workers struck and seized the company's plant in Pyeongtaek, holding it from May 22 to August 5, 2009, during which management resorted to severe tactics, shutting off power and water and denying medical care, while riot police forcefully suppressed the action.[84] Twenty-six workers died after the strike from suicide or disease after they were terminated from their jobs.[85] Driving the final nail in the coffin, the Korean Supreme Court affirmed the legitimacy of the layoffs in 2014,[86] overturning a lower court's ruling earlier in the year.[87]

Revenge circulates. We might think of these deaths as the extradiegetic continuation of the open-ended circulation at the end of *Sympathy for Mr. Vengeance*, even further down the road than the horizon toward which the RAA drives off. Another episode in what increasingly seems a long downturn, Korea's IMF Crisis seemed far from over in 2009. Although we often understand the historical event as ending with the payback of the loan in 2001 and the earlier than expected return to growth,[88] the significant restructuring of the economy put in place a series of conditions that made recursions like the Ssangyong case more likely, a recursion that Hyun Ok Park describes not as exceptional but as "paradigmatic."[89]

Since Kim Young-sam's epiphany about the relative value of *Jurassic Park* and Hyundai cars in 1994, movies and automobiles have become analogous export products, but Kim's classification of film as a semimanufactured product is ultimately a ruse. The industry practices of Korea's IMF Cinema were certainly closer to those of a service industry (its former classification) and dependent on low-wage labor. As stars began to earn higher salaries, production output decreased, and production budgets increased, the vast majority of workers in the industry saw minimal compensation. In 2004, a year before workers in the industry were able to unionize, the average monthly income for a production staff worker was 618,000 *wŏn* ($544), despite working on the average fourteen hour days.[90] Even midlevel staffers with experience only managed one million *wŏn* ($880) per month.[91] As intellectual property, the business model focused on extracting monopoly rents. Jeremy Valentine has written that "culture industry activity is organised around the practice of 'value skimming,'" which profits off of positional advantage.[92] The Korean government's branding efforts under the banner of *Hallyu* in the post-IMF period thus enact the strategy of the French wine trade, in David Harvey's account, adopting standards of authenticity like "appellation contrôlée" in order to secure "the uniqueness upon which monopoly rent can be based."[93]

Anticipating the collapse of Hanjin Shipping in August of that year, a 2016 article published in *The Economist* catalogs the recent losing streak in Korean industrial exports, citing declines in petrochemicals, steel, shipbuilding, and, indeed, automobiles, all of which were facing stiffer competition from China and Japan.[94] The optimistic title of the article, "Films Are the New Stars," had seemed to promise reprieve but also wishful thinking. Indeed, snappy title notwithstanding, the article contained a significant caveat: "But cultural and fashion businesses are no less volatile and vulnerable to global trends than ones that make stuff out of lumps of metal. . . . Even a more diverse export base is not enough to protect South Korea entirely from the chill winds blowing across Asia."[95]

Empires end. Such chill winds should feel familiar. In her book *Cinema at the End of Empire*, Priya Jaikumar argues that popular British and Indian films of the 1930s, in this late colonial period, "embodied the ambiguities, possibilities, and fears generated by two historical paradoxes: that of colonialism's moral delegitimization before its political demise and that of its persistence in shaping modern postcolonial societies well after the end of formal empire."[96] Although framed in moral terms, these twin paradoxes create the dynamics of a vicious circulation in which an unsustainable construct, namely the British Empire, pulls the colony into its orbit so thoroughly that its influence outlives imperial rule itself. In the face of such chilling winds, cinema's task, for Jaikumar, was to record the energies that attended to the stubborn persistence of the colonial legacy. Korea's IMF Cinema similarly attends to the analogous neocolonial relationship between the United States and the Republic of Korea, late in the autumn of American empire. We should of course be wary of differences: instead of a colonial system of occupation and tribute, the present arrangement is brokered by free-trade agreements and IMF structural adjustments. Nevertheless, the postcolonial problem abides in the client state, as does the analogy between India with respect to the British Empire and Korea with respect to that of the United States. In both cases the overdetermined orbits of vicious circuits elide something that they can't quite contain, in which two facts seem beyond reproach.

Revenge circulates. Empires end.

Concrete Memories
Historiography, Nostalgia, and Archive
in *Memories of Murder*

Toward the end of *Memories of Murder*, Detective Cho (Kim Roe-ha)—a comic, but disturbing, sidekick—learns that he must have his leg amputated. A few days earlier, an innocent former suspect had driven a rusty nail into Cho's leg in the course of a drunken brawl. Left untreated, the leg becomes infected with tetanus. The irony is clear: Cho—a thug with a badge and little formal training—is fond of cruelly kicking suspects and even covers his boot with fabric to prevent scuffing. The ailment is thus clear symbolic punishment for this appendage of state violence. But whereas Cho quickly receives the appropriate punishment, justice is far more elusive in the film's central murder case, in which the killer is never caught. This striking displacement signals not only the film's ambivalence toward generic convention (i.e., the officer of the law becomes the object of its discipline) but also its deployment of crime as a figure for state violence. This violence pertains, furthermore, not only to Korea's authoritarian past but also to its present.

Memories of Murder is perhaps the period's most forceful articulation of the sense of historical rupture caused by the economic transformation brought on by the IMF Crisis. Arising out of the period's shock, the film's concern is largely methodological, asking how we might begin to understand a sudden historical change, still too immediate to process with the clarity of hindsight and the effects of which were still viscerally present in everyday life. The film's strategy is to attempt this engagement at the broader scale of Korean historiography. Rather than identifying the culprit for the immediate changes in these years, which remain beyond local comprehension, the film folds in millennial economic transformations into the larger historical transition in the Republic of Korea from authoritarian to democratic governments as an attempt to place the present within larger timescales. Additionally, it runs the entire period through a genre experiment, as the object of detective investigation, asking a quintessential post–IMF Crisis question—what happened?—as part of an exercise that is native to the genre of crime fictions—who did it? To the extent that we might posit the particular form of epistemological uncertainty that inheres in the classic detective story as a modality of the dismayed reaction by many after the Korean IMF Crisis, *Memories of Murder* employs genre to query history.

Despite many permutations since the nineteenth century, which have made it difficult to delimit generic characteristics too narrowly, a formal constancy persists in the detective story in its propulsion toward knowledge, even as that category becomes troubled. The abiding relevance of Todorov's description of the dual structure of classic detective fiction, driven by the disparity between the veiled story of the crime and the emergent story of the investigation,[1] ensures a predilection for a particular kind of backward-looking teleology: investigation moves forward toward a knowledge that is finally a reconstruction of the criminal past. Even in manifestations that refuse to satisfy this impulse, there remains at least a provisional, if disappointed, nod toward this past-oriented, forward movement toward justice and punishment as ideal forms of juridical closure.[2]

Clues are what propel the investigation, and as Franco Moretti has argued, clues are not *facts* but rhetorical figures representing multiple possibilities of signification in moments of semantic ambiguity that the detective must work to reduce. The task of the detective is to "dispel the entropy, the cultural equiprobability that is produced by and is a relevant aspect of the crime" and "to reinstate the univocal links between signifiers and signifieds."[3] The fact is a stabilized clue that forecloses myriad possibilities of signification in order to ascribe meaning. As such, it is the increment by which the uncertain past can be reclaimed as knowledge and the impetus for narrative movement. Moretti's spin on genre fiction echoed a slightly later but related discussion among historians about the problem of historical representation of what had recently come to seem like an unknowable past after the linguistic turn, as Western high theory pivoted toward culture in the 1990s. Empiricists arguing for dour examinations of primary sources found antagonists in poststructuralists speaking of history as the "work of construction rather than of discovery."[4] The abiding question of historiography became its own possibility, different answers for determining attitudes about facts: empiricists believed plainly in judgments "about the past in which historians agree,"[5] while poststructuralists retorted that historical facts "are always refracted through the mind of the recorder."[6]

Caught in the crosshairs between these problems of genre and historiography, *Memories of Murder* is preoccupied with the way in which detection might model historical inquiry.[7] The symbolically punished policeman with whom we began becomes symptomatic of a larger inversion in the film, which stages the detective story as failed historiography. Facts are hard to come by in *Memories of Murder*; the investigation consists of a series of vigorously pursued trails that ultimately reach dead ends. But though it would seem that the film might wish to bank toward antiempiricism, it does more than worry postmodern Möbius strips. Based on the actual story of what is often described as Korea's first serial killer (who was never caught), the film instead interweaves a criminal narrative with a retrospective meditation on the particular history of postauthoritarian Korea. The period represented in the film is a crucial period in this history, coinciding with the end of Chun Doo-hwan's military dictatorship in 1988. The appearance of violent crimes in the sleepy rural village in which the film is set serves, then, as synecdoche for the vexing emergence of Korean postindustrialism. The years that bracket the film, 1986 and 2003, coincide with Korea's emergence into a globalized economy, a time when crimes against the body politic seem less visible than in an era of dictators and serial killers. The crimes of the state become imbricated with the business of the state. As a somewhat representative figure of that shift, Detective Park transforms from small-town detective to urban businessman over the years, though the film elides the specifics of the transition. As in *Oldboy*, in which the protagonist, Dae-su, is imprisoned for fifteen years, roughly from the end of the authoritarian government until the film's release (1988–2003), *Memories of Murder* paradoxically foregrounds this period, including the IMF Crisis, by skipping over it. Whereas *Oldboy* compresses the period into a split-screen montage, *Memories of Murder* more radically omits the intervening years entirely, jumping from late in 1987 and picking up the story again in 2003. This elision in both films gives historical change the effect of suddenness; it is something we awake to discover, much to our surprise and confusion. And although historical change is stark, any explanation for it remains unavailable as the crime scenes expand, not spatially but temporally. History comes to seem simultaneously immanent and inaccessible, and the theoretical problem of historiography becomes how to recover a material history from the distressingly oblique sensorium that follows in the wake of the IMF Crisis.

Memories of Murder frames this problem as a genre question, beginning provisionally within the clichéd terms of the mystery-thriller. We thus see a familiar clash between a streetwise detective and a scientific technocrat, a clash that just as familiarly resolves into a relationship of mutual respect. There are false leads, chase scenes, young women in danger. Furthermore, any crime procedural enthusiast will immediately recognize the harsh interrogation-room scenes, gruff police chiefs haranguing the detectives for their screwups, tense witness interviews, cordoned-off crime scenes ringed with curious onlookers, and the graveyard humor of grizzled veterans. Nodding even more explicitly to lowbrow generic conventions, the detectives at one point halt a brutal interrogation to watch, with the suspect, a popular television cop show called *Inspector Chief.*

But as we settle into the pleasures of the formula, the film loses interest in its own commitments. As the cycle of murder and subsequent investigation turn increasingly episodic, the film replaces one temporality with another as teleology gives way to serial indeterminacy. The familiar will-to-truth of the detective plot loses its momentum and dissipates, as if to reveal that we were never moving toward an end but rather wandering aimlessly in one of the large rural fields that the film's cinematography captures lovingly in steady, wide-angle gazes. These transformations are definitive but subtle. As the murders pile up, the investigation stalls, and as the events proceed, they seem to repeat rather than progress. Plot gives way to episode with each step on this steady continuum betraying the false promises of suspense.

Too rooted in Korean history for abstract universalizing,[8] *Memories of Murder* is also not a *metaphysical detective story* of the sort that foregrounds abstract philosophical questions through the mental peregrinations of its investigators.[9] Steeped in ambivalence rather than suffering, neither does it seem to fit neatly into the robust tradition of Korean trauma films, as exemplified most powerfully in Lee Chang-dong's *Peppermint Candy* (*Pakha Sat'ang*, 2000), which cites Korea's history of traumatic experiences in colonization, war, and dictatorship.[10] Beyond tweaking the Hollywood crime thriller to suit a Korean context, *Memories of Murder* makes a cleaner break, first enthusiastically embodying and then apathetically jettisoning generic conventions. Bong's film arrived at a moment around the millennium as a series of what might be termed postmodern Hollywood genre films became highly visible in the global marketplace—for example, Quentin Tarantino's *Pulp Fiction* (1994), Bryan Singer's *The Usual Suspects* (1995), and David Lynch's *Mulholland Drive* (2001). But whereas these American films amp up generic conventions until they hyperventilate, *Memories of Murder* casually discards them, shrugging off any obligations for closure and disappointing the built-up anticipatory suspense. In a baiting progression, genre isn't just bent; it's abandoned.[11]

As the film empties out the epistemologies of detection that it initially employed as generic armature, the violent crimes cease to serve as occasions for trauma, strangely functioning instead as objects of nostalgia, not because the murders themselves become somehow retroactively celebrated but because they mark a past in which both investigative detection and historical memory seemed possible. *Memories of Murder* thus registers a broader anxiety about how current events will be processed into historical knowledge, given the attenuated status accorded to the fact, demonstrating the limits of understanding history as a problem of signification. The genre of detective fiction and the historiographic practice it subtends both become understood as epistemological strategies that attend to their objects by dilating on their own representational capacities, which invariably prove insufficient because they obfuscate rather than reflect the violence of which they are presumed to be traces. Both become preoccupied, instead, with the lenses through which they look, but because the objects of their analysis are ultimately inaccessible, we learn that the lenses don't matter.

In this vacuum the film identifies an alternative historiography attentive now to a more expansive sense of the crime and to that which remains unseen, which becomes understood as ontological despite its inaccessibility; the murderer remains invariably *out there* (a young girl has seen him years later), just as the missing years of Korean history remain immanent despite the failure of representational strategies to make them visible. If the revelation that Keyser Soze's (Kevin Spacey) narrative at the end of *The Usual Suspects* is fabricated casts into doubt the ontological status of the film's entire story, then *Memories of Murder*, in contrast, cannot explain away the blunt fact of violence that produces both literal and figurative corpses. History abides despite its unrepresentability. And because the lenses fail, the film invokes other figures of materiality, specifically film apparatuses and institutional forms like bureaucratic records and print media, in order to provide history with a firmer ontological scaffolding.

In signaling such a historical desire, these invocations in the film ultimately lead us to a concrete history, I will suggest, in the form of a history of concrete. A subtle, but persistent leitmotif throughout the film—the first corpse is found, for example, in a concrete irrigation ditch—is its preoccupation with the various sites of REMICON (or ready-mixed concrete) production throughout the town from the rock quarry where raw materials are mined to the factory at which the concrete mixture is produced. In serving as a persistent backdrop for the action of the film and, more to the point, for the crime scenes, these sites link the film's historiographic ambitions at a moment of political upheaval in 1987 to an important economic transformation that persists through the post-IMF period. This attention to concrete parallels the film's broader move away from the preoccupation with a singular culprit, pointing instead continually and in various ways to the historical processes and systematic relations that inflict far more harm than the sociopath in the film who evades capture. As we will see, the film's interest in the history of this industry in Korea has everything to do with its vision of its own medium and of the political economy that extends out of its apparatus.

Kind of Plain, Just Ordinary

In the course of the hospital scene a striking detail registers briefly on the screen. Because Cho has no family, Detective Park (Song Kang-ho) must approve the surgery. As he signs the requisite paperwork, we quickly see on the form that the date is October 20, 1987 (fig. 3), almost a year from the date of the opening scene of the film, October 23, 1986, when the first corpse is discovered in the concrete ditch, and precisely the one-year anniversary of the murder itself. Here, the camera lingers over the detail for a moment in a tight shot of the document. This is a prominent trope in the film, close-ups of documents and newspapers that situate the viewer in the chronological trajectory of the investigation. As the filmic apparatus coincides in this moment with the apparatus of bureaucracy—screen becomes paperwork—we get a fact, marking an important, though

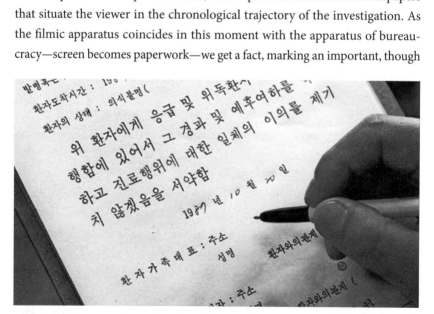

FIGURE 3. The camera lingers briefly over hospital paperwork for Detective Cho's operation in Bong Joon-ho's *Memories of Murder* (CJ Entertainment, 2003).

diegetically unacknowledged, anniversary: precisely a year has passed since the first murder occurred. Admittedly, this is a disappointing fact.

But given the difficulty that the detectives in the film have ascertaining facts, the plain appearance of such a fact as a date is arresting, particularly in the bureaucratic form of a hospital document. In contrast to the rarity of dependable investigative facts in the film, dates are provided with regularity, not only extradiegetically on the screen but also diegetically, particularly through shots of print media. Painfully aware of the public antipathy toward the police in the period (especially in the decade following the notorious Gwangju Uprising in 1980), the police chief is constantly reading about his murder investigation in the Seoul-based *Chosŏn Ilbo*, Korea's oldest and largest newspaper, since the events in this remote rural village have garnered national attention and police activity in general has become scrutinized. In one of the newspaper shots, the camera focuses in on a story that presents the facts of the investigation. At the top edge of the screen, which coincides momentarily with the newspaper page, we clearly see the date with an account of various key, often embarrassing, moments in the investigation there below. Through such shots, and through the customary rehashing of dates in the course of police work, we get a sense of Walter Benjamin's shopworn description of "homogeneous and empty time,"[12] which, as Benedict Anderson's equally familiar account suggests, is most powerfully exemplified in the form of a newspaper.[13] In *Memories of Murder* the fact of time, as presented both in news media and on the bureaucratic hospital document, is ultimately marked not just as indeterminately empty but, more radically, as banal—an artifice that is ultimately insufficient for scaffolding any teleological structure, be it nation or justice.

The film's lack of closure has to do, of course, with the desire to remain true to the original unsolved murders on which the film is based—the so-called Hwaseong serial murders, in which ten women were killed in just under five years—but it is also significant to recall that the main narrative of the film ends late in 1987, significantly choosing not to narrate the ongoing investigation of the subsequent murders, which continued until 1991.[14] In so doing, the film's time frame becomes more neatly linked to the end of Chun Doo-hwan's military dictatorship and the beginnings of democratic globalization. The film thus aligns its folds to the seams of Korean history in the terms Michael Robinson has summarized: "The year 1988 is generally accepted as a watershed between a long period of military intrusion in South Korean politics and a shift toward more open, liberal democratic governance."[15] Instead of following the subsequent murders, the film climaxes (anticlimactically) at the point where the main suspect is proved innocent, a moment that registers the absolute failure of detection, including both Detective Seo's (Kim Sang-kyung) modern scientific method and Detective Park's homespun approach.

We find out in the *dénouement*, set in 2003, when the narrative picks up years after the climactic moments of the investigation, that Detective Park has quit his job and become a juice-maker salesman, living with his family in a modern apartment, perhaps in Seoul, like many formerly rural residents who migrated to Korea's capital and economic center. Crucially, the film has also leaped entirely over a significant period of Korean history, picking up after the fact. We see that Park has adopted a more corporate style of dress, eats sitting at a table with chairs instead of on the floor, and has trouble drawing the attention of his children away from video games and cell phones. On a sales trip, the former detective returns to the countryside and sees the field where the first corpse was discovered back in 1986; he tells the driver to pull over. Wandering wistfully to the old crime scene, he finds a young girl who tells the former detective that she had seen a man not too long before looking into the same concrete irrigation ditch. When the girl had asked this stranger why he was looking, he had told her that he did something there years ago and had come back to take a look. Realizing that this young girl can identify the murderer, the former detective asks what the man looked like, with a cautious glimmer of the old investigative curiosity lighting his face. But the girl disappoints: "Kind of plain," she says, "just ordinary."[16]

In contrast to *Peppermint Candy*, which moves successively backward from the present to the 1980 Gwangju Uprising as the violent origin of the protagonist's trauma, *Memories of Murder* remains unwilling to understand the intervening years between the present and the authoritarian 1980s as part of a trauma narrative that privileges a primal past. As signified by the return to the mise-en-scène of the film's opening, with its oscillations between tight shots of faces and wide shots of landscapes,[17] we have not progressed much from the beginning. Facts have not accumulated, and history remains blank: we still have no satisfactory way to make sense of experience. The former Detective Park pauses for a moment to absorb the information; we see an extreme close-up of his face as he looks directly into the camera before the image fades to black; then the credits roll against a black background for a moment before a final wide shot of the field emerges.

The sequence also reprises the opening shot of the film, which focuses closely on the face of a boy in the field who himself is focusing intently on a small insect perched on his finger. An instance of close looking that contrasts against the wider views of the landscape that we see in this scene, the shot suggests that the open field is not unintelligibly indeterminate but filled with particulars (i.e., grasshoppers). The shot of the inquisitive young boy leads into the scene in which Detective Park examines the first corpse, which he finds hidden in a covered segment of an otherwise open irrigation channel. The enclosed concrete space forms a small dark enclosure about the size, appropriately, of a coffin. The detective leans in to look at the corpse in the narrow, enclosed space and then looks up at the boy, who sits perched on the concrete directly above the corpse. He peers quizzically back at Detective Park. The decomposing corpse as evidence of a brutal crime contrasts with the childish innocence of the boy, unaware of the corpse beneath him. Park barks at some noisy children nearby, and the boy begins to parrot everything he says, even mimicking Park's facial expressions, in a typically Bongian comedic moment that unexpectedly redirects the emotional energies of the tragedy at hand.[18] The scene ends with a shot of the vast open field as the opening credits appear, in a similar manner as the film's closing credits, which also roll against the backdrop of the field.

But whereas the opening scene is a study in contrasts—between the enclosure of the irrigation ditch and the vastness of the field, between the harsh temporal finitude of the corpse and the spatial infinity of the horizon, and between the innocence of the unaware child perched directly over the corpse and the criminal perversity required for such a brutal rape and murder—the final scene lacks what Fredric Jameson has described as "comparatist perception."[19] If the opening scene turned on a series of oppositions, the final scene depicts Park as a solitary, confused, and distressed figure, standing alone in discomfort with the knowledge given to him by the young girl, who, unlike the young boy in the opening scenes, does not serve as a contrasting figure. This final scene thus expresses Jameson's sense of unnoticed dispossession, as though the consequence of never arriving at narrative and juridical closure and of breaching the genre has prevented the recent past from becoming recorded as history.[20] The wide-open fields function here as repositories for the unsettled anxiety left behind by the failure of detection in the film.

Indeterminacy, however, is an unsatisfying conclusion for a story that begins with a corpse. In the final scene Park gazes at a would-be object of nostalgia, the wide-open rural space that earlier signified a premodern way of life, but here it is bereft of these associations. In gazing at the open field, Park is not nostalgic for a time and place; rather, following his interaction with the young girl, he is reflecting on the past, on the murder investigations, and on a life that he no longer lives. It is crucial to note in this context that the particular form of memory that the film's Korean title signifies, *chuŏk*, implies nostalgic fondness. But if nostalgia replaces detection and investigation as a kind of compensatory mode of looking at the past, it is an unusual form of nostalgia, one for violent death. Park's gazing on the open field might then be described as a scene of *chuŏk* in this sense; he is nostalgic for murder. As a moment of awakening and coming to consciousness, the complex operation is one that holds the fondness of nostalgic remembrance in tension with horrific violence. It is a nostalgia that is incapable of ambivalence toward its object.

In contrast to Derrida's account of nostalgia as a kind of compulsive home-sickness,[21] the film posits nostalgia (for murder, for violence) as an alternative mode of attention. If globalization has ushered in an amnesiac regime, then nostalgia has become a strategy for attending to what is unrecoverable from the past. Furthermore, affixing murder as the object of nostalgia seems to mitigate the ambivalence toward the object at the heart of nostalgia. In a discussion of Wong Kar-wai's *Happy Together* (1997), Rey Chow articulates nostalgia in similar terms, as "not simply a hankering after a specific historical past" but rather "a condition that can never be fully attained but which is therefore always desired and pursued."[22] Focusing more on emotional convergences between people, what it means to be happy together, Chow's specific context is different, but the nostalgic imperative she describes—"pursuit of what is ultimately unreachable"—is the same. This is a nostalgia not for murder itself, not for a return to violence or even for a time and place, but for the kind of attention that murder demands.

Pressing the Police

Further pursuing its interest in historiographic inquiry, *Memories of Murder* offers a concrete figuration of this nostalgia's imperative in its depiction of the press in the film. Significantly, the period of these murder investigations was also a time when the state's tight grip on the press during the Chun Doo-hwan administration finally loosened under the pressure of antiauthoritarian student protests. As John Kie-chiang Oh has suggested, "the scale and nature of demonstrations in the summer of 1987," a period that coincides with the height of the investigation in the film, "were unprecedented."[23] In fact, *Memories of Murder* might be understood as a canny treatment of the central driving tension behind these sweeping changes, the opposition of student groups to police brutality in particular. Detective Cho's amputation is a clear commentary on the issue of police brutality, but the film registers this issue more subtly elsewhere. A riot erupts at one point, for example, and policemen, led by Cho and his vicious right foot, suppress the crowd. At another point we hear a brief news broadcast on a television in a restaurant about the trial of Mun Kang-je, a policeman charged in Incheon for torture and sexual assault, before Cho throws a bottle through the screen and starts a fight with the patrons of the restaurant, who were disparaging Mun and the police in general. Finally, the conflict between the police and the primary suspect of the film—a boyish man with soft hands who attended a four-year university (a crucial point of class distinction)—reflects the kind of conflicts that were erupting between police and prodemocracy student demonstrators all around the country.

Press freedom in this period, in some ways, can be understood in direct relationship to the police, as the force that checks this arm (or foot) of state power through an investigative method ironically borrowed from the very institution it monitors. In this narrative of failed detection, the investigative function seems to pass from police to press, as does its relationship to social justice. Skepticism about the police has made them the object of discipline and no longer its purveyors. Although the film does not narrate Detective Seo's inspiration for coming to the small rural town as a volunteer for the investigation (he is not assigned), it is likely that he is motivated by stories that publicized these rural crimes to urban audiences in the press. Korean newspapers in this period were, in fact, given the right to place correspondents in rural areas, and the kind of press coverage that the film depicts in this murder case would have been less likely before these newly accorded press liberties. Although he is a police officer himself, Seo also represents, by virtue of his very presence in the countryside, the power of the press in the public imagination in this period. Of course, the global media in the age of deregulation is often appropriately regarded as a conspiratorial force with movements of late capitalism, and it is quite easy to dump the representations of the news in the film onto the scrap heap of postmodern amnesia. To be sure, the press in postwar Korea is notorious for its (often coerced) complicity with the state and *chaebŏl* power,[24] but at this historical moment, and in relation to the police, it figures differently, as part of an era marked by an emergent freedom, which allows, if only temporarily, the checking of state power.

It is worthwhile at this point to review the dates presented in the film. Cho's hospital visit occurs on October 20, 1987, which is itself the precise one-year anniversary of the first murder. The FBI lab report that Detectives Park and Seo receive in the climax of the film shows that the request for tests was sent a day after Cho's surgery, on October 21, 1987. This is the scene in which Seo, on learning that the latest victim is a young girl that he had met through the course of the investigation, loses his patience and sheds his commitment to scientific method (as well as any concern for habeas corpus), dragging the main suspect forcefully from his home to a remote railroad tunnel where he plans to mete out justice. Before Seo can finish the job, Park arrives with the paperwork from America that contains the results of DNA tests, which the detectives had earlier requested because the technology did not yet exist in Korea. Confident that it will confirm his suspicions, Seo tears open the envelope and examines the document. We see a close-up of the document over Seo's shoulder, and we catch a glimpse of the date on which the request was sent to the laboratory.

Although the date of the climax is not explicitly given, one might fairly estimate—factoring in bureaucratic delay, international mail time, and rural postal service—that this FBI document arrives to the Korean countryside around a week or so after the original request was sent. Let us approximate that the climactic scene of the film takes place on or about October 29, 1987. (I am, of course, taking liberties here but not too drastically.) This date is also an auspicious one in modern South Korean history, the date on which the government's Constitution was officially and extensively amended to provide for democratic reforms and to limit the power of the military in national government. Though the official end of the Chun Doo-hwan administration came later, the constitutional amendment provided the legal grounds for this profound transformation. In other words the climax of the film coincides almost precisely with a fundamentally transformative, though not often commemorated, moment in national history, the specifically *bureaucratic* end of the authoritarian regime. The unlikely spectacle of dramatic paperwork in the film's climax reflects, then, another document drama simultaneously occurring in governmental chambers. Although the filmic moment is one of tragedy and confusion, depicting the ultimate failure of the investigation, the simultaneous historical moment is one of optimism.

One of the most crucial elements of this constitutional amendment was article 21, paragraph 2, which guaranteed both a free press and the right to free assembly.[25] While it is fair to point out that corruption along with the forces of global capitalism foreclosed on any reasons for optimism for the press fairly soon after this period, the film nevertheless finds something worthwhile to preserve. Bits and pieces of the news media and its documentary possibilities are quietly omnipresent; police events are always accompanied by their representation in the press, often to the frustration of the police. Of course, the press in 1987 from the perspective of the present no longer signifies an unqualified optimism. As represented in the Showbox thriller *Inside Men* (*Naebujadŭl*, 2015), the Korean media in the intervening period, as well as the global media in general—losing much of its autonomy from moneyed interests in the frenzy of deregulation and corporate consolidation in subsequent years—has done much to disappoint those heady days of enthusiasm.

But rather than attempting to recuperate the press itself as a mechanism for restoring some sense of historicity, *Memories of Murder* preserves not its institutions but its function, claiming this capacity, not for newspapers or for journalism in general but for its own medium. In this respect one might draw a parallel between the policies of the 1980s that ushered in a new era of press freedom and the confluence of governmental policies and material conditions in the late 1990s and early 2000s that relaxed censorship and gave creative film-makers opportunities to explore their craft with relatively little interference. *Memories of Murder*, of course, was made in this context. One characteristic of this moment in Korean cinema is the ability of serious, challenging cinematic art to appeal to a broader public and to achieve commercial success.[26] This was made possible by a combination of factors, including the easing of governmental oversight of content combined with increased government financial support, the withdrawal of *chaebŏl* interest from the film industry due in part to the IMF Crisis, and the emergence of venture capitalists that were less intrusive in film-making itself and more conducive to artistic freedom.[27] Like the reemergent press with respect to the end of the authoritarian government in the late 1980s, the renaissance of Korean film at the millennium is both a response to and product of crisis conditions.

A brief scene in the film suggests this parallel between newspaper journalism and film in ontological terms. After the early blunders in the investigation the police chief reads in the *Chosŏn Ilbo* about the changes made to the investigative team. We see a close-up of the newspaper, which he is reading while walking (fig. 4). The chief turns the page by slapping the paper shut, shifting one page from the right to left hand, and then reopening it. This is, of course, a fairly standard way of turning

FIGURE 4. A sequence of shots shows the police chief reading the newspaper in *Memories of Murder* (CJ Entertainment, 2003).

large newspaper pages, especially if one is standing. But at precisely the moment when the page turns, there is an odd, arguably unnecessary cut to the next shot.[28] That is, instead of holding the camera steadily on the paper while the chief turns one page to reveal the next one, there is an extraneous cut that divides the shot into two discrete parts, as if to suggest a material equivalence between the newspaper's page as a unit of information and a spliced segment of film. The second shot, after the cut, is, in fact, reframed to magnify the effect. Although the sequence depicts a continuous moment, the cutting of the scene suggests the discontinuities of montage. In addition, in the upper right-hand corner of the shot we see the steady blur of a train passing by, its continuous movement and distinct whirring sound reminiscent of a film projector. Furthering the connection, the next shot shows the chief, still reading the paper, from the other side of the passing train, rehashing the historical intimacy that cinema has enjoyed with railroad technology since its inception.[29] We see the chief flicker in between the passing wheels, another image that is suggestive of the mechanisms of film projection and of zoetropes, which are often cited as a protofilmic technology.

Finally, at the end of this succession of progressively wider shots, we see the chief walking through precisely the same street scene depicted in the newspaper image in the second shot of the sequence, with the town's concrete factory in the background (fig. 5). This final shot of the sequence thus depicts the chief inhabiting the same image in filmic space that we have just seen in print. We see

FIGURE 5. Shot of the police chief reading about the investigation in the newspaper alongside a shot of the chief walking through the same scene that is depicted in the newspaper photograph in *Memories of Murder* (CJ Entertainment, 2003).

another version of this cross-medial self-reflexivity also in the previous image, in the first newspaper shot in the sequence of the scarecrow figure that serves as a memorial and warning of one of the early murders. This is an iconic image in the film and one that appears on at least one version of the cover for its US DVD release. At the very moment that the audience is invited to view the print media at work in monitoring the actions of the police, we are also presented with an imaginary conflation of film and newspapers, as if the two media were somehow fundamentally alike, not just in social function but also in the ontology of their apparatus. And though this connection is suggested as a formal similarity, it implicitly extends to their political function as well. This medium self-consciousness, which positions film in relationship to news media, extends to the latter's capacity, however short-lived, for social critique.

As much focused on the historical period it leaves blank as the one it explicitly depicts, *Memories of Murder* thus positions cinema in relation to late capitalism as similar to the position of the press toward military dictatorship in the period it chronicles. In both cases, although it is the government that relaxes the strictures under which these enterprises operate, motivated by public pressure, the Korean press in the 1980s and Korean film at the turn of the twenty-first century appropriate the power to check the very institutions that granted it opportunity in the first place. But if film can perform the same function that the press provided in the late 1980s, it can also suffer the same fate. The film thus refrains from any triumphalism: the investigation remains a failure in 2003, just as it was in 1987. Instead, it is preoccupied with specifically the material apparatus of film and journalism, which it links not just in their respective institutional histories but in their ontology, both of which in turn find correlates with bureaucratic apparatuses. And although it remains inaccessible in the film, such gestures function to circumscribe an ontological archive in which history persists despite the failure of our attempts to ascertain its content.

The Concrete Present

Memories of Murder takes the occasion of the police procedural to shift historiographic methodology, from one focused on hermeneutic codes toward concrete materialism, and it literalizes this turn by foregrounding the history of Korean concrete production as a figure for broader political economic shifts. The argument here overlaps with Timothy Bewes's critique of Fredric Jameson's cultural turn: "The domain of culture, in Jameson's thought, does not merely foreshadow the Messianic new world; it replaces it. . . . Marxism, in Jameson, is hereby reinvented as pure method."[30] *Pure method* for Bewes inheres in the relegation of revolutionary thought to the realm of culture and the substitution of social struggle with textual hermeneutics. The pull away from clue-semiotics in the film and its concomitant effort to recover alternative sites of ontology outside of the investigative genre paradigm adheres to the Lukácsian logic Bewes favors, which wrests historical materialism from linguistic-turn preoccupations. In his own methodological claim-staking essay, writing contra the critique of *symptomatic reading* that Stephen Best and Sharon Marcus outline in defense of *surface reading*,[31] Bewes offers an account of *reading with the grain*. An alternative to the Jamesonian political unconscious—regarded here as "a hermeneutic structure, denoting an economy of presence and absence"[32]—Bewes suggests a reading practice via Benjamin that seeks out "that which in the work is 'seared' by reality, by moments of 'intentionlessness,' what in photography Benjamin calls the 'optical unconscious.'" Bewes continues that such a practice is only possible with a practice that inquires "not simply of the text as encountered material object, but of the event of its production *inseparably from* the event of its reading, a reading with an eye to *the reading that the text itself makes possible*."[33]

Bewes's methodological gambit echoes not only Benjamin's account of photography but the oft-quoted passage from the second version of "The Work of Art in the Age of Its Technological Reproducibility" about film's pedagogical capacities: "*The function of film is to train human beings in the apperception and reactions needed to deal with a vast apparatus whose role in their lives is expanding almost daily.* Dealing with this apparatus also teaches them that technology will release them from their enslavement to the powers of the apparatus only when humanity's whole constitution has adapted itself to the new productive forces which the second technology has set free."[34] These lines sum up what the essay itself takes pains to track, that is, the complicated ways in which history becomes manifest in film via the apparatus of its production, as well as the need to think of film as one of numerous apparatuses that index the productive forces that constitute them in a variety of manners. We remember the loss of aura as a thesis statement, but perhaps at the expense of the essay's quite lengthy taxonomy of film's social ontology, the various sites of intentionlessness seared into the medium: for example, film's production of exhibitional value and diminishment of ritual value, its demand for acting oriented toward the image rather than the character, the wide accessibility of its means of reproduction, and its deepening of human apperception. These and other qualities are presented in illustrative comparisons with other media and discursive traditions that also detail their various tensions and overlaps with film: theater, painting, magic, surgery, photography, architecture, and psychoanalysis. Through this comparative taxonomy of symptomatic forms, Benjamin supplements the pedagogical vision of film in the quoted passage above, suggesting that the apparatus before the audience trains them to sense the adjacencies of larger, more nefarious systems, not because they are metaphoric substitutes but because they are materially determined by the same conditions. He is of course writing during the crisis of fascism's horrific ascension in Europe in the 1930s, and, significantly, the filmic apparatus is not merely analogical to the rapidly expanding vast apparatus that enslaves but, rather, derives from precisely the same overlapping material conditions that produce it and are thus seared into it.

Miriam Hansen describes these sections not as taxonomic but as "arranged to suggest alternating camera setups or, to use Benjamin's words, a 'sequence of positional views.'"[35] Following this logic, Benjamin's essay foregrounds relations established between different apparatuses and different media. For Benjamin, film makes political economic apparatuses visible because they are not analogical but adjacent. Filmic apparatuses train us to seek freedom from "enslavement," not by offering a definitive archetype of systemic oppression that transfers from one apparatus to the other but by teaching us to notice and adapt "to the new productive forces" that an engagement with technology helps us appreciate. Hansen describes the effect as a triangulation: "By placing film at the intersection of three different trajectories—the fate of art and the aesthetic under industrial capitalism; technology and sense perception; mass politics—the essay constructs the significance of film in terms of the logics of each of these trajectories and makes it the locus and medium in which they intersect."[36] Benjamin's method, then, relies on triangulation to strengthen corroborating evidence; strong correlation closes the gap to cause.

Following in this Benjaminian mode as characterized by Hansen, *Memories of Murder* reorients the decoder of genre toward apparatus for a historiographic purpose. The resulting orientation toward historical ontology follows, then, not from any homology between apparatuses but through a series of material triangulations or the "intersection of three different trajectories" in Hansen's terms—most significantly in this case film, journalism, and bureaucracy—which reproduce the kind of relations that inhere in Benjamin's remediating logics. One version of these triangulations—film, photography, and crime—comes together in a scene early on in the investigation when Detective Seo puts in a late night at the police station. The lights have been turned off because of an air-raid drill; we hear a siren in the background and a voice on a loudspeaker that barks out procedural instructions. Holding a flashlight that here invokes film projection, Seo exhibits fidelity to his catchphrase throughout the film, that "documents never lie," flipping through a series of documents pertaining to the case. In one sequence he flips through a series of similar photographs depicting the murder victims. Not unlike a flip book, the series of stills is suggestive of the individual static images that make up a strip of film, another invocation of the filmic apparatus that we can now place alongside previously discussed invocations of protofilmic technologies in *Memories of Murder*.[37] Although Seo proceeds to examine each image and document with care and deliberation, he is ultimately unable to make sense of the clues. His flipping through the images and documents, however, by rehearsing in miniature the realization of early motion picture experimentation into more advanced film technologies, imagines a synthesis between archival and filmic modes, as if the filmstrip with its sequence of frames were becoming the place where these bits of evidence might be stored. Eventually his eyelids begin to get heavy, and he nods off for an instant. Rather than resolving into coherence in Todorovian fashion through the synthesizing figure of a genius detective, the fragments of this investigative archive hold a kind of ontological value that persists in the machine itself, finding its most robust formulation in cinematic apparatus. The value of this material archive persists independently of Seo's witness as he falls asleep, as if the machine-cum-archive could run on its own.

Although Seo examines a kind of archive imagined in relation to the history of filmic apparatus, the scene places less emphasis on the unavailable answers and more on the careful attention implied by the archive and medium, not the sleepy detective. In turn, the apparatus of attention becomes the focal point of this scene, offered against the background of the wailing siren of the evacuation drill proceeding on the street below, which situates the apparatus in a specific historical context. Neither Seo's fidelity to scientific professionalism nor Park's shamanistic approach is ultimately effective, but effectiveness seems finally less important than the archival apparatus that accumulates around them. In the absence of reliable historical memory, we are left not with Derrida's archive fever, a "compulsive, repetitive and nostalgic desire . . . to return to the origin, a homesickness,"[38] but rather nostalgia for murder that is immanent but unrevealed.

The scene seems to give form to Benjamin's photographic optical unconscious, fantasmatically isolating that which, to lean on Miriam Hansen's formulation, was "encrypted into the image that nobody was aware of at the time of exposure."[39] Thus, against modernity's deleterious effect on human temporal experience, film holds the potential to archive, in Mary Ann Doane's terms, "a 'lost' experience of time as presence, time as immersion."[40] Inseparable from the broader modern project of rationalizing contingency, the historical value of film for Doane, as it is for *Memories of Murder*, inheres in its particular openness to historical contingency.[41] The film thus produces a similar effect as Eugène Atget's photographs of deserted Paris streets, which Benjamin describes, apropos of the current context, as if they were "scenes of crime." Benjamin's assessment of Atget seems, indeed, to fit *Memories of Murder*, serving as "standard evidence for historical occurrences, and acquire[ing] a hidden political significance. They demand a specific kind of approach; free-floating contemplation is not appropriate to them. They stir the viewer; he feels challenged by them in a new way."[42] For Benjamin, Atget's photographs hold an evidentiary rather than representational logic. Though adjudication of guilt remains impossible from what is visible, something has happened here, even if we don't know what it was. The film, of course, contains many crime scenes of its own, littered as it is with ruthlessly discarded corpses—not just those of the murderer in the film's diegesis but also those of Korean compressed capitalism. And like Atget's photographs, they contain an imperative for historical inquiry, even though they may lack the necessary information to act on it. *Memories of Murder* thus claims for film a privileged view of the post–IMF Crisis moment, just as print media took on that role in the late 1980s toward the postauthoritarian moment. The film thus attempts to archive *presence* as a fundamental feature of a historiographic methodology suitable for a historical moment, like the post-IMF period in Korea, when familiar epistemologies fail, but crisis conditions demand more than aesthetic satisfactions. It attempts what Miriam Hansen describes as "the apprehension of cinema's place in a materialist phenomenology of the present."[43]

The dynamic Hansen observes operates in the film in more concrete terms, specifically in its subtle but persistent foregrounding of literal concrete production, and even more specifically in its REMICON, or ready-mixed concrete. The film's central suspect is an employee at the town's concrete factory, which produces REMICON, as are many of the characters in the film. We see the factory in the background, including in the previously discussed sequence of the police chief reading the newspaper at the train crossing, and up close in establishing shots throughout the film, including a fairly extended shot of a concrete mixer before we meet the primary suspect of the investigation. One of the murders occurs, in fact, in the shadows of the REMICON factory, as Seo explicitly points out in his analysis of the crime scene, and we later return to this same site following yet another employee of the concrete company who, aroused by their sexual nature, returns to the scene of the crime to masturbate. When the detectives run after this man, furthermore, thinking that he may be the killer, the man leads them on a long chase from the REMICON factory all the way to the quarry where the raw materials for the concrete are extracted from the earth.

If 1987 was a crucial year in the political history of Korea, it also marked an important turn in its concrete history, one that signaled a larger transformation in Korean political economy. Concrete had been an important export up through the early 1980s. Its industrial precursor, cement-making, had been an important stepping stone since the 1960s for Korean heavy industries toward more complicated and profitable economic pursuits.[44] But by the period depicted in the film, concrete production was intended for the domestic construction boom in the late 1980s, which witnessed the massive construction of new infrastructure (bridges, highways, etc.) and new apartment buildings like the one Park lives in with his family at the end of *Memories of Murder*,[45] many of which forced local residents out of their longtime homes. We see the costs of this new housing boom in the 1988 independent documentary *Sanggyedong Olympic*, which depicts the life of the residents of a neighborhood in Gangnam that was cleared to make way for the infrastructure for the 1988 Olympic games in Seoul, an event that often marks the end of an authoritarian regime and the beginning of Korea's rise as a global economic power. It also displaced seven hundred thousand people from their homes.[46] Nominally directed by the legendary independent filmmaker Kim Dong-won, the film was actually equally made by the displaced residents themselves, who were given video cameras to document what was happening to them. Though they resisted leaving, they were coerced by thugs hired by government officials and business interests and then further harassed when they attempted to settle elsewhere.[47]

As the detectives chase the man into the quarry, we see them run under a banner that encourages the workers to work more efficiently in the name of a national construction effort (fig. 6). The banner cites the Korean Ministry of Construction, a government program from the early 1960s that had promoted national construction efforts, but in the time frame of the film, such citations of nationalist programs were not so much references to explicit state programs but more general invocations of developmental nationalism. The banner the detectives run under is thus one that marks the very transition the concrete industry was undergoing in the period, moving from a logic of industrial developmentalism to one that was linked to the rent-seeking ventures of the upcoming real estate boom. To be sure, concrete production is certainly an industrial activity, but its turn toward a domestic focus in the late 1980s indexes the first step in a larger transition of Korean political economy.

FIGURE 6. Ministry of Construction banner at the town's concrete mine in *Memories of Murder* (CJ Entertainment, 2003).

Concrete and film are thus not just analogues of one another; the parallels be-tween them arise because both are produced within the same material conditions, as was the case for adjacent apparatuses for Benjamin. Following a triangulating pattern, both manifest the trailing edges of deindustrialization in a transitional economy that encompasses older developmentalism while simultaneously giving way to the postindustrial orientation of the FIRE industries (Finance, Insurance, Real Estate). From the unnamed serial killer to Chun Doo-hwan to real estate speculators, the progression of criminals becomes more inchoate and thus even more elusive, not just because we can't figure out the killer's identity, as is the case in the film, but also because they become increasingly a part of a systemic, and now not merely serial, problem in which criminal agency becomes diffuse. The film's focus on 1987 and 2003 thus complicates the familiar bildungsroman of Korean democracy in all of its triumphalism with a less salutary story about its deindustrialization. Ultimately, then, the conceit of the unsolved murders in *Memories of Murder* allows for a more expansive version of what constitutes crime, one in which the killers remain concealed while the victims proliferate.

Company Men

Salarymen and Corporate Gangsters
in *Oldboy* and *A Bittersweet Life*

In a moment of repose near the end of *Oldboy* (*Oldŭboi*, 2003) after all the violence, Oh Dae-su (Choi Min-sik) seeks the help of a hypnotist to forget the recently acquired knowledge that his new lover is actually his long-lost daughter. When the hypnotist instructs Dae-su to imagine himself back in the room where the film's bloody climax had just wrapped up, the film explicitly depicts the content of Dae-su's semiconscious imaginings as the hypnotist's voice leads him to the window: "When I ring my bell, you will be split into two persons." We hear the bell, the room goes dark, and we see Dae-su's reflection in the window. "The one who doesn't know the secret is Oh Dae-su," she continues; "the one who keeps the secret is the monster."[1] As part of her method, she directs the monster to walk away and die. The Dae-su that remains, however, the one who does not know the secret, is surprisingly not the embodied figure that occupies the physical space of the apartment, as we might expect, but the blurry reflection in the glass, a dim, degraded image of Dae-su's face that abides as residuum despite the departure of its embodied referent (fig. 7).

Oldboy explicitly references the Korean IMF Crisis in the late 1990s as the historical background for this emptied-out figure when we see government officials signing the bailout agreement in a neatly edited montage during the incarceration scene, a montage that compresses the highlights of a larger story about Korean global capitalism into a few minutes of screen time. Comprising the years that he was forcibly removed from Korean history, and the same years that *Memories of Murder* omits entirely, Dae-su's incarceration calls attention to the dramatic effect of the period by leaving it absent. But unlike the deliberate vagueness of *Memories of Murder*, *Oldboy* focuses on a specific and iconic figure of the post-IMF moment that functioned as synecdoche for crisis victims writ large, the salaryman. If the most immediate changes brought on by the crisis and bailout restructuring were massive corporate layoffs, then the salaryman was

FIGURE 7. Dae-su's reflection in *Oldboy* (Show East, 2003).

the most conspicuous figure in this drama, not least because of the frightening rise in suicides among the demographic, most famously accomplished by jumping off the bridges crossing the Han River in Seoul. *Oldboy* thus begins with a scene of Dae-su at the police station, dressed in the familiar corporate garb of those of his group and drunk from the kind of stress-release drinking typical of salarymen. It is no coincidence, furthermore, that immediately on his release, Dae-su (only temporarily) saves a man in a business suit who is about to jump off a building. This displacement from Dae-su to the stranger on the building reflects *Oldboy*'s larger move from a focus on a specific figure to the situation that determines it. While it is tempting to think of the monster that walks away from Dae-su as his job, *Oldboy* presents his situation more abstractly. Although it resembles the relationship between the salaryman protagonist and his CEO antagonist, the perverse relationship between Woo-jin and Dae-su invokes this scene of literal employment under the larger rubric of the power dynamic implicit in the credit relationship that epitomizes the changing economic conditions of the period—particularly in cases of overwhelming indebtedness—at the level of both interpersonal and interstate relations. The salaryman in this systemic schema becomes, more than a sympathetic victim, a pivotal discursive site that indexes a larger problem in the wake of the IMF Crisis.

Illustrating the plight of such men in a short story originally published in 2005 called "The Salaryman," Krys Lee employs a kind of second-person naturalism to universalize the protagonist's broader milieu in a manner that echoes *Oldboy*'s abstraction away from literalism. She describes the situation: "Just last month, after his company released him, an acquaintance of yours drowned off Seongsu Bridge in the Han River. The truth of his suicide was muzzled so his wife and children could subsist on the life insurance money. Nightly the nine o'clock news parades such stories. These clips, rare to Korea before the 1997 IMF Crisis destroyed the job-for-life policy, are suddenly so ordinary that when you attended your acquaintance's funeral, your mourning felt like forgery."[2] Following the formula, two pages later, the protagonist is laid off. After a few more pages he loses hope in the meager prospects offered at the local employment center and falls into a despairing life of homeless struggle at Seoul Station, an iconic site for IMF-crisis suffering. And though the story ends before the protagonist suffers the same fate as that of his acquaintance, his fate seems clear. For Lee as for *Oldboy*, the salaryman is a quintessential victim of the IMF Crisis, and a figure that occasions thought about broader social patterns.

Taking up this diagnostic invitation, the trope of the residual reflection seen at the end of *Oldboy* reemerges almost immediately in Korean IMF Cinema to index what comes to seem a parallel labor situation in specifically *kkangp'ae* (gangster) films, most notably just two years after the release of *Oldboy* in Kim Jee-woon's *A Bittersweet Life* (*Talk'omhan insaeng*, 2005). In Korean, such criminal organizations and the men who work for them are usually called *geondal* or *jopok*, while the term *kkangp'ae* refers more to street hoodlums and their gangs. I have chosen the term "*kkangp'ae* film" to highlight a central characteristic of many of these narratives: the aspiration of the lowly protagonist for something like corporate rising. Although the *kkangp'ae* is a thug at the bottom rung of the ladder, these narratives tend to focus on the few who are able to rise above grunt work and humble origins by joining the managerial class. To venture a generalization, pre-IMF *kkangp'ae* films, particularly those interested in criminal organizations, tend to focus on class mobility in general (as in Lee Chang-dong's 1997 film *Green Fish*), while post-IMF *kkangp'ae* films tend to locate this mobility specifically within a structure modeled on large businesses (as in Yoo Ha's 2006 film, *Dirty Carnival*).[3] A shift in degree rather than kind, elevating one's class position becomes subsumed within the problem of climbing the corporate ladder. Such a ladder is rendered somewhat literally, for example, in the 2015 Korean television drama *Last* (*Laseuteu*), in which the top members of a criminal organization are actually numerically ranked and governed, accordingly, by a rigid hierarchy that allows for challenges up and down the rankings. In similar fashion, post-IMF *kkangp'ae* films interrogate corporate work by locating it in something that is like, but not quite, a corporation, in which the *kkangp'ae* figure, like Dae-su, resembles, but is not quite identical to, the salaryman. In

Jang Sun-woo's classic depiction of the rise and fall of a salaryman in *The Age of Success* (*Sŏnggongsidae*, 1988), the idealized figure of the salaryman abides the protagonist's fall. After a meteoric rise in the firm, Kim Bang-chul (Ahn Sung-ki) ultimately fails to live up to the image; crucially, however, the image itself remains valorized when Kim's spot is taken by another upstart. In contrast, in *Oldboy* and *A Bittersweet Life* it is the sustainability of the salaryman as a category that is degraded, a degradation figured by the residual reflection. These are in a sense glass-ceiling narratives (epitomized by residual figures on glass) in which the limit point is not, say, stagnation in middle management but death.

In *A Bittersweet Life* Kim Sun-woo (Lee Byung-hun) is a former *kkangp'ae* now in a high-level position, the duties of which include everything from accounting nightly receipts to managing the club's staff, though he does have to revert to beating up unruly patrons from time to time. Despite the apparent security implied by his favored position in the organization, he is cruelly punished for failing to carry out the murders of the boss's cheating girlfriend and her lover. Upset by this unexpected devaluation of his devoted service, Kim retaliates, and in depicting the ensuing body count, the film reprises not only the revenge narrative of *Oldboy* but also its iconic reflection scene. After Kim's death, the film flashes back to a shot of him looking out the window of the club that he manages before all the trouble began, focusing on the dim reflection in the glass without his actual body in the foreground (fig. 8). The camera eventually switches to a position opposite him now outside the window where we see him shadowboxing (another nod to *Oldboy*) and then finally back to the image in the glass before the credits roll.

FIGURE 8. Sun-woo's reflection in *A Bittersweet Life* (CJ Entertainment, 2005).

This tweak on the residual reflection in *Oldboy*, as reflecting the face of a dead *kkangpʾae* instead of an absent body, becomes increasingly prevalent in subsequent Korean films in this subgenre. A film that depicts the corrupt intimacy between Korean government, journalism, and organized crime, *Inside Men* (*Naebujadeul*, 2015), for example, reproduces this iconic moment a decade later, in fact, with the same actor, Lee Byung-hun, in a similar role. The shot also appears at the end of Im Sang-yoon's *A Company Man* (*Hoesawŏn*, 2012), another film about a criminal organization that is fashioned after a corporate workplace. As in *A Bittersweet Life*, the film flashes back in dénouement, in this case to a moment long ago on the subway, as a young, less-jaded Hyeong-do (So Ji-sub) prepares for a job interview at the company where he will work for the remainder of his life as a hit man. As in *A Bittersweet Life*, the shot is residual in these cases, not because the body is physically absent as it is in *Oldboy* but because it either captures the reflection of a dead man in a flashback occurring immediately after his death or else foreshadows death as an eventuality. Each of these three films specifically depicts dead gangsters who had progressed to management in their respective organizations enough to think of themselves as company men, no longer upstart thugs, having faithfully devoted their service to a criminal firm, which is imagined to function identically to its more legitimate corporate counterparts.

The bloody endings in these films play out the tension that these characters seem to encompass, between violent criminal and diligent salaryman. In so doing these *kkangpʾae* films about the dream of rising toward the impossible ideal of the salaryman help contextualize Dae-su's fall from corporate to criminal world. Indeed, the criminal organization becomes understood as the only place in which the desire for the life of a salaryman can persist in a residual afterlife given the transformations in corporate employment practices brought on by the IMF Crisis.[4] Both *kkangpʾae* films and *Oldboy* idealize and render this life impossible; and the failure of the characters to occupy the position of the salary-man indexes the historical shift in which such possibilities become foreclosed. The residual image at the end of *Oldboy* and reprised in *A Bittersweet Life* thus reflects the salaryman's diminishment and newly felt precarity in a post-IMF era of exploding unemployment.

This chapter will thus focus on these two films in generic relation to the post-IMF *kkangpʾae* film. By rendering *kkangpʾae* as explicit employees within the hierarchy of an explicitly corporate criminal organization, *A Bittersweet Life*'s homage to the *Oldboy* residual shot realizes a tension that is latent in Park

Chan-wook's film. On the one hand, Dae-su's diligent investigation, though compulsory and forced by Woo-jin's insistence, models a specific form of labor, that of the devoted salaryman working for a large corporation, despite the fact that Dae-su is not actually an employee of Woo-jin's company.[5] On the other hand, what we might call Dae-su's *work*, the work of investigation, consists also of a good deal of violence, and thus resembles the kind of duties, more bitter than sweet, that Sun-woo must ultimately revert back to in *A Bittersweet Life* despite newer managerial responsibilities.

Both Dae-su and Sun-woo might be described as performing *irregular* labor (*pijŏnggyujik*). Invoking here the technical sense of irregularity—low-wage, short-term work without benefits—the term becomes important in the post-IMF period, when irregular labor increased sharply in Korea, leaving the promise of lifetime employment, a once defining characteristic of *chaebŏl* work, a legacy of the past. A key element of the IMF's restructuring program was labor flexibility, and the unusual nature of work for both Dae-su and Sun-woo figures the new instability that the implementation of this directive brought to the lives of workers. By 2014, as stated in a Ministry of Employment and Labor report, more than half of the workers employed by *chaebŏl* were considered irregular.[6] The depiction of devoted, if irregular, labor in the space of illegal business in these films thus lays bare what remains only just beneath the surface in Korean corporate culture: fictions of corporate decorum are fantasies because the boss would rather kill than pay.

We should not fail to observe, however, that the residual reflection is also a reification. The salaryman functions to subsume the larger issues of the IMF Crisis into a tidy figure that broaches broader, systemic issues even as it narrows the perspective through which such issues are viewed. Although the salaryman functions as a discursive linchpin for the Korean labor structure in general, the implicit focus of the figure on white-collar male employment occludes a much broader fallout. By drawing our focus toward individual rather than systemic pathologies, it is a figure that simultaneously elides the full reach of the socioeconomic dynamics it encompasses. The chapter will thus conclude with a comparative analysis of Filament Pictures' *Helpless* (*Hwacha*, 2012), in which the conditions of insurmountable debt that occasions a revenge narrative in the previously discussed films produces, instead, a survival story in which the fantasies of agency in the former genre give way to the resignations of the latter.

Requiem for a Salaryman

Historically, the figure of the salaryman was an ideological construct, in which the nesting of labor into nationalism allowed corporate ambition to be understood as patriotic sacrifice, its material rewards notwithstanding. This powerful ideological apparatus was buttressed by corporate life itself at the *chaebŏl*, the massive state-supported conglomerates given tax and market advantages to compete on a global scale,[7] which actively appropriated a Confucian heritage. Controlled by powerful families and passed down from fathers to sons, these *chaebŏl* famously operated on a patriarchal model in which salarymen were promised lifetime employment. Using Hyundai as an illustration and North Korea as an analogy, Bruce Cumings has suggested the extremes to which working for a *chaebŏl* inspired and demanded deep devotion: "The typical Hyundai worker drives a Hyundai car, lives in a Hyundai apartment mortgaged by Hyundai credit, gets health care from a Hyundai hospital, sends his children to school on Hyundai loans or scholarships, and eats his meals at Hyundai cafeterias. . . . In the same way that Kim Il Sung built a Confucian-influenced hereditary family state in North Korea and called it communism, the Korean *chaebŏl* have built large family run hereditary corporate estates in Korea and called it capitalism."[8]

Although this was all largely fantasy, the appropriation of familial and Confucian discourses for the sake of capitalist expansion became a potent cocktail because it placed modernity on a continuum with traditional values, such that fealty to one's job felt like devotion to one's family and country. Modernization became a seamless continuation of the past, not a rupture. This is not to say that all workers bought into this paradigm or that financial considerations were irrelevant, but the discursive fantasy of the *chaebŏl* did idealize work, and this fantasy pertained especially to salarymen, whose relative proximity to the actual families that ran the *chaebŏl* magnified the power of discourse. Carter Eckert has made sense of this ostensibly odd coupling of modernity and tradition, rooting the marriage in late nineteenth-century Korean reformist scholars "steeped in a long neo-Confucian tradition that emphasized communitarian values and were interested in capitalism primarily as a way to augment the wealth and power of the country to save it from imperialist domination."[9] Lacking any tradition that valorizes personal profit and the individual pursuit of wealth (Adam Smith and John Locke), Korean capitalism, Eckert argues, instead stressed the unselfish, "nationalistic orientation" of its enterprise.

Because of this ideological scaffolding, the IMF Crisis was not only an economic catastrophe but an epistemological rupture as well.[10] The massive layoffs represented not only a breakdown of the economy but also a breakdown of corporate paternalism. During the crisis there was a prevailing sense that the *chaebŏl* had overreached and required restraint. But in fact, what seems to have happened as a result of IMF-mandated restructuring might be narrated as a corporate bildungsroman: the *chaebŏl* that survived bankruptcy *grew up* by rationalizing its strategies, ruthlessly cutting inefficiencies (particularly in labor), and becoming more streamlined for global competition. Hyeng-joon Park and Jamie Doucette have demonstrated that, far from being chastened under the rallying cry against cronyism, the *chaebŏl* have grown tremendously in wealth and power since 1997, becoming more smoothly integrated into the flows of transnational global capital.[11] This newly minted transnational flexibility also meant that the *chaebŏl* could continue on without the atavistic burden of nationalist duty. In retrospect, the IMF bailout restructuring demands gave *chaebŏl* cover for their subsequent transformation.

In the opening sequence of *Oldboy*, the inebriated Dae-su is immediately recognizable as one of an army of men put to work for the *chaebŏl*. At the time, the actor who played Dae-su, Choi Min-sik, had made a mark for his role as a laid-off salaryman in *Happy End* (*Haep'i endŭ*, 1999), a film about a man whose wife has an affair with her former lover. The emasculated protagonist figures the pervasive humiliation endured by many former salarymen through a period of unemployment that, for Choi's character, seems to have no end, despite his diligence in trying to find another position. Interestingly, *Oldboy* borrows some key features from the film, including the use of a picture album to narrate the arc of a transgressive sexual affair (extramarital in *Happy End*, incestuous in *Oldboy*). Also, the framing of Dae-su for the murder of his wife echoes the plot device at the end of *Happy End*.

Salarymen like those portrayed by Choi Min-shik were asked to sacrifice, working long hours for the *chaebŏl* and, by extension, for the nation.[12] Befitting such a figure, Dae-su turns to work in response to Woo-jin's manipulative game. Beginning from his imprisonment after the initial period of shock and despair, Dae-su becomes dedicated. He sheds flab from his body, digs through the wall with a chopstick in hopes of escaping, and fills notebook after notebook with earnest confessions. Once freed, he pursues the mystery set before him by Woo-jin with singular determination, not hesitating to torture someone for information or to fight thugs.[13] Apropos of the film's emphasis on displaced figures of labor, the iconic fight scene that takes place when Dae-su returns to the prison facility is memorable for its strange, protracted quality. Nearly three minutes in length with no cuts, the scene moves left to right through a long hallway and thus has a comic strip feel, appropriate given the film's derivation from a Japanese *manga*. The fighting feels more like physical toil than it does in the typically fast, dizzying choreography of Hollywood action films. The scene even contains numerous pauses in the action during which Dae-su doubles over and gasps for air while his adversaries lie writhing on the ground before the fighting resumes. In a promotional interview, Park Chan-wook explained that the shot took two days and seventeen takes, leaving Choi Min-sik exhausted, since it had to be performed in its entirety for each take.[14] In a nation that once boasted the longest workweeks in the world, the fight scene emblematizes Dae-su's salaryman work-centered orientation.

It is no surprise, then, that Woo-jin, the scion of a rich family and a figure of corporate authority in the film, has a heart problem. Although the film leaves the details of his professional life unaddressed, by all appearances he has assumed authority over the family business. He lives in the penthouse of a tall glass building, more like a corporate office than a home, and is followed around by business advisers.[15] So even though Dae-su's career as an actual salaryman ends with his abduction at the beginning of the film, his life from this point on seems nonetheless bound and framed by Woo-jin's authority, which Dae-su ultimately affirms at great personal expense. Indeed, Dae-su's protracted labor at Woo-jin's behest might be read as a cynical rejoinder to the promise of lifetime employment that proved empty after the IMF Crisis. At one point in the climax of the film Dae-su calls out to Woo-jin in remarkable language: "*Ŭrŭshin hoejangnim!*" The subtitles of the film's DVD edition translate the phrase as "Sir! Boss!" The Korean word *hoejang* refers, however, not just to any boss, but usually to the head of a *chaebŏl*, and the suffix *-nim* turns the address into an honorific. Not a form of address often used metaphorically, it might translate more literally as "Awesome Chairman!" Thus, at this crucial point in the film, Dae-su addresses Woo-jin in the very manner that a salaryman would address the chairman of the *chaebŏl*, revealing in stark terms his understanding of their relationship and of the specific type of authority that Woo-jin wields, despite the crucial fact that Woo-jin was never his actual employer.

Oldboy addresses the discursive instability that characterized life in *chaebŏl* employment at this transitional moment, at which workers were motivated, as

Kang Su-dol puts it, "either by appealing to the older kinds of patriotism, or by laying stress on flexible adaptation to 'the times of globalization and information.'"[16] If the *chaebŏl* historically cloaked the demands of profit in the guise of older Confucian practices that foregrounded familial relations, then the film enacts a somber parody of these historical practices in Dae-su's perverse labor, through which he becomes a subordinate character in Woo-jin's family drama. Different in this respect from his counterpart in *A Bittersweet Life*, Dae-su's only indirect relationship to the figure of authority (i.e., he is not a literal employee) redirects emphasis toward his abstract condition in a changing economy rather than in his specific circumstances. Framed in this manner, Dae-su's labor comes to play out a deep-seated anxiety about the efficacy of work and the autonomy of the laborer in the wake of the IMF Crisis. His efforts, however diligent, are already accounted for by Woo-jin's plan.

Punch the Clock

Dae-su's prolonged incarceration as the central framing device of the film gives him the impression of a man out of time upon his release. Repeating tropes of compressed modernity that are common in Korean cinema, he constantly notes differences between the 1980s, when he was abducted, and the postmillennial present of the film.[17] But Woo-jin's directives to Dae-su function to bind Dae-su to the ticking clock: he is given only five days to discover the reason for his incarceration, until July 5, which turns out to be the anniversary of the suicide of Woo-jin's sister (and also the unmentioned anniversary of the first battle of the Korean War in 1950). This paradoxical relationship between the out-of-time, open-ended anachronism, on one hand, and the harsh teleology of suicide, on the other, emerges in a remarkable scene toward the end of the film in which Dae-su finally begins to remember the past incident that was the revenge plot's origin.

In a scene that I've described elsewhere as an *embodied memory*,[18] the film casts the older Dae-su counterfactually as a literal witness to the events as they occur and to his own younger self.[19] Through this device the film depicts Dae-su's remembrance of Soo-ah, Woo-jin's sister. We see a young Dae-su horsing around on a set of playground parallel bars, trying to get the attention of the young woman, who pulls out a book to read. In plain view during an extended medium shot, the book is the trade paperback edition of Karen Kukil's *The Unabridged Journals of Sylvia Plath* (fig. 9), which was not published until 2000. Given that

FIGURE 9. Soo-ah anachronistically reading Karen Kukil's *The Unabridged Journals of Sylvia Plath* (2000) while talking to a younger Dae-su in *Oldboy* (Show East, 2003).

the flashback takes place years before the actual publication of the book, the choice is blatantly anachronistic; the book does not exist at the time Soo-ah is supposed to be reading it. Otherwise quite careful with period details, the film's choice of books seems intentional. This anachronism, however, is balanced against a thematic coherence: the edition of Sylvia Plath's journals proleptically evokes Soo-ah's suicide, which would come not long after the time frame of the flashback, by linking Soo-ah's fate to Plath's death in 1963. Although Dae-su is a walking anachronism, his labor at Woo-jin's behest faces a harsh temporal limit that is linked to the tragic finality of Soo-ah's suicide.

It is ultimately in the context of this temporally inflected domination that we might locate the film's preoccupation with clocks. One of the few items that Woo-jin gives Dae-su on his release is a watch, and the film takes pains to display timepieces of various sorts, including in the opening credits, where the letters that form names rotate like clock mechanisms. Though these appear often in seemingly stray shots, the most prominent example is the film's use of a mechanical flip calendar to count down to Dae-su's deadline, which is, of course, a manifestation of Woo-jin's directive and thus a symbol of his final authority over Dae-su's life. By the end of the film, we learn that Woo-jin is always one step ahead, having anticipated almost every action and accounted for any resistance. Dae-su's release from prison, for example, seems at first like an escape. After fifteen years Dae-su finally breaks through the outer wall of his cell and feels the rain falling outside. But immediately following what seems like an accomplishment, he is suddenly released by his captors without warning or explanation. Crucially, he does not achieve the goal, which is instead bestowed on him as if a gift. This becomes a common pattern throughout the film. Dae-su's sublimated forms of labor (chopstick digging, trauma investigation) are never productive and are always thwarted or anticipated, already accounted for by a power that circumscribes his actions. Although motivated by the desire for revenge against Woo-jin, Dae-su's actions end up affirming Woo-jin's power.

Woo-jin's revenge against Dae-su enacts a revisionist displacement of blame for his sister's suicide to absolve himself, driven by the fantasy that Dae-su's shame might subsume his own. Woo-jin's sister was rumored to have been pregnant with her brother's child, and through Dae-su as a conduit, Woo-jin revises the story in counterfactual terms: "Your rumor grew so out of proportion that Soo-ah being pregnant became a rumor. My sister got sucked into that rumor and began believing it. So her period stopped and her belly began to swell. . . . Your tongue got my sister pregnant. It wasn't Woo-jin's dick. It was Oh Dae-su's tongue." Dae-su's incestuous relationship with his daughter, forced by hypnotic suggestion, is thus intended to double and replace Woo-jin's incestuous relationship with his sister, as if Dae-su's reenactment allowed Woo-jin to forget his own culpability. Dae-su is thus made to suffer for the trauma of a family that is not his own.

At the film's climax, furthermore, Dae-su falls to his knees before Woo-jin, begging that Mido be spared the news that she is his daughter. "I have committed a terrible sin to your sister," he says to Woo-jin, "and I was very wrong to you." For a moment he slips out of character, cursing Woo-jin, but soon resumes supplication. After reverentially calling him *hoejangnim*, Dae-su goes on to humiliate himself: "If you want me to be a dog, I will," while frantically scrambling around on all fours, barking and wagging an imaginary tail. He then licks Woo-jin's shoes while Woo-jin holds a handkerchief in front of his face, trying to contain his laughter. Most important, Dae-su cuts off his own tongue, and it is only after this gesture that Woo-jin finally spares Mido. It is not enough for Dae-su to debase himself; he must also comply with the discourse of the *chaebŏl*, one that revises the past both to control the salaryman and to absolve the *hoejang* of guilt. The sign of supplication also validates Woo-jin's revisionism. Dae-su's tongue becomes the guilty member that gets castrated in order to comply with Woo-jin's version of the facts, and Dae-su becomes a nightingale without a song.

A similar dynamic animates *A Bittersweet Life*, in which the now trusted gangster-manager, Sun-woo, is asked to deal with a personal issue, the matter of the boss's girlfriend, who is having an affair. Instead of killing the couple as the boss had directed, Sun-woo orders them to stop seeing each other and pretends that nothing happened. When the boss learns of his employee's disobedience, the formerly valued employee must be punished, and the boss gives his reasons:

> Years ago, a smart young man was working for me. One day I got him to do a simple job. I guess he thought it was no big deal. He made a mistake. Thinking about it now, it wasn't such a serious mistake. I could have just told him off and let it go. But he was kind of strange. He wouldn't admit it was his fault. He said he didn't do anything wrong. He could have been right. It might have been my fault. But what are families for? If the boss says you're wrong, then you're wrong even if you didn't really do it. Then it's over. Period. But that guy lost his hand. One promising guy's life ended just like that one morning. This time, one hand is not enough.[20]

As in *Oldboy*, the employee is duty-bound to confirm the boss's accounting, even when the boss is at fault. Although the boss seems to be reaching for an older Confucian logic, his reference to family merely implies the dominant contemporary corporate logic in which the hierarchies of work determine truth. Notably, two modalities of temporality animate these comments and echo Woo-jin's account of revenge. The first is teleological, beginning with a misdeed and ending with the employee's admission of guilt (then it's over). The second is recursive. The boss's comments here initially refer not to Sun-woo but to a predecessor. Sun-woo's case only comes at the end of his comments: "This time." Despite Sun-woo's diligence and talents, then, we learn at this moment that even smart young men are eminently replaceable.

A similar account of temporal authority persists in *Oldboy*, in Woo-jin's explanation for his twisted revenge plot. In a narrative in which revenge indeed circulates, it is Woo-jin who orchestrates this proliferation, all the action branching off his own primal scene. The displacement of guilt over his sister's suicide onto Dae-su and the subsequent revenge this displacement requires takes the form of compelling Dae-su to commit incest unwittingly with his own daughter—as if Dae-su were not merely the witness to Woo-jin's taboo relationship with his sister but also the cause. It turns out that, though the arc of revenge seems teleological leading up to the big reveal at the end of the film, the need for revenge requires recursive satisfaction. As he explains to Dae-su: "I've been watching over you for fifteen years. I fared well thanks to you. I wasn't bored or lonely. Seeking revenge is the best cure for someone who got hurt. Give it a try. The loss of fifteen years.

The pain of losing your wife and child, you can forget all this. Once again, revenge is good for your health. But what happens after you've revenged yourself? I bet that hidden pain will probably come back again."

For Woo-jin, revenge is not a cure but a panacea—a deferral rather than a solution. At the end of the film, when Dae-su realizes that his lover is his daughter, and Woo-jin's revenge is complete, the pain returns. After his game is done, Woo-jin steps into the elevator and immediately remembers the scene of his sister's suicide so thoroughly and so viscerally in another embodied memory that he imagines himself returning to the original event, holding out his hand after his then-falling and now-absent sister. The past now emerges forcefully as a flashback into the present. We see this trope, in which the past and present coincide not only psychically but also physically, at a few crucial moments in the film where the line between the present and remembered past dissolves entirely, as does the line between the ontological and the work of memory. On the ride down the elevator, lost in the flashback, he shoots himself.

As is the case for Sun-woo, Dae-su's labor is not measured by accomplishment. He is not credited, for example, for figuring out the mystery of Woo-jin's elaborate plan, just as Sun-woo is given little credit for years of loyalty. Rather, in both cases, it is the labor's *recursion* that matters. In Sun-woo's case loyalty does not accrue but has to be proven endlessly. Furthermore, it is easily replaceable. In Dae-su's case the moment that Woo-jin's revenge is accomplished is the moment in which revenge's capacity to defer pain ceases. Although described by Woo-jin as a *cure*, it is merely a palliative. Decidedly nonproductive, Dae-su's work, as is the case with Sun-woo as well, is ultimately service labor, geared toward the satisfaction of needs in perpetuity.

Service labor and irregular labor are not identical categories, of course, but they are overlapping historical phenomena in Korea, both of which rise significantly after the IMF Crisis. Already high since at least the early 1990s, irregular labor spiked from 27.4 percent of the working population in 2002 to 37 percent in 2004, though it stabilized around 34 percent shortly thereafter, with the absolute number of workers in the category increasing from 3.8 million in 2002 to approximately 6 million in 2011; wage differentials between regular and irregular workers widened significantly in this period, as well.[21] As recently as March of 2017, statistics showed that about a quarter of Korean wage earners were engaged in low-wage work and that the figure had not changed significantly in a decade.[22] Meanwhile, as in many postindustrial Western economies, the service sector grew proportionally in Korea during this period, up to 56 percent of the economy's total value and 65 percent of its employment by 2005.[23] Attentive to this trend in Korean work culture, Storm Pictures Korea released a film in 2017 called *Part-Time Spy* (*Pijŏnggyujing t'ŭksuyowŏn*), in which even the National Security Agency must employ temporary contract workers.

Such numbers constitute the background of the preoccupation in *Oldboy* and *A Bittersweet Life* with the changing nature of labor after the IMF Crisis; and both films are cynical rejoinders to the disappearance of lifetime employment and the rise of temporary, contract work. In this context both films might be regarded as macroeconomic glass-ceiling narratives, in which not an individual but a whole labor class confronts its limit. No longer the archetype of middle-class stability, the salaryman becomes reduced to residuum, and because the figure was once so central to the national capitalist imaginary, the transition is experienced as historical rupture. The final reason that the salaryman bleeds so easily into the realm of the *kkangp'ae* in these films is that both come to be defined by their disposability.

It is no wonder, then, that at the end of *Oldboy* Dae-su seeks the hypnotist to help him forget. The desire, in fact, seems more broadly characteristic of the post-IMF moment. Released in 2003, *Oldboy* follows on the heels of a pair of Korean films that depict the desire to be free of trauma's recursions.[24] Produced on a shoestring budget and featuring the actor who plays Mido (Kang Hye-jung) in *Oldboy*, Moon Seung-wook's *Nabi* (2001) is an independent film that tells the story of Anna Kim (Kim Ho-jung), a Korean woman who has lived most of her life in Germany. She returns to Korea through a tourist agency that specializes in the *oblivion virus*, which allows those that are infected with it to forget their traumatic past. Set in a science fictional, postapocalyptic Seoul, the story follows Anna's search, accompanied by a pregnant tour guide and a taxi driver, an orphan who picks up random passengers in hopes of finding his birth family. She eventually learns that she had already been infected with the oblivion virus years before and that this is not her first such trip to Korea nor her first dealings with the tourist agency. Also released in 2001, *Flower Island* (*Ggot seom*) depicts the journey of three women to an island far from Seoul, where Ok-nam (Seo Ju-hie), the group's de facto leader, knows a woman that can help them forget. The women are strangers to one another, and each is burdened by horrific memories. When they finally arrive on the island, however, the treatment focuses on Yu-jin (Lim Yu-jin), a former opera singer who has lost her voice to cancer, along with her will to live. It is possible that *Oldboy* borrows at least two elements from *Flower Island*. The first is the pair of angel wings that the youngest woman, Hye-na (Kim Hye-na), keeps with her, and which she wears in the film's theatrical poster. Second, in a scene that anticipates the hypnotist's second-person directions to Dae-su in *Oldboy*, Ok-nam's "angel" friend hypnotizes Yu-jin at the end of the film to help her forget her pain. Neither of these films explicitly refers to the IMF Crisis, but both refer to the same despairing sensorium in which forgetting seems the only desirable option.

These films thus contrast the tradition of Korean trauma films in which the past must be confronted and processed. An iconic example is Lee Chang-dong's *Peppermint Candy* (1999), which moves progressively backward from the protagonist's suicide to the origin of his trauma, the 1980 Gwangju massacre, where, in the course of doing his military service, he accidentally kills a student protester.[25] Lee's film is similar in this respect to the related subgenre of amnesia films, like *The Long Kiss Goodnight* (1996), *The Bourne Identity* (2002), and *A Moment to Remember* (*Nae Mŏrisogŭi Chiugae*, 2004), which cast the recovery of a lost past as necessary for psychological well-being, even if the possibility for healing becomes remote. In contrast to such narratives, Dae-su seeks to forget so that he can live unburdened by the knowledge that his lover and his daughter are the same person. The past quite literally walks away and dies, leaving a residual self with literally no knowledge of its painful secrets. The end of the film thus enacts the fantasy that the painful aspects of the past might be simply jettisoned so that one might live free of trauma. The implicit wish at the end of *Oldboy*, as it is in *Nabi* and *Flower Island*, is that forgetting provides the necessary conditions for survival through a Nietzschean reshaping of trauma in a dream of living *unhistorically*.[26]

The logic of this dream is inseparable in these films from the logic of flexible labor. Dae-su is similar to Leonard Shelby (Guy Pearce) in Christopher Nolan's *Memento* (2000), for whom forgetting also seems to promise a new beginning. Both are diminished, out-of-time company men in high-concept plots whose central devices render memory problematic;[27] both also approach their unusual investigations as if they were work. A former insurance fraud investigator, Leonard famously cannot form new memories owing to a condition resulting from a brutal attack in which his wife was murdered. But rather than gaining satisfaction with the realization at the end of the film that his wife's murder has already been solved, Leonard remains committed to his day-to-day puzzles, which become serial rather than teleological. Like Dae-su, he becomes less concerned with repairing traumatic issues and more preoccupied with management strategies for dealing with what now seems irreparable damage. Both thus opt finally for an unheroic persistence within the dream of living unhistorically, following the rhythms of a ticking clock that parses life into manageable increments, forgoing entirely any interest in the roots of the problem, much less the grander scales of history. Early in the film, when he is first imprisoned, we see Dae-su succumbing to gas coming out of the pipes in his cell. From an already subservient kneeling position, he falls off the bed, unconscious. It turns out that this is a gas with a history. As the subsequent voice-over reveals, it is the same type of Valium gas used by Russian soldiers on Chechen terrorists during the siege of the Dubrovka Theater in Moscow by Chechen separatists in 2002. Russian soldiers pumped it in hoping for a bloodless suppression but, tragically, used too much, and the separatists along with approximately 130 hostages died. The idea that history is lodged in a gas that induces the *loss of consciousness* indicates a deeper irony. Rather than seek revenge on the system that has destroyed his life, a resigned Dae-su seeks merely to carve out a modest existence within a new world order, hoping to survive the crash against a glass ceiling that always seems to be lowering.

Mirrored Histories

The abdication of historical consciousness that adheres to this resignation with flexible logics authorizes the kind of revisionism at the heart of Woo-jin's revenge plot; and the authorization of this revisionist impulse is figured in the film by its specific depiction of how mirrors function. In the manner of the emptying out that accompanies the residual images in the film, mirrors and other reflective surfaces in *Oldboy* and *A Bittersweet Life* are troubled sites, marking moments of psychic crisis, as if reflection were both literally and figuratively too painful. In *Oldboy* Dae-su is constantly breaking them, usually just prior to losing consciousness. At a moment before the final climax in *A Bittersweet Life*, Sun-woo peers into a bathroom mirror in dismay, gathering up his resolve in an instant when self-recognition loses its automatic quality. In these scenes, as in the residual shots, priority is given to the reflected image over its referent. A particularly frank example of this occurs toward the end of the film when Dae-su finally confronts Woo-jin face to face in Woo-jin's apartment, through a mirror that mediates their interaction (fig. 10). This is the scene in which Woo-jin offers Dae-su his

FIGURE 10. Woo-jin talking to Dae-su through a mirror just before the film's climax and the same conversation no longer mediated by the mirror in *Oldboy* (Show East, 2003).

revisionist account of his sister's pregnancy, addressing Dae-su not face-to-face but through a mirror while he changes his clothes, which becomes then a figure of mediation through which the past event becomes distorted. We see Woo-jin standing before the mirror, and in the shot we see over his shoulder from behind, his own reflection to the right, and Dae-su's still farther to the right. As Woo-jin's figurative reflection succumbs to revisionist urges in his version of the story, reflection turns into refraction, and historical fidelity disperses.

The visually complex sequence begins as Woo-jin, standing in his underwear, steps in front of the mirror and says, "Looking in the mirror reminds me of that day," referring to the day long ago when Dae-su had witnessed Woo-jin and his sister incestuously engaged, a scene that had involved Soo-ah holding a hand mirror. The camera abruptly zooms, seemingly without cutting, into a tight close-up of the reflection of Dae-su's face, while pivoting slightly to center Dae-su in the frame, in which he appears to be looking directly at the camera. We know that the impossible shot is a trick because a camera directly pointed at a mirror would reflect the camera itself, which we do not see. As their conversation proceeds and as Woo-jin gets dressed, the scene plays with a variety of devices to depict their interaction in such a way as to emphasize further the fact of technical mediation. At one point Woo-jin turns around to face Dae-su, and we see the reflection of his back in the mirror. There are also a few shot/reverse-shot sequences between Woo-jin's face or his body and a tight close-up of Dae-su's face; we can tell that we are no longer looking at a reflection because of the position of Dae-su's head relative to the pictures in the background or from the orientation of the pictures themselves when Woo-jin pulls them off the wall.

There are other cues in these shots that help us discern whether or not we are looking at a reflection—the direction of the buttons on Woo-jin's shirt as he fastens them or the brand name on his belt as he buckles it—but because they come so quickly in succession, we struggle to tell the difference in this shell game that confuses referent and reflection. At one point the camera takes the point of view of the mirror itself, facing Woo-jin and Dae-su, a change that we notice because Dae-su is now standing on the opposite side of Woo-jin. And as Woo-jin leads up to the final revelation about Mido's identity and his complicated machinations to achieve revenge, the editing, appropriately, gets even more complicated, with a series of wipes, bleeds, and split-screens as strategies for assembling past fragments into a coherent narrative. But rather than piercing through the distortion, the formal preoccupation with Dae-su's face in this sequence ultimately seems to engage in the same sort of cover-up that Woo-jin performs in his plot to fashion Dae-su into a scapegoat for his own misdeeds. All of these images or reflections, including the residual shot with which we began this chapter, hide what becomes visible in wider frames, not just the basic diegetic fact of Woo-jin's final culpability but also the more general priority given to corporate interests. The preoccupation with Dae-su's residual image at the end of the film signals, then, not only the diminished agency of the salaryman in the period but also the material priorities given to *chaebŏl* interests, which are manifested in everything from the fundamental transformation of labor in the period to the operation of reflective surfaces, as if the *chaebŏl* power extended all the way from complicit governmental policy to physics itself. Like any good shell game, this one is fixed.

In this context we might note the film's acknowledgment of the radical expansion of ostensibly legitimate business in the period into the realm of criminal activity. If characters like Dae-su and Sun-woo reveal the line between secure salaryman and irregular laborer to be a tenuous one, then these films seem also to suggest that the difference between corporate transaction and illegal transgression may be similarly ambiguous. Indeed, criminal enterprises in *Oldboy* and *A Bittersweet Life*—privately run prisons and weapons dealing respectively—are extensions of more legitimate enterprises. Woo-jin pays for a new facility for the owner in exchange for the role he plays in Woo-jin's plot. The owner of the prison facility not only has an inordinate number of employees but also a clear sense of his business's focus, which the owner reviews for a client over the phone, including free transportation for stays longer than six months and referrals to similar businesses with slightly different specializations. The prison owner, in fact, is played by the same well-known character actor (Oh Dal-su) who plays the gun dealer's lieutenant in *A Bittersweet Life*. His boss in the latter film, the weapons dealer, is on a first-name basis with the other bosses in the film and even takes the time to run through responsible gun assembly with Sun-woo. Sun-woo's boss, despite his criminal past, runs a number of legitimate businesses as well.

The overlap between criminal and legitimate businesses in these films, another form of uncomfortable mirroring, reminds us, in turn, that it is not uncommon for *chaebŏl* executives to resort to *kkangp'ae* muscle. In 2008, CJ Group chairman Lee Jay-hyun, for example, was implicated in a complex blackmailing scandal that involved a contract killer hired by a company accountant.[28] That same year, Hanwha chairman Kim Seung-youn was charged for hiring thugs to avenge the mistreatment of his son by the employees of a bar in Seoul.[29] He received a light sentence and was eventually pardoned, only to be jailed four years later for embezzlement.[30] In this context it is perhaps a natural fit to reach for the figure of the *kkangp'ae*, one of the more historically visible forms of contract labor, as a way of registering the transition from salaryman to irregular worker.

Most pertinently for these films about indebtedness and revenge, arguably the most problematic expansion of traditional businesses into the territory of organized crime in this period occurred through the legitimization of high-interest loan-sharking practices. Once a mainstay venture of organized crime, it became more pervasive in legal business operations, at first in the form of high-interest credit card lending in the years immediately following the IMF Crisis. Hoping to stimulate domestic consumer spending, government agencies deregulated the industry considerably during those years, permitting credit card advances and loans, removing corporate borrowing limits, and eliminating ceiling ratios that capped account balances.[31] This wave of deregulation predictably encouraged irresponsible lending practices, for example, the granting of minors' credit cards without parental consent.[32] The protagonist of *The Scam* (*Chakchŏn*), a 2009 film about stock market rigging, for example, uses credit card loans to build up capital for his initially disastrous career as a day trader in this period. On a larger scale the nearly immediate result was snowballing household debt, as well as credit defaults,[33] peaking in 2003 when the largest credit card company in Korea, under the LG umbrella, became illiquid and required a bailout.[34] Although the immediate fire was extinguished in 2004, household debt has continued to rise in Korea through the time of this writing. Credit card lending has not only remained a problem;[35] legal and illegal informal lending, once the purview of loan sharking gangsters, has also expanded in Korea in the form of *third-tier lending* (*daebuŏpch'e daech'ul*). This system is operated by private entrepreneurs outside of the traditional *kkangp'ae* profile who charge exorbitant rates (more than 30–40 percent and in some cases up to 100 percent).[36] We might think of the so-called credit card crisis of 2003, then, as debt shift, an effort by government agents to displace onto the domestic economy the pains it had experienced at a macroeconomic scale, a protocol that initiates its own cascading sequence of debt escalation. In a similar debt shift, Woo-jin's indiscretions become Dae-su's trauma, which, in turn, becomes more vicious with each cycle.

That Dae-su wishes to forget this realization at the end of the film reminds us that the salaryman, while serving as an entry point into a broader historical discourse about socioeconomic transition, functions finally as a reification that ultimately forecloses a view of the systemic relations that it begins to broach. As a way to consider what the line of analysis begun in *Oldboy* and *A Bittersweet Life* might look like without such reification, this chapter concludes with an examination of Filament Pictures' *Helpless*, which tells the story not of a gangster figure but of his victim, as manifested in the mysterious Kang Seon-yeong (Kim Min-hee). The fiancée of an upstanding young veterinarian with his own practice, Seon-yeong seems destined for a life of middle-class comforts until one day the truth comes out of her troubled financial past. Although it began with a modest credit card debt, her troubles begin to balloon; we learn she had to take on loans to pay her debts and then high-interest subprime loans, fueling the vicious circuit that leads her further into precarity. Though pointing to the inadequacy of the salaryman as a representative figure of post–IMF Crisis victimization, Seon-yeong remains an extension of this figure, insofar as her experiences mark the explosion of a middle-class dream in Korean society in the period. Kang Seon-yeong is a character that, like Dae-su and Sun-wo, is forced to rely on her ingenuity and eventually turns to violence, but she does so in pursuit of survival instead of revenge. As a financial agent who had tried to help Seon-yeong explains later to her husband, Seon-yeong's experience was a common one in the period: "That's pretty much standard course."[37]

But beyond simply detailing the struggles of middle-class bliss upended by fiscal irresponsibility, *Helpless* directly portrays the historical connection between these high-interest loans and the notorious *kkangp'ae* business model in Korea of loan-sharking. Although the later bank-led credit system lacked the explicit brutality of gangster violence, it closely hewed to its predecessor's business model. Both were finally more interested in creating perpetual debt than in being paid back. In the classic *kkangp'ae* scheme the endgame is much more

than the handsome profit guaranteed by interest rates; instead, it targets a significant asset, like a home or a business or, perversely, a daughter who could be put
into prostitution. For the credit card company the point was to cause perpetual
indebtedness that would create dependable revenue streams from debtors who
were simply paying the interest and no principal every month. And as in Annie
McClanahan's account of the US context, because the debt in many of these cases
was incurred not for the sake of discretionary spending but for basic survival,
debtors had no choice but to pay.[38]

Helpless bridges these two related business models (credit cards and loan
sharking) in the figure of Seon-yeong, who turns out not to be Seon-yeong at
all but a woman named Cha Gyeong-seon, whose father had taken loans from
loan sharks to deal with financial problems after the IMF Crisis. Seon-yeong, it
turns out, is the name of a woman whose identity Gyeong-seon had stolen and
whom she had killed as part of a plot to live finally free of her father's debt. After
her father had skipped town, the *kkangp'ae* had identified her as the primary
debtor and harassed her husband's business until she, too, tried to leave town.
The *kkangp'ae*, however, catch her at the bus station and force her into sexual
slavery. Furthermore, we learn that Gyeong-seon had identified the real Seon-
yeong as a useful target for her scheme because of the latter's credit card debt. In
the figure of Gyeong-seon posing as Seon-yeong, two modes of predatory lending
come together, the violent brutality of the *kkangp'ae* and the more calculated but
equally violent credit card company. The effect of precisely this synthesis defines
the experience of the victim (who in turn becomes a murderous aggressor) in
Helpless. Although this one is separated from the events of 1997 and 1998 by a
generation, the story ends, as many IMF stories do, with a suicide.

Helpless and *Oldboy* both blend revenge narratives with survival stories,[39] in
which the subject has no recourse to take measures against the overwhelming
force of her antagonists, against whom she is ultimately, indeed, helpless. Facing such dire circumstances, Seon-yeong turns toward weaker prey from whom
she extracts a means to subsist. Like Dae-su at the end of *Oldboy*, Seon-yeong
wishes merely to survive, but because of the debt stacked against her, she must
turn monstrous to do so, seeking out precarious women whose place she can
take in an example of vicious circulation that harkens the zero-sum dynamics of
Park Chan-wook's *Sympathy for Mr. Vengeance* as described in my introduction.
Echoing the hypnotist's division of Dae-su into residuum and monster, she tells
her one-time fiancé near the end of the film, "I am not a person. I'm garbage."

What turns her into garbage is mounting debt in the hands of creditors who want much more than to be paid back.

Here at last is the crucial connection between all of the films discussed in this chapter: in focusing on the relationship between creditor and debtor, they all expose that the real intent of the creditor is not merely to extract money from the debtor but to create a situation of perpetual indebtedness. Seon-yeong's helplessness casts light, then, on the quality of Dae-su's indebtedness to Woo-jin in *Oldboy*. Like Gyeong-seon's debt, Dae-su's responsibility to Woo-jin is based on little that is real. In both cases it is only fully realized by the power of the person that imagines it into being—be it through traumatic displacements or ballooning interest rates—imposed on a precarious person who has lost the means to mount any defense. Irregular labor, service work, and subsistence debt are all fruits from the same rotting tree. Against such violent aggressions, however sublimated, the only realizable desire is the modest hope for survival. Revenge is taken not against the aggressor but against someone else further down in the spiral of vicious circulation.

Segyehwa Punk

Subsistence Faming and Human Capital
in *Looking for Bruce Lee*

Blake Schwarzenbach's lyrics for Jawbreaker's "Boxcar," off the American punk band's third album, *24 Hour Revenge Therapy* (1994), respond to an accusing interlocutor, who polices punk values in the manner of a schoolyard tattletale: "You're not punk and I'm telling everyone." In rebuke, the song defies punk orthodoxy—"Save your breath, I never was one"—scripting individuality in more radical forms and recasting punk as reactionary Puritanism before returning the sing-songy taunting in kind: "One. Two. Three. Four. Who's punk? What's the score?[1] In 1994 Schwarzenbach's reversal might have been read more skeptically, however, as apologia for Jawbreaker's recent commercial success. Late that year, the band signed with the major label Geffen Records, much to the disappointment of punk purists. Though it was written and recorded before their move, "Boxcar" becomes a retroactive justification for a punk band becoming a corporate entity to a community invested in the band's initial success. The problem is not *being* punk; it's *remaining* punk.[2]

Coinciding precisely with the post-IMF period, the appearance of punk in the late 1990s and early 2000s in the Republic of Korea is fraught with similar contradictions, not least of which is the fact that punk had itself by then become a global commodity. Because the Korean iteration blends rebellious counterculture and globalized privilege, the problem of remaining punk articulated in "Boxcar" is a precondition. On the one hand, Korean punk critiques what it perceives to be a stultifying culture. On the other hand, the flow of punk culture into Korea, dubbed *Chosŏn* punk (after the traditional name of Korea), was facilitated by affluent youth who were able to travel to the West for the first time in large numbers during the 1990s. As Stephen Epstein has suggested, Korean punk does not share with its Western origins a sense of working-class frustration and disenfranchisement.[3] Its atomized rebelliousness is more individual than social; gestures on the order of parental defiance supplant politicized calls for anarchy.[4] This is far from a story of a pure Western form devolving into a diluted facsimile, however, since Western punk rock by the mid-1990s had already become a viable commercial form.[5] In this mass marketing, the rebellious conceits of early practitioners had reified into affectation, and Korean punk simply mimics these later Western iterations, which supplant "urban working-class frustration" with "American suburban alienation, boredom and depression."[6] Accordingly, the Korean punk is not the salaryman's foil, as one might assume, but rather an elaboration on the way in which the sociological transformations brought on by the IMF Crisis manifest themselves in a different demographic, one of two—namely youth and women—that were specifically ignored in the dominant post-IMF discourse, which tended to foreground the plight of middle-class men.[7] In this chapter and the next I will examine films that consider these groups and the fantasies they engage to both explain and disavow their material circumstances.

In the post-IMF context, the punk youth figure is not so much about the counterculture as it is about access and entitlement, regarding the salaryman not as a sellout but as unfairly advantaged. Like later iterations of Western commercial punk, Korean punk might be better characterized not by radical politics but by what Bill Brown terms *radical consumption*, in which "existentialist struggle replaces both class and ethnic conflict in a classic case of the embourgeoisement of mass-cultural and cross-cultural novelty."[8] Examples of radical consumption abound in Kang Lone's *Looking for Bruce Lee* (2002), an anomalous film in Korea's IMF cinema. Coming off as sloppy hackwork, Kang's independent production (his only film to date) is a bizarre footnote in what Youngmin Choe terms *hallyu cinema*, a cinema that foregrounds "the flows of capital, material goods, and cultural products that epitomize the hallyu phenomenon."[9] A chaotic composite of idiosyncratic fragments with only the loosest of plots holding it together, the film is part rock documentary that follows around the successful Korean punk band Crying Nut and part mystery, with Crying Nut's bass player, Han Keong-rok, filling the role of detective for a series of murders (at which the killer leaves behind photographs of Bruce Lee) that coincide with Crying Nut performances. It is also (amazingly) part avant-garde art film inspired by French New Wave Cinema and part ethnographic documentary, complete with interviews of Seoul residents of non-Korean ethnicity who speak on behalf of Korea's vexed multiculturalism.

While the surprising continuity between the salaryman and punk unsettles an easy binary, the more significant implication of this relation is its indication of an expansive systemic transition in the period that encompasses both experiences of contemporary life. Moving now still farther away from the epicenter of wealth as figured by the *chaebŏl*, to which the salaryman was more proximate, the punk's inquiry becomes less about the attribution of blame and more about obtaining a wider view of social machinery. When Han looks to the camera in the opening shot of the film and asks in English, "What happened?" he shifts from the detective's interest in finding the criminal (whodunit?) to the question of how young people in particular go about inhabiting the new global economy, a question that becomes pressing in the shadow of a catastrophic financial crisis that arrives just in time to imperil their opportunities to enter the workforce.[10] Kim Young-sam's globalization policy, *segyehwa*, was nearly a decade old when the film was released; the punk's milieu is already the global marketplace. If *Memories of Murder* and *Oldboy* were surprised to find that once securely discrete spaces (small town, family, nation) had been infiltrated by world systems, *Looking for Bruce Lee* begins with a more jaded disposition that assumes that no dependable local structures remain in a world defined by competition. *Chosŏn* punk is a misnomer: this is *segyehwa* punk.

To make sense of the complex interplay of disparate actors and interests in *segyehwa*, *Looking for Bruce Lee* employs a key device of Korea's IMF cinema: the self-reflexive depictions of the filmic apparatus as a representational strategy for making sense of the political-economic structures that became visible in everyday life in that tumultuous moment. And beyond simply engaging in this signature activity of the period's cinema, the film does so with a certain abandon, seeming to generate analogous forms compulsively and in excess. In incorporating too many different modes of visual representation—from stylized art film to low-budget video documentary—the film offers a chaotic model of an imaginary globalized economy with all of its confluences and conflicts. As a transnational cultural icon born in the United States and who made films in Hong Kong,[11] Bruce Lee (the object of a previous era's radical consumption) becomes a sign of this economy's intensity and dissonances,[12] under which the film mimics the tangled networks, multivalent cathexes, and disparate cultural locations that make up global markets. From the point of view of a radical consumer, the film presents its own mess as object form for the mess of globalization, to the degree that it seems not just authorized but authored by globalization itself.[13]

The *segyehwa* punk's milieu is spectacular in the Debordian sense, in which "appearing" supplants "having" as the central ethos of consumption, thereby radicalizing the domination of the economy over social reality, which becomes increasingly shaped according to the logic of the spectacle.[14] The film blends punk and global aesthetics so radically that the two become indistinguishable from one another, yet this attempt to visualize the workings of globalization by way of film apparatus yields primarily a fantasy of its operations instead of the truth of political economy. Although bathed in the countercultural affect native to punk cultures, the film's vision of globalization is not a critical one but is offered, instead, as projective wish-fulfillment—an attempt to articulate new possibilities for creative achievement while eliding the very workings of the unequal system that the fantasy itself makes partially visible. *Segyehwa* punk wishes to enter the global marketplace, not explode it.

At the same time, however, the critical value of *segyehwa* punk inheres in its inability to articulate globalization without recursively indexing the objective contradictions that it wishes to disavow, contradictions that remain stubbornly seared into the fantasies. *Looking for Bruce Lee* does, indeed, celebrate the logic of global entrepreneurialism as central to the punk imagination, but because it must emerge in a material context defined by precarity, it becomes legible as a smaller-scale survival tactic in a labor environment increasingly oriented toward human capital and not as a mode of large-scale capital accumulation. In this environment the only alternative to poverty seems to be celebrity. I will call this *subsistence faming*.

A rejoinder to the idea of human capital as traditionally understood, human capital in the context of subsistence faming is no longer preoccupied with adding value or success; rather, it is a means of navigating the brutal challenges of late capitalism and includes a measure of self-deception. As Annie McClanahan has argued with respect to US economic history, human capital for thinkers as different as Michel Foucault and Gary Becker is "not a *critical* category" or "a description of material reality" but rather an *ideological* category, in which remaking "the subject in capital's image" does "little to capture either labor on a global scale or the condition of the US under- and un-employed."[15] My intention is not to minimize the difference between the meager output of farmers attempting to live on their crops and celebrities flush with cash but rather to highlight the way in which both enterprises in the present context share an all-or-nothing sensibility. Though the rewards are theoretically more considerable (if more unlikely) in the present case, both engage severe downside risk.

Marking the material limit of this ideology, *Looking for Bruce Lee* is an independent film that worries the problem of independence for both the rebellious teen against a backdrop of mounting youth unemployment and household debt, by staging a human-capital fantasy—that punk rock becomes a way to master the global marketplace. We learn, however, that this is not the escapist fantasy of the disillusioned worker who dreams of leaving the rat race behind but a fantasy of participation that aspires to enter the world of work rather than depart from it. Ultimately, then, the critical value of the fantasy is its unsustainability: the false promise of the *segyehwa* punk only thinly veils the fact of a collapsing job market in which the pursuit of celebrity and other entrepreneurial forms becomes a means of basic survival. Subsistence faming indexes not a refinement of the apparatus facilitating upward mobility but the expansion of the precariat in Korea's youth demographic that was beginning in the period and has only become more visible in subsequent years. At the same time, it offers an explanation for the distinct antirevolutionary current in contemporary Korean countercultural thought in the persistence of this ideological fantasy despite the stubborn material conditions that make the fantasy both necessary and impossible.

Punk Speed

Performed early in the film, Crying Nut's iconic hit "Speed Up Losers" (the Korean title is "*Mal Tallija*," or "Let's Run like a Horse") expresses the temporality of rebellion as the kind of punk tempo parodied by Schwarzenbach's "one, two, three, four." Often screamed at the beginning of a song by the singer, the familiar call in punk rock songs in synchronizing musicians also hails an intensity, in which driving rhythms, distorted guitars, and hoarse vocals express defiance writ large. In this vein "Speed Up Losers" turns on the repeated exhortation of its chorus, "Run like a horse," whose prescription for speed is panacea for contemporary frustrations. If Korean modernity emerged too fast, then the retort is even faster. Toward the end of the song, lead singer Park Yun-shik proclaims the exigencies of intransigence in the imperative: "In this world, we can only run. / What else can we hope for?"[16]

To illustrate the point, the scenes of the band's performance at Drug (the club at the epicenter of Korean punk rock) are crosscut with shots of a strange man wearing a trench coat, pink spandex shorts, and some sort of codpiece. He flashes a group of school girls and begins to run. If the political significance of running were not already clear, the accompanying dramatization brings it home in no uncertain terms, playing out the vulgar allegory form of 1980s American music videos. Though we are troubled by the notion of a heroic flasher, the conceit is that he is a rebel breaching decorum and is thus chased around by a Buddhist monk, a policeman, and a man waving a South Korean flag, bald figures of tradition, authority, and nationalism, respectively. To run like a horse is to resist interpellation.

Another scene early in the film further develops the stance when the band sneaks into the bathroom of a corporate building to apply hair product. (It is unclear why the location is desirable, except as a stage for irony.) On their way out, they are stopped by the building's security guard, who makes them kneel uncomfortably and berates them with the pithy maxims of postwar Korean corporate nationalism, the American roots of which are marked by an allusion to John F. Kennedy's famous inaugural address: "You kids just consume and shit? People working hard for our country's productivity use this building. Same applies for the rest rooms. And it's punks like you that deflate our economy like a flat tire. What does productivity mean to you? Think not what your country can do for you, but what you can do for your country!"[17]

Against the guard's unflattering assessment of punk political economy, speed provides an antidote to nationalist discourse in the form of a subversive energy that refuses co-optation by the corporate state as labor.[18] When the band arrives at the chorus in the Drug performance, the youthful crowd breaks out into a mosh pit, and slam dancing (to play out the semiotics) becomes a Weberian parody—a display of nonproductive enthusiasm. As Jean Baudrillard has described as a consequence of accelerated modernity, however, the risk of speed is ahistoricism: we are propelled to an "escape velocity" that flies us "free of the referential sphere of the real and of history."[19] If running like a horse outruns authority, then the cost is a clear view of the landscape. The dilemma is that the escape from the state-sponsored, false historical narrative exacerbates rather than repairs the problem.

Although Baudrillard looms, the film resists postmodern ahistoricism by turning continually to the material history of film itself. In this parallel context the film explicitly links the punk's running horse to that of Eadweard Muybridge's Zoopraxiscope, often considered a precursor to film projection technology, which proved in 1878 that all four horse's hooves left the ground simultaneously as it ran, a phenomenon that became visible to the human eye only through Muybridge's device. In one of his voice-overs, in fact, Han directly alludes to Muybridge: "While searching for the criminal, I met many people along the way, but the only information I could get from them were their personal memories. As we can't distinguish every gesture of a running horse, it's impossible to link all the

encounters into one story. It's like trying to remember all 24 frames in one second."
For *Looking for Bruce Lee* the film apparatus holds a good deal of explanatory
power: the impossibility of seeing every gesture of a running horse is like the
impossibility of seeing the full picture of a crime, which becomes analogous,
somewhat tautologically, to the impossibility of seeing the individual frames of
modern industry-standard film technology. The limitation of human apprehension of the mechanical apparatus also becomes analogous to the impossibility of
linking "all the encounters into one story," and in this analogy we see the film's
attempt to link the filmic apparatus to the mechanisms of globalization.

The reference to Muybridge also cites a particular tradition of film criticism
that foregrounds medium-specific ontology. Although comprising photographic
elements, or so goes the account, film technology hides its material condition—
the fact that it is composed of individual stills—by synthesizing individual photographs into the illusion of movement. As Garrett Stewart puts it: "Ruptures
overlooked: that's film for you."[20] Stewart regards evidence of the photogrammatic
particularly in freeze-frame shots as self-reflexive moments in which the projection on the screen seems materially coherent with the image imprinted on the
film.[21] Whereas punk rock is blinded by the very form of speed that energizes
it, film here is imagined to have the capacity to see that which speedy projection
elides, an awareness of the machinery, and we may further extrapolate that seeing
history amid speed is akin to seeing the photograph in the film. The film thus
attempts to update Muybridge's technology in the theoretical mode of Stewart
in order to make sense of global flows, implicitly tweaking Stewart's aphorism:
Ruptures overlooked: that's globalization for you.

Oriented toward such an inquiry, Han's search for the murders involves talking not to potential witnesses but, rather, to people who know something about
the world outside of Korea (i.e., immigrants or native Koreans that have traveled
abroad). More anthropological than criminological, his detective work seeks to
understand the social effects of globalization. The very first witness he interviews
is a Korean "bohemian" who might be better described as a radical consumer of
all things Indian: he has traveled to India, dresses himself and his female companions in Indian clothes, and listens to sitar music in a room decorated with
Indian accoutrements. Later, after encountering an Asian woman who speaks to
him in German and who reappears later in the film inexplicably fanning herself
with a copy of Giuseppe Zigaina's *Pasolini et la mort*, Han remarks: "There's been
an increasing number of strange people around here. It's too weird." Through

such interactions it becomes clear that *segyehwa* comes to inform the method of investigation, the object of which is not murder at all but global patterns. Although in the film *weird* seems to refer simply to foreigners in Korea, Han's term also names what Steven Shaviro describes as a "radically unfamiliar and irrecuperable" sense of "intense anxiety and dislocation," which is particularly symptomatic in "a world that is too complex and far-flung to be totalized on the level of any grand narrative . . . and at the same time too intricately intercon- nected to be treated linearly, or atomistically."[22]

Amid the film's weirdness, ruptures are ultimately hard to overlook, and they remain particularly exposed in the closing sequence, in which Han wakes up from a dream about a performance and turns to his right to face the camera. Behind him we see a poster of François Truffaut's French New Wave classic *The 400 Blows* (*Le quatre cents coups*, 1959), a film that is also about youth culture.[23] In a subsequent allusion to the final scene in Truffaut—in which the film's protagonist, Antoine Doinel (Jean-Pierre Léaud), runs away from a youth detention center in a famously long tracking shot before turning at the last moment to face the camera directly— *Looking for Bruce Lee* depicts the band running toward the audience away from a *koshiwŏn* (a study center for the Korean Civil Service Exam), echoing Antoine's institutional escape. The final shot then cuts to a young Filipina. Looking into the camera, she says, "I am doing OK" in Tagalog without subtitles (using the honorific, *po*) before asking in English, "You can understand what I mean?"

On one hand, the sequence as a whole blends liberal multiculturalism, punk antics, French New Wave Cinema, and youthful exuberance into a happy cocktail that takes less than a minute of screen time. On the other, the polite phrase in Tagalog, the silent dreamed performance, the discomfited waking, the acknowl- edgment of the camera in Han's turn, and the odd invocation of Truffaut point to moments of uneven stitching where even the homogenizing power of glo- balization is strained. The Filipina's presence onscreen as the film's final shot, in particular, invokes not just an ostensibly happy global multicultural subject but also the most dominant figures of Filipinas in contemporary Korean discourse— namely nannies, migrant brides, laborers, and entertainers—who are frequently the marginalized objects of the more exploitative, violent, and abusive aspects of globalized Korea.[24] Her presence reminds us that the majority of the interviews of foreigners in the film are of South or Southeast Asian descent (though the darker sides of their stories remain occluded) and that Korea's multiculturalism is largely a by-product of its need for cheap service labor. Her use of the English word *OK*, a word with a particularly idiosyncratic American etymology and perhaps the most assimilated American English word in the world,[25] might refer not just to her ostensibly happy disposition but the material complexity that globalization works so hard to expunge.

10,000 *Wŏn* and the 880,000 *Wŏn* Generation

Closing a circle opened by Chris Marker's 1959 photo-travelogue *Coréennes*,[26] which documented Marker's trip to the Democratic People's Republic of Korea (a.k.a. North Korea) in 1957, the homage to his *La Jetée* (1963) at the midpoint of *Looking for Bruce Lee* is perhaps the film's weirdest section. A photomontage of stills in the manner of Marker's iconic art film, the sequence begins with Han repeating his earlier reflection about the impossibility of distinguishing every gesture of a running horse as the image of a long wall in Seoul (likely the boundary of palace grounds) shot from a moving car appears and then freezes. And as the final of these lines is uttered in voice-over ("It's like trying to remember all 24 frames in one second"), the film shifts into this drama of high-cinematic self-reflexivity. Accordingly, Kang's version of Marker's *photo-roman* appropriates Marker's visual style and emphasis on filmic apparatus, what Stewart describes as "the photographic strip's becoming film track,"[27] adding a sepia-toned treatment to the images befitting the scene's discordant Victorian mise-en-scène.

Just before the film shifts into the photomontage, we see a long shot of Han on the street. As the camera pulls back, a cello player on the roof emerges in the immediate foreground; we see only the back of her head and the tip of the cello resting on her shoulder, while just below, the figure of Han remains visible in the background (fig. 11). This colored, moving image then freezes into the first still in the homage sequence, which in juxtaposing the aesthetics of the long shot and the close-up in a single shot calls attention to the central problem of Han's investigation. He witnesses plenty of detailed evidence from up close—first-person testimonies, curious phenomena, and idiosyncrasies that make up the everyday life of Seoul—and he recognizes the proverbial big picture, that is, the aggregate perspective required to catch a serial killer. What seems lacking is the relationship between the two scales. In a sharply focused and centered long shot juxtaposed to a soft-focused and marginal close-up, the disparate figures seem to occupy altogether different planes of existence. Although they coincide within a single frame, their relation is not transactional, and what seems missing is the mediating context that might clarify the relation between the two.

It's like trying to remember
all 24 frames in one second.

FIGURE 11. First still in the Chris Marker homage sequence in *Looking for Bruce Lee* (Drug Films, 2002).

The sequence continues when Han climbs the stairs of the building on top of which the cellist sits. When Han reaches the roof, he meets another woman, who is dressed in Victorian garb. This "creepy lady," as Han describes her, is reading a Korean translation of Julia Kristeva's obscure 1998 detective novel *Possessions* (retitled for the Korean edition as something like *The Devil That Is Possession*).[28] Disoriented, he asks her a series of questions: "What are you doing now?" "Did you see the strange girl on top of the roof?" "Did something happen here too?" As Han asks these questions, we see a series of stylized close-ups of both Han and the woman, who begins to tell the story about how she met the love of her life when he walked by one day, zealously waving around Kristeva's novel. Claiming to be an "equalist" and proselytizing an absurdly masculinist perversion of poststructuralist feminism, he criticizes the young woman's legs, saying cryptically, "Your legs are the cause of your own loss of rights." For some inexplicable reason, the woman falls immediately in love and decides that in order to marry this man, she will have to cut off her left leg. The man later shows up with another woman who also has attractive legs, now claiming to have been cured of his aversion. When the "creepy lady" finishes her story, she is alerted by the rooftop cellist that the man and his new paramour have arrived. Shifting from an account of a memory to the present, the scene also shifts here from tragedy to revenge, as the strange woman proceeds to splash acid on her rival's face. As a third act, the homage sequence ends with photographs of a dancer crosscut with images of the strange woman lying motionless on a barren hillside. It is unclear whether she is dead or merely forlorn, but the dancer's movements express the strange woman's despair. The only part of the entire homage sequence that employs moving images, a rejoinder to the woman's blinking eye in *La Jetée*, this final dance element, significantly, is performed by a member of the polymathic film director Kang's experimental dance troupe MongolMongol, a reference to which we see later in the film when Han stands before a poster for a performance by this group called "My Wonderful Left Hook" (fig. 12), featuring an image of a cellist that appears to be the same cellist from the film.[29]

Although the homage sequence acknowledges aesthetic debt within an act of cosmopolitan radical consumption, it also functions as something like a self-reflexive branding exercise, a kind of high-art product placement, within the context of a film that is itself in large part something of a promotional venture, a band rockumentary. Constituting a kind of *mise-en-abyme d'commercialisation*, it is a promotional video nested inside a promotional video. And despite the high-low disparity between avant-garde modern dance and punk rock, both serve as entry points to the marketplace of human capital. In the film, transnational homage modulates from the payment of an aesthetic debt into angiography for the routes of global consumer flows in

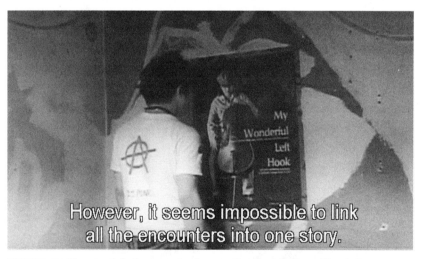

FIGURE 12. Han stands before a poster for a performance by Lone Kang's dance troupe, called "My Wonderful Left Hook," in *Looking for Bruce Lee* (Drug Films, 2002).

which Marker's filmic aesthetics circulate along with Victorian iconography, deconstructive feminism, and modern dance. The Kristeva example demonstrates, furthermore, that this global circulation is ambivalent to the original political or cultural context: a minor Kristeva novel not only stands in for her theoretical work but also justifies female mutilation to secure heteronormative coupling. Circulation authorizes such strategies of appropriation. Kang's homage thus functions as a form of spectacular consumption, in which what is demonstrated is not wealth but a connoisseurship whose precondition is a marketplace in which American punk rock, French New Wave Cinema, and Hong Kong kung fu are equally accessible.

Such a global system characterized by promiscuous transnational circulation produces an imperative toward self-promotion because the relationship between individual and market comes to be defined by human capital, and the individual worker within an entrepreneurial context comes to be understood as a kind of appreciating asset. As Michel Feher has put it, workers "do not exactly own their human capital; they invest in it."[30] The advantages of such a system come at a cost: "while they can considerably alter their human capital—by means of either diversifying or modifying their behaviors and social interactions—they can never sell it. In short, rather than a *possessive* relationship, as that of the free laborer with his or her labor power, the relationship between the neoliberal subject and his or her human capital should be called *speculative*, in every sense of the word."[31]

The Marker set piece works through the implications for young adult labor within globalization, particularly in the context of growing national focus on Korean culture industries from the mid-1990s onward as a strategy for realizing new revenue streams and employment sectors.[32] Entrepreneurialism in such a context gains an air of optimism, particularly when buoyed by state funds. The Korean Film Council (KOFIC), for example, was founded in 1999 under the Kim Dae-jung administration and given significant funding to support industry growth.[33] But such optimism can also obscure another characteristic of models of labor that center on human capital. In contrast to accounts like those of Gary Becker and Theodor Schultz,[34] which foreground the advantages of human capital without acknowledging a labor market in which one has no choice but to acquire it, subsistence faming in *Looking for Bruce Lee* marks a labor situation in which the *only* opportunity for self-reproduction seems to be celebrity. Feast or famine, the middle ground between alternatives collapses.[35]

While popular music has perhaps always been a means for poor or working-class youth to rise in class, subsistence faming in post-IMF Korea, particularly with the rise of K-pop, specifically becomes inextricable from a troubled job market for young people. Near the end of the movie, Han refers to this context, confessing in voice-over that he can only earn ten thousand *wŏn* a day in Seoul (about ten dollars) and that it is difficult to live that way in that expensive city. "But if I have numerous fans," he continues, "if I can perform in front of a large audience, I'll be ok." The mention of ten thousand *wŏn* here connects to an earlier scene in which Han describes a nightmare in which he is paid precisely that amount to be an extra in a film, hanging on a cross as Jesus Christ. After painting wounds on his body (wounds that are later echoed in the Bruce Lee sequences) and the bodies of his bandmates, who are also extras in the scene, the film crew ignores them and eventually leaves them to die, still affixed to the crosses. In both cases, getting paid only ten thousand *wŏn* is to be a sacrificial lamb for the new economy (the crosses are no coincidence). The only alternative is to refuse the bit part and to cast one's lot for a starring role.

As we saw in the previous chapter, this period saw a dramatic increase in the number of *irregular workers* (part-time, short-term, contract workers), who lacked job security and benefits,[36] further encouraging workers to reimagine themselves according to market logics. No longer something to be avoided in the quest for security, risk becomes a mark of boldness and bravery. This broader context clarifies the leitmotif in *Looking for Bruce Lee* of the bloody claw marks on Han's body, which are borrowed from the iconic finale of Bruce Lee's *Enter the Dragon* (fig. 13). Crucially, these claw marks are understood not as records of past experiences but as a means to appropriate Lee's iconic celebrity. Han's proudly displayed wounds reimagine the nature of the wound itself. In marking the transfer of risk from the corporate body to that of the worker, a transfer experienced as liberating, Han's wounds become understood as self-branded trademarks, not marks of vulnerability as they were in the movie-extra scene.[37]

Luc Boltanski and Ève Chiapello have described such changes as components of what they call the new spirit of capitalism.[38] Eschewing older hierarchical models, a flatter system of corporate management developed based on the idea of a network, which privileges connectivity and flexibility. Employees become autonomous actors engaged in a series of *projects*, with the workplace becoming the site of personal development rather than Fordist repetition. The security of longtime employment characterized by a structure of promotion is relinquished

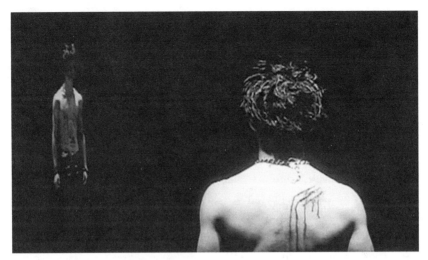

FIGURE 13. Han's Bruce Lee wounds in *Looking for Bruce Lee* (Drug Films, 2002).

for the sake of the immaterial human capital in which workers accumulate experiences as they progress. Though a response to antiauthoritarian management strategies, the new network model ironically allows the new company to be more ruthlessly efficient and perfectly comfortable with an increasingly temporary workforce.[39] Although the French model may have differed from the Korean one, IMF-mandated structural reforms similarly created an environment in which flexible labor and the social psychology that attends it become the norm.[40]

Such changes had a nearly immediate impact, giving rise to what economist Woo Seok-hun and journalist Park Gwon-il dubbed in 2007 the 880,000 *wŏn* generation, and their term quickly became a buzzword in Korean public discourse.[41] Named after the per-month minimum wage at the time (approximately US$750), the generation consisted of twenty-somethings whose work experiences were defined by conditions of irregular labor. Even those who graduated from good universities saw few prospects and were denied access to the middle-class comforts enjoyed by previous generations of Koreans.[42] Although these young people were the subject of griping by older generations—in a similar manner that American millennials are sometimes criticized—Woo and Park's insight about a "structurally disadvantageous position" proved prescient in a youth job market that has only worsened since the book's publication. The mentions of ten thousand *wŏn* per day in *Looking for Bruce Lee* refer to this context, as do the various examples of youth dissatisfaction that have gained the public eye since, like the "Hell *Chosŏn*" discourse and the "I am not OK movement,"[43] both of which were expressions of youth dissatisfaction over contemporary Korean life. Although the various efforts in the film to organize hope and ambition according to the logics of human capital require a disavowal of such dissatisfaction, they are ultimately immutable.

Pop Star / Pro Wrestler

The economic frame in which subsistence faming became a phenomenon was wide-ranging enough to produce a filmic subgenre in Korea's IMF Cinema. Films under this rubric, like *Looking for Bruce Lee*, thought comparatively about work and creative enterprises. Here I will look at a small cross-section featuring figures that echo *Looking for Bruce Lee*'s pairing of musicians and martial arts fighters in pop stars and professional wrestlers in three films: Yim Soon-rye's *Waikiki Brothers* (*Waik'ik'i pŭratŏsŭ*, 2001), Kim Jee-woon's *Foul King* (*Panch'ikwang*, 2000), and Park Je-hyun's *Oollala Sisters* (*Ullala ssisŭtŏjŭ*, 2002). The point will be to gain a wider sense of youth culture in the period and the way in which it engages with the question of work.

Although it shares with *Looking for Bruce Lee* an inquiry into the idea of rock music as labor, Yim Soon-rye's *Waikiki Brothers* is a very different kind of film. With a deeply naturalist sensibility, the film depicts the life of Sung-woo (Lee Eol), guitarist and lead singer for the eponymous band in the movie, as bereft of glamour. Once successful, the band has fallen on hard times after the IMF Crisis, and each gig is worse than the last. If their own depressing experiences weren't sufficient for diagnosis, we explicitly hear a news report on a car radio at one point that the unemployment situation in the nation has not improved. Reluctantly, the band takes a gig in Sung-woo's hometown of Suanbo, a once-popular but now faded resort town. Eventually, every other member of the band quits, and Sung-woo's attempt to keep his career afloat becomes increasingly difficult. At his lowest moment Sung-woo plays solo for an audience of drunk businessmen engaged in bawdy exploits in a karaoke hostess bar. During the set, one of the men forces Sung-woo to strip naked like the members of the drunken audience, and he is forced to finish his set in humiliation, with only his guitar to protect his modesty. Persistent if affectless throughout the entire film, Sung-woo's musical performances are depicted as manual labor. He is a competent musician, perhaps even gifted, but rather than highlighting his talents, the film documents his toil in nightclubs. Like *Looking for Bruce Lee*, the film features many scenes of extended musical performance, but the effect of these extended sequences is not at all promotional in quality. Rather, often shot in stationary medium shots with few cuts, they seem to self-consciously align screen time with real time to underscore the labor expended to make the music. It looks and feels like work.

Kim Jee-woon's *Foul King* depicts the work life of Im Dae-ho (Sung Kang-ho) in similar terms, although the daily misery and humiliation Dae-ho experiences at his job fall more in line with expectations of life as a bank employee. One of the two lowest performing workers in his company, he is often the target of his manager's abusive rebukes, the worst of which is the manager's tendency to put him in a vicious headlock.[44] Dae-ho dreads his job and becomes attracted to professional wrestling when he stumbles on a gym specializing in it, not least because he thinks it might help him escape his boss's grip. Originally, the gym owner is resistant but relents when he finds himself in need of a wrestler that specializes in dirty tricks (a foul king), a role that he deems perfect for Dae-ho. Dae-ho eventually gains some proficiency, and his training in the ring helps him find self-esteem outside of it. Wearing his wrestling mask, he beats up a group of thugs who had taunted him earlier in the film and (though with less success) confesses his love to his office crush.

His newfound confidence and self-satisfaction contrasts with the experience of his fellow low-performing bank employee, Choi Doo-sik (Jung Woong-in), who is asked to sign off on a shady deal worked up by his manager and an associate. Ultimately refusing, he burns the loan documents, deciding to accept the consequences. As the pressures mount for Doo-sik, Dae-ho in contrast becomes increasingly comfortable. Significantly, pro wrestling is ultimately not an alternative to work in a corporate atmosphere but a way to work successfully in it. If playing rock music in *Waikiki Brothers* becomes a form of manual labor, then the physical toil of pro wrestling becomes the physical manifestation of the mental strength necessary for corporate forms of combat—a better way to work, not a reprieve. Dae-ho does not begin a new career so much as he obtains tools for success at the bank. Accordingly, the film ends with a shot of Dae-ho, wearing not his wrestling tights but a suit and walking confidently in Jongno, a business center in Seoul.

Park Je-hyun's *Oollala Sisters* offers an unlikely synthesis between pop star and pro wrestler when the (also eponymous) singing group in the film is hired to perform before an under-attended professional wrestling match sponsored by the World Wrestling Association of Korea. After the performance the promoter of the event offers to pay the women in the group to wrestle as well, replacing a pair of no-shows. Desperately short on cash, they reluctantly accept, and comedy ensues. Albeit absurd, their choice is not so puzzling, given that they face default on a high-interest loan from a loan shark and the loss of their club to a rival club/conglomerate across the street intent on turning the land on which the Sisters' club sits into a shopping mall. A desperate attempt to repair this dire situation, their group, the Oollala Sisters, is a pop group formed under conditions of massive debt, for whom the possibility of success as a musical act is understood to be the only way of paying back their loan. Another example of subsistence faming, there is no middle ground between bankruptcy or K-pop stardom. Although they do become a successful lip-sync act for a while (none of them can sing),[45] their efforts are thwarted by the underhanded machinations of the rival club owner, and it is ultimately a legal gambit that saves their club, when Eun-ja (the leader of the Sisters) realizes that the rival owner owes her a fortune in back-dated interest payments. The homology between musical success and financial prosperity persists, however, at the end of the film when we learn that after saving their club, the Oollala Sisters become a huge sensation, this time as pop singers (they have apparently learned how to sing), even winning a prestigious industry award for best female group, as if their success as musicians (and indeed singing ability) were a logical consequence of healthy bank accounts.

The first of these films is quite different from the other two in that the weight of social realism in *Waikiki Brothers* is heavy in the face of the comic commitments in *Foul King* and *Oollala Sisters*. The former never loses sight of the fact of tragic decline, whereas the latter pair of films works precisely to veil such inevitabilities. But even though these comic films are highly committed to their enabling fantasies, both prove determined by precisely the same downward forces that *Waikiki Brothers* acknowledges more openly. *Oollala Sisters*, for example, might be considered an early representation of not only K-pop celebrity but also (to expand the ubiquitous prefix) K-political economy. By the film's release in 2002, the so-called *K-pop slave contracts* had not yet become so visible in the mass media, but they certainly had become prominent as a media corporation practice.[46] In these arrangements young performers seeking stardom were forced to commit to exploitative terms that would secure their labor for years of difficult training, consent for painful body modification (including plastic surgery), and image control, all in exchange for only the faint possibility of fame. Furthermore, even if a performer or group were to become a hit, the production company would receive the majority of the profits. Historically speaking, the spectacle of K-pop performances is also a spectacle of labor exploitation. Not only do less than 1 percent of applicants become trainees for prospective groups but also only 5 percent of these trainees eventually make it into a band.[47] Furthermore, the ensemble nature of most K-pop bands allows for the devaluation of the individual performer's leverage and a business model in which companies actually plan for the obsolescence of their bands from the moment they take the stage.[48] The unlikely success of the Oollala Sisters (remember they were very recently a lip-sync band because they were terrible singers) imperfectly occludes a system in which the vast majority of aspirants fail.

Similarly, in *Foul King* Dae-ho's rise in self-esteem, though it will correspond to impending financial success (as the final shot of the film perhaps implies), also corresponds to the jettisoning of his troubled coworker, Doo-sik, as a concern. Although the film had drawn on the comparison of the two friends, who were also the worst employees in the bank, we never see Doo-sik again in the film just past the halfway point when he quits his job and Dae-ho's wrestling career accelerates. If both *Foul King* and *Oollala Sisters* tell stories about characters beating the odds, they can only do so by minimizing a parallel story about why those odds are so long in the first place. And although the comic form demands such elisions, Doo-sik's thwarted story line lingers as synecdoche for a larger tragedy about the newly precarious condition of wage labor in the post-IMF period.

Fists of Finance

Looking for Bruce Lee shares with *Foul King* the intuition that fighting to enter and rise in the workplace is best understood in literal terms. Hence, Han imagines himself not as a professional wrestler but as a martial arts fighter in the mold of Bruce Lee, and fighting becomes understood as analogous to professional development as a rock star. In one of the final scenes in the film (fig. 14), a shirtless Han mimics Bruce Lee in the climactic scenes of *Enter the Dragon*, walking through a darkened hall of mirrors, a direct allusion to the final scene between Lee and the evil villain (coincidentally also named Han). By this point Han (the bass player) has become ambivalent to the crime—but in looking for Bruce Lee (and not the Bruce Lee killer), Han has incorporated his object. In a dramatization of iconography, the dreamlike *Enter the Dragon* scene also functions as a clearinghouse for many of the disparate figures that appeared heretofore in the film, especially from the Marker homage, which become allegorically subordinated to a now

FIGURE 14. Mimicking Bruce Lee in *Looking for Bruce Lee* (Drug Films, 2002).

more important human-capital bildungsroman about Han's career. This shift in emphasis becomes clear in a subsequent voice-over in which Han proceeds to speculate about what would happen if he were to solve the crimes: "the whole world will concentrate their full attention on me. There will be a rush of interviews. Maybe they'll even ask me to talk about my new music. I think it may be the most crucial moment to decide the kind of music I will make in the future." As becomes plain, the investigated crime ceases to be understood as a social problem and becomes, instead, an opportunity for publicity. Han thus imagines himself undergoing a change through his *Enter the Dragon* performance from upstart musician into a successful economic actor; and part of the deep identification with Bruce Lee in the scene leading up to this revelation entails the transformation of his own body into an iconic image.

Appropriately, a pair of live-concert-footage scenes from the 2000 Busan International Rock Festival, at which Crying Nut plays its hit "Circus Magic Clowns," brackets this *Enter the Dragon* scene. Here, the band plays on a large, professionally lit, outdoor stage (in stark contrast to the cramped, dark conditions earlier at Drug), in a venue with both corporate and governmental sponsorships. The song is self-referential, about the band traveling and playing to adoring audiences, proclaiming in its refrain, "We are Crying Nut, gentlemen on a journey." It also seems to announce the transformation of this band during its meteoric rise as it enters the marketplace ("Speed Up Losers" was, for example, used in a well-known ice cream commercial). Although the English title uses the word *clowns*, the more literal translation of the word *yurangdan* in the Korean title is *wandering troupe* (or *nomad*). But in contrast to Jinying Li's account of carnivalism as a way "to allegorize the abstract crimes of finance capital,"[49] the decidedly carnivalesque tropes in the song, more Monkees than Sex Pistols, is mobilized here instead in their defense.

The structural reforms undertaken during the Kim Dae-jung administration in the wake of the IMF Crisis and the problem of mass unemployment reflected a shift in the ways in which young people conceived of their relationship to the job market. After having witnessed *chaebŏl* lay off large numbers of employees, betraying promises of lifetime employment, many younger job seekers, particularly those with IT skills, opted to take on more risk in start-up companies.[50] Designed to help firms maintain profit levels in a postdevelopmental context, this shift in the orientation of labor, not coincidentally, was the result of one of the primary demands of the IMF bailout package for labor flexibility.[51] This transition is important because it entails not only a change in the kinds of jobs sought by young people in Korea but, more fundamentally, a change in this labor's orientation.

This shift in the nature of labor, in which workers are no longer tied to a company for the long term, leaves its mark in "Circus Magic Clowns" and in *Looking for Bruce Lee* in general. Reimagining precarity as a punk virtue, the punk rocker becomes an ideal irregular worker. He realizes Alan Liu's imperative, that work must be *cool*, a term that Liu describes as "an attitude or pose from within the belly of the beast, an effort to make one's very mode of inhabiting a cubicle express what in the 1960s would have been an 'alternative lifestyle' but now in the postindustrial 2000s is an alternative *workstyle*."[52] Far from countercultural, the Korean punk rocker tames wild forms of energy (run like a horse!) into the kind of frenzied *activity* in Boltanski and Chiapello, or *zaniness* in Sianne Ngai,[53] both of which are terms that describe the affective energies suited for new economy labor. Appropriately, Boltanski and Chiapello describe the ideal figure of new economy not as an owner but as an artist, one who is not only "freed from the burden of possessions and the constraints of hierarchical attachments" but also is "a network creature . . . the realization of whose projects demands costly, heterogeneous and complex arrangements."[54] By locating surplus energy in its expressions of frustration with authority, punk rock captures otherwise-wasted labor power and, ironically, allows one to indulge in countercultural fantasy while simultaneously underwriting new-economy careerism. It does not so much sell out as buy in.

It is important to recognize, however, that the context for such a valorization of wild energy is the chronic oversupply of labor in Korea's creative industries (as in the K-pop example), with low wages and precarious living and working conditions being the rule, despite explicit government attempts to expand the economic sector.[55] The film captures the irony of punk buy-in in a set piece, which is essentially a music video for the song "Homeless," by the Korean punk-rap group Johnny Royal. The narrative of the scene recounts a visit by one of the members of the band to Yeouido, the island neighborhood in Seoul that is an investment banking district and home to the National Assembly. Ending with an image of a beckoning Bruce Lee projected onto the facing of the National Assembly Building (fig. 15), the song itself is propelled by the repetitive chorus: "We are homeless, homeless. It's time to stand up and fight." The song refers less to literal homelessness (recall that Korean punk is characterized by relative privilege) than to a feeling of disenfranchisement. The discourse of homelessness in this period was very specific, referring to dispossession, perhaps even recent dispossession (as in by the IMF Crisis); and the concerns of the long-standing homeless, outside of the IMF context, never really come into view.[56] In this context Johnny Royal's claim of homelessness might be read as an ironic claim of entitlement to state support. Punk rockers (and rappers) in this milieu are not anarchists but stakeholders. The beckoning image of Bruce Lee projected onto the National Assembly Building in this context is an interpellation that hails only a select group.

FIGURE 15. Bruce Lee beckoning projected onto the National Assembly Building in Seoul in *Looking for Bruce Lee* (Drug Films, 2002).

Fingers and Moons

In *Enter the Dragon* (1973) Bruce Lee's character famously delivers a lesson to a young pupil that is reprised in *Looking for Bruce Lee* as a voice-over: "Don't think. Feel. It is like a finger pointing a way to the moon. Don't concentrate on the finger or you will miss all that heavenly glory." The conceit is: To think when fighting is to be overly concerned with mechanics; whereas to feel is to appreciate one's relationship to the cosmological whole in which mechanics fall naturally in line. Since 1973, we have seen this trope deployed to different ends, even in critical theory. For Eve Sedgwick, the finger *is* the moon and vice versa within a Buddhist pedagogy about the symbiotic relationship between means and ends.[57] More irately, Bruno Latour reaches for aphoristic validation in his critique of contemporary sociology: "A (surely fake) Chinese proverb says that 'When the wise man shows the moon, the moron looks at the finger.'"[58]

Although we appreciate Sedgwick's embrace of Buddhist sentiment and gently chide Latour (the proverb is not fake),[59] Bruce Lee's deployment of the aphorism in *Enter the Dragon* seems part of a different pedagogy, one in which fingers fold into fists and the point of all that heavenly glory is to kick some serious ass. Its subsequent appropriation in *Looking for Bruce Lee* becomes an orientation of the individual in relationship to the global at a moment of state-endorsed globalization in more commercial forms of combat. Becoming Bruce Lee for Han entails, then, projecting himself into a global imaginary, an act that simultaneously generates the global as an effect. A finger pointing at the moon, Bruce Lee becomes means by which a fictional sense of the global is effected and given form, synthesized out of disparate parts with ruptures overlooked.[60] In misrecognizing themselves as masters of this new economy rather than its pawns, workers validate the very financial mechanisms that undermine their security and at the same time fuel atomization at the very site at which a collectivity might form.[61]

In this respect the timing of both *Enter the Dragon* and Lee's death in 1973 is conspicuous. Here Lee's iconic digit becomes a world historical index finger, something like Arrighi's *signal crisis* of the US empire, the inaugural moment for the new financialized economy, pointing to the moon of Brenner's long downturn, for which *segyehwa* is an epiphenomenon.[62] Indeed, the dragon seems to enter at the very moment when industry departs. Reflecting this moment when Western firms, including motion picture companies, reached abroad for larger revenue streams, *Enter the Dragon* was coproduced with the Hong Kong–based

Golden Harvest Films by Warner Communications (formerly Warner Bros. and not yet Time Warner), which was pursuing a more "rationalized" strategy that emphasized finance and distribution (deemphasizing production) as part of a larger structure that included television, music, and video games.[63] For Warner Communications, which had infamously passed over Lee in favor of David Carradine for the lead role in its TV series *Kung Fu* in 1971,[64] Bruce Lee was not a product but an investment.

Furthermore, the marketplace became more diffuse after Lee's death in 1973 when a robust subgenre of *Brucesploitation* films emerged in East Asia, starring imitators with similar names (Bruce Li, Bruce Lai, Bruce Ly, etc.).[65] The titles of these films often (un)imaginatively riffed on Lee's existing catalog—*Enter Three Dragons* (1978), *Re-enter the Dragon* (1979), *Enter Another Dragon* (1981), etc.—including Lo Wei's *The New Fists of Fury* (1976), which was a failed attempt to market Jackie Chan as the new Bruce Lee, following up on Chan's brief appearance in the original *Fists of Fury* (1972). Another was a very forgettable Korean film called *Bruce Lee Fights Back from the Grave*, originally released as *Visitor of America* (*Amerik'a pangmun'gaek*, 1976), made by Lee Doo-yong, a prolific director of *quota quickies*, so named because they were designed to satisfy minimally the requirements of protectionist film policies.[66] Taking advantage of the martial arts craze in Korea from the late 1960s through the early 1970s,[67] *Bruce Lee Fights Back from the Grave* starred a Korean taekwondo instructor turned actor named Jun Chong, taking the name Bruce K. L. Lea for the role. We might think of the Brucesploitation industry as an attempt to profit on the human capital that Lee had left in circulation in a secondary market as a consequence of his early death. In taking on the appearance and martial arts gestures of Bruce Lee, then, Han in *Looking for Bruce Lee* seems to engage in a belated act of Brucesploitation, and the best analogue for Han might not be Bruce Lee himself but the many ersatz imitators. If the punk rocker is an ideal subject of new-economy flexible labor, then the Bruce Lee imitator might serve as its uncanny mirror, reflecting a market in which the hero (and labor) is eminently replaceable by those eager to fight for the scraps.

Read as a figure of *segyehwa*, the finger/moon relation also indexes the changing discursive function of *independence* in the new world economic system defined by rampant free trade. After World War II the United States played a central role in the formation of multilateral trade agreements known as the General Agreement on Tariffs and Trade (GATT), which formed the basis of global trade from its establishment in 1948 until the 1990s. These somewhat liberal policies, designed to lower the impediments to interstate commerce in the context of a dominant US economy attempting to shore up Cold War alliances, were not "free trade" policies in the traditional sense.[68] But in the context of declining US industrial profits, the explosion of international trade, and the increase in economic competition beginning in the 1970s,[69] the United States began to rethink its multilateral trade policy orientation, seeking more regional and bilateral agreements, with the 1994 North American Free Trade Agreement (NAFTA) among the United States, Canada, and Mexico marking a full turn to this new orientation to Free Trade Agreements (FTAs). One of these FTAs was the highly controversial agreement with the Republic of Korea that finally went into effect in 2012 after a nearly decade-long process of negotiation and approval. The most explicitly controversial element of the FTA was the provision about the import of American beef, which sparked volatile protests in Seoul in 2008,[70] but also included was a significant weakening of the Korean film quota system. Although it finally formalized the economic relation between the two countries, we might understand the FTA as a response to the evolving interdependent relation between the two nations (with the US taking the lead) within the context of a much more complicated global economic system in which questions of geopolitical independence become increasingly entangled with complicated arrangements of alliance and affiliation. As we scale successively outward from punk rocker to human capital to flexible labor to postprotectionist trade policies to transnational world economic systems, we see that fingers seem to have no choice but to be oriented toward moons. The *segyehwa* punk is a symptom of a larger contradiction.[71]

During the ROK-US negotiations beginning in 1998 about loosening the protectionist orientation of the Korean motion picture quota system until Korean authorities finally relented in 2006 as part of the negotiations for the US-ROK FTA, the ambivalent position of Korean independent film became a focal point. In arguing for a kind of protectionist anti–free trade independence, as Young-a Park argues, groups like KIFA (Korean Independent Film Association) found themselves in the odd position of advocating, de facto, the rights of Korean blockbusters, films that they eventually felt were not deserving of their advocacy.[72] In the original negotiations between the ROK and the US in 1998, when anti-American sentiment was high because of unpopularity of the IMF bailout package, KIFA's advocacy for maintaining the quota system seemed like an extension of 1980s-era anti-Americanism and dovetailed with the nationalist spirit of the moment. But in the early 2000s, when the negotiations persisted, and as the fervor of the immediate aftermath of the IMF bailout waned, KIFA became more ambivalent. In the intervening time the Korean blockbuster *Shiri* (1999) had become a huge hit in domestic markets, famously beating out the Hollywood blockbuster *Titanic* (1997) in box office receipts. Faced with the prospect of defending mainstream rather than independent cinema and advocating for market independence rather than political independence, KIFA's opposition lost its fervor.[73]

In this context independent cinema in Korea came under the similar pressures that the Korean economy did in general during the IMF period because of the pressure by US agents, who were in turn facing their own economic challenges. Both Korean groups struggled to maintain their independence in the face of deeper complicities that came increasingly to the surface. The fight over quota system protectionism became a miniature version of the broader scale market liberalization that the IMF bailout later formalized as economic restructuring. Political independence was, of course, a dominant concern in its twentieth-century history, beginning with Japanese colonialism in the first half of the century and moving into successive waves of American military, political, and financial forms of imperialism, but the problem becomes more difficult at the end of the American century, more complex than simply making way for an ascendant China.

It is no surprise, then, that the term *independent film* (*dongnip yŏnghwa*) during the 1990s was obfuscating rather than clarifying. Park argues that by the mid-1990s, the term *independent film* had subsumed terms like "*undong yŏnghwa* (activist films) *minjung yŏnghwa* (people's films),[74] and *minjok yŏnghwa* (national films)," which "suddenly seemed antiquated and irrelevant under the new civilian rule in Korea."[75] Park's study is particularly valuable for the way it tracks the transformation of activist filmmaking in Korea in the 1980s, which foregrounded communal production and distribution methods and was intimately tied to the period's militant labor movement.[76] This activist tradition began to dissipate in the independent film organizations of the 1990s,[77] facing the challenges of maintaining the original ethos in a rapidly changing industry, in which independent cinema became increasingly dependent on film festivals and intertwined with moneyed interests who were ambivalent about the roots of the tradition.[78] Indeed, as Nohchool Park has suggested, the phrase "'independent cinema' was proposed to capture the new contour of people's cinema in an age of de-politicization."[79] In this emerging context, in which new directors often made independent films simply to gain visibility for more commercial projects, the growing ambivalence of independent filmmakers and independent film organizations like KIFA in the post-IMF period reflected a larger ambivalence about the notion of independence in general in Korean public discourse. Distant now from the political usage in colonial times, *independence* instead becomes a clumsy synthesis into which populist activism fades.

Accordingly, *Looking for Bruce Lee* is an independent film as nouveau quota quickie, one that, in its rush to market, converts independence into personal rather than communal concerns. The punk's mastery of the flexible-labor job market and his embrace of human capital is not merely ironic complicity but is symptomatic of the larger socioeconomic restructuring from which IMF restructuring also follows. The independence of the *segyehwa* punk and the post-protectionist state is no longer about autonomy but rather about negotiating complex networks of affiliation to the greatest advantage as the kind of survival strategy that inheres in subsistence faming. Youth culture becomes an extension of emerging global dynamics: to imagine oneself as Bruce Lee is both to see oneself as symptomatic of a new brutally competitive economic regime and to embrace its terms. It is finally no surprise that the *segyehwa* punk must disavow the political economy from which he springs; the logic of human capital rests fundamentally on such a disavowal. For the *segyehwa* punk, looking at the moon becomes indistinguishable from a blinkered preoccupation with the finger, a way of seeing that rests on the prohibition of more pressing forms of inquiry. Such a position entails both a recognition and a refusal of the new material conditions of post–IMF Crisis life in Korea and in the world political economy that the punk imagines to inhabit.

One, two, three four. Who's punk? What's the score?

The Surface of Finance
Digital Touching in *Take Care of My Cat*

Following Hae-joo (Lee Yo-won) on her long commute from a working-class neighborhood in Incheon to a brokerage firm in the wealthy Seoul neighborhood of Apgujeong, the opening credit sequence of Jeong Jae-eun's 2001 film *Take Care of My Cat* might be read as a microcosm of Hae-joo's attempt to rise above humble roots and enter the world of global finance. A mere vocational high school graduate from the less prestigious satellite city, Hae-joo is doubly abject at the brokerage, where her supervisor openly refers to her as a *value-deficit* employee, a categorical label that no amount of hard work can overcome. Although both share an ambitious spirit, we might ultimately see Hae-joo in contrast to Tess McGill (Melanie Griffith) in the 1988 20th Century Fox romantic comedy *Working Girl*, which depicts the rise of a working-class young woman from secretarial pool to executive boardroom through a swamp of gendered and classed expectations. While Hae-joo certainly shares Tess's up-by-the-bootstraps spunk, her glass ceiling remains inviolable, whereas Tess's shatters.

Even more sadly, of the five friends from Incheon in the film, Hae-joo's limited prospects are the brightest. Citing the twin crises of youth and women's unemployment in the post-IMF period,[1] the film is a coming-of-age narrative in which any apparatus of upward mobility becomes unavailable.[2] The underemployed orphan Ji-young (Ok Ji-young) lives in a ramshackle hovel that is deteriorating even more rapidly than the health of her aging grandparents with whom she lives. Tae-hee (Bae Doona) works listlessly without pay at her parents' sauna business, trying to shrug off the inequities of her patriarchal family. The ethnically Chinese twins, On-ju (Lee Eun-jo) and Bi-ryu (Lee Eun-shil), sell trinkets on the mostly empty streets of Incheon's Chinatown. Their shut-in grandparents refuse to answer the door for their own granddaughters when they try to bring a package from their mother, who has long-since left Incheon. In this post–IMF Crisis milieu, when jobs were particularly scarce for their demographic,[3] the young women occupy positions near the bottom of the economic ecology. Unlike the capital and commodities moving in and out of their historic port city, for which authorities were rapidly trying to build a new infrastructure at the very same moment, the women remain left behind by an economy shifting further away from the developmental model that characterized Korea's rapid growth in the second half of the twentieth century.

Incheon is to Seoul in the film as Coketown is to London in Raymond Williams's account of Charles Dickens. Whereas "London could not be described in a rhetorical gesture of repressive uniformity" because it encompassed a complexity that "was not, in any simple way, physically apparent," the industrial city of Coketown offered an order and a system that "were indeed quite visible on the surface." It is not just that the city's rapid emergence around an industrial boom meant that its streets and housing "were systematic and uniform" but also that the new industrial towns "were organised around their decisive places of work— usually a single kind of work—in ways that London never had been or would be."[4] Although existing in a different modality, the Incheon of *Take Care of My Cat* is largely presented as a place defined by trade and transport in an industrial context. Despite the existence of historical layers that differ from Coketown (e.g., Incheon's Chinatown), the film's vision of Incheon seems uniformly defined by its sites of traditional labor.

This vision comes under some pressure with the building of the new airport. Although the Incheon International Airport appears only obliquely, it remains a spectral presence in the film. Built in time for the FIFA World Cup tournament, which South Korea cohosted with Japan in 2002, and opening in 2001 (the same year that Jeong's film was released), the airport was initially conceived after the 1988 Seoul Olympics, when the older Gimpo Airport was deemed insufficient. Contemporary in design and a recipient of numerous awards, the airport became one of the busiest in the world. A complex befitting a world financial capitol, it greets international travelers with the gleaming face of global technomodernity and an optimism befitting the sentiment associated with Incheon as the site of General MacArthur's tide-turning offensive in 1950 during the Korean War. The opening scene of the film, in fact, references MacArthur's famous gambit when the young women sing "Farewell Nak-dong River," a song that commemorates this event. Still wearing their high school uniforms, they giddily celebrate the end of their school years by the water's edge at the Incheon port, against a backdrop of cargo containers and shipping cranes. Even before the airport was built, Incheon was the nation's second largest naval port behind Busan and the endpoint for a large rail infrastructure designed to move products to and from these global access points. But because Incheon could now function as an even more multimodal hub (air, sea, land), the new airport reflected the increasing global orientation of the Korean economy. Infrastructural development in the area has further taken the form of large-scale urban development to provide growth environments for new economic ventures oriented toward foreign capital, including a number of Special Economic Zones.

The film, however, is not so sanguine about these new developments and the possibilities they afford. Despite the focus on new infrastructure in the region at the time, the representation of the airport in the film is surprisingly elliptical. Instead of loving wide-angle flyovers and slow pans across duty-free shopping and food courts, we see only a few indirect allusions: a shot of a shuttle bus on its way to the airport, two shots of planes taking off and landing, and a fairly tight shot of Ji-young and Tae-hee looking at departures screens in the film's final moments as they prepare to leave Korea for some unannounced destination. Although the new economy emerging around them holds a good deal of promise for the region, these opportunities seem unavailable to the characters in the film. For these five young women, sites of the new economy ironize rather than address their socioeconomic precarity as they enter adulthood.

In this milieu the film is preoccupied with the problem of work in the post-IMF era, specifically for young women. If the task of the *segyehwa* punk was to master the logics of an economy shifting away from their interests, then the young women here gauge to what extent these new daunting structures can accommodate their existence at all. The IMF experience certainly influenced their trepidation. Women were not only disproportionately affected by postcrisis unemployment trends, but they were also ignored by post-IMF public policy, which focused more on men and treated the employment status of women as a secondary concern.[5] The IMF Crisis period thus became a moment in which state policy, committed to structural reforms, effected a retrenchment in gendered labor. Even more radically than in the previous chapter, these young women have to imagine themselves as entering the global marketplace, not as instruments of labor but as figures of capital, a task that requires that they increasingly see themselves as immaterial. This fantastical option, furthermore, occludes (unevenly) the fact that their only real alternatives in this economy are the more precarious forms of service labor,[6] including a fate that is only obliquely alluded to in the film: commodification in sex trafficking.[7]

A crucial diagnostic gesture in the film is the representation of this gendered precarity in sublimated form as a fear of technological obsolescence. More specifically, the anxiety about a vanishing mode of gendered labor becomes reimagined as a problem of technological remediation. As Jay David Bolter and Richard Grusin have defined this primary characteristic of new media, *remediation* is "the representation of one medium in another."[8] The term encompasses not just the effort of new media to absorb older media but also attempts by older media, as in the case of *Take Care of My Cat*, to "reaffirm their status within our culture as digital media challenge that status."[9] Riffing on W. J. T. Mitchell's elegant description of *ekphrasis* as "verbal representation of visual representation,"[10] their articulation of remediation in the present context helps us track the film's effort to think through the problem of economic adaptation in the film (i.e., the inability of the young women to succeed in the new economy) as a problem of technological transition and opens a way of thinking conjointly about technological and economic obsolescence.[11] Just as airports replace shipping ports and digital networks replace airports, new-economy labor models in the film make older categories of work and workers obsolete.

Take Care of My Cat is particularly interested in digital technology, most specifically in relation to cellular phones. Ironically, though the handheld device is central to the new technological economy that promises a brighter future, it also becomes a means by which the young women can grasp their own obsolescence. A related modality of this precarity, then, is an anxiety about connection, one that blends social, technological, and emotional senses of the word. Beyond lacking college degrees, all of them (to different extents) lack familial support and connections. At one point Ji-young, an orphan, is turned down for a job in accounting because she has no parent to vouch for her. With only each other to rely on, Bi-ryu and On-ju live without their mother, who resides in Japan; Tae-hee comes from a more traditional nuclear family, but her father is ambivalent about her aspirations, favoring his sons instead; Hae-joo's parents, who divorce during the course of the film, only appear in brief glimpses and are displaced by Hae-joo's older sister, who in turn leaves Seoul. Despite the fact that the film's setting is a logistical hub, the young women severely lack access. In fact, they seem to perform their condition late in the film, when they are locked out of the house where they are having a get-together. The closest the film comes to depicting organized labor, they dig a hole (a metaphoric grave) in which to lie together in order to stay warm.

To address the connection anxiety, the young women engage in what we might term *digital touching*, a tautology that encompasses both the forms of intimacy allowed by new communication technologies and the older sense of touching with one's fingers, or digits.[12] In the film these two senses overlap as part of a larger effort to consider the imbrication of the tactile and technological as modes of intimacy in late capitalism. Offering a means of mattering in a world where these young women become increasingly immaterial,[13] the handheld device becomes a way of holding hands, both a prosthetic charged with the task of feeling and a mode of redressing the marginalized figures who carry them into an otherwise apathetic milieu. This compensatory material presence in the film, however, also functions paradoxically to disarticulate the young women from the material structures of the new economy. As personal relationships become mediated by digital technologies, the young women, susceptible to obsolescence, become the objects of remediation as well.

Window Cartography

At the end of the initial title sequence, Hae-joo pulls open the blinds at the brokerage firm to reveal a global map, which consists of large black squares resembling enlarged pixels (fig. 16), simultaneously unveiling both the geographic coordinates of the global economic regime depicted in the film and its technological inclinations. As the camera offers a wider view, we gradually see that these pixels specifically form the southern half of Europe and the northern half of Africa. The film's title appears in Korean script at the end of this shot, fitting within the northern border of Africa, with the English translation diagonally above in the blank spaces that correspond with the Mediterranean Sea and the Indian Ocean. But as the camera pulls back and as Hae-joo finishes raising the blinds, we realize that the map is not affixed to the windows as it first appears but rather to an initially unseen glass partition positioned closer to the camera that separates the position of the viewer from that of Hae-joo and the distant windows. Self-reflexively figuring the literal film screen, clear surfaces like this one, which separate viewer from diegetic scene, constitute a repeated trope in this film that either delimits fictive space or serves as sites for extradiegetic digital inscription. In addition, these surfaces also figure the sites of contemporary Korean finance and digital modernity,[14] giving form to economic structures that became more prominent after the IMF Crisis in Korea but nonetheless remained difficult to see, not least because we look *through* and not *at* them.

FIGURE 16. End of the title sequence featuring the view from the office windows at the brokerage firm where Hae-joo works in *Take Care of My Cat* (CJ Entertainment, 2001).

Slyly then, the film's title sequence gives form to the otherwise invisible economic infrastructures of the moment as the map begins to function as a cartographic window, its primary coordinates formed not by its organization of land mass but by its framing of the view outside, behind the map. A masked cartography, we need to look through and not at the map's explicit forms. When we look in this way, we see three important signifiers emerge from behind in the Seoul cityscape, each of which the camera takes pains to frame in the map's empty spaces by moving slightly to its left as it pulls back. First, just off the northwest coast of Africa we see a sign for Anycall, the name of Samsung's cellphone division during the period. At the time of this film's release and through the next decade, the usage rates for cellular in the Republic of Korea were among the highest in the world. In the context of a newly deregulated communications industry, the ROK proved to be a nation of early adopters, even ahead of Western markets.[15] Appropriately, cellular phones figure prominently in the film. The young women constantly use them, often beyond their appointed functions (in one case as a cat toy). Although the narrative takes place before the introduction of smart phones, the usage of cell phones in the film anticipates the way in which the new technology will become part of the fabric of everyday life, particularly as a social networking instrument.[16] At one point, the poorest of the five, Ji-young, upgrades to a better model using money that she has borrowed from Tae-hee, even though her financial situation is becoming increasingly desperate. In this regard it is notable that the film lists among its corporate sponsors in the closing credits SK Global, one of the largest telecommunications companies in Korea. The technology, and the capital that backs it, seems indeed inescapable.

The film focuses particularly on text messaging, still an emerging technology in 2001 but already widely adopted in Korea ahead of the international curve. The young women, in fact, might be considered part of the *ŏmjijok* (thumb tribe phenomenon), a neologism used to describe the multitudes of Korean youth who embraced this new technology with enthusiasm.[17] In the film, cell phone use alleviates the most alienating aspects of contemporary life, with texting working to produce compensatory connections, digital touching, as the friends drift apart after graduation. A remediation effort, the depiction of texting in the film represents an early attempt in media history to represent this technology, a later version of which becomes prominent, for example, in the American Netflix serial *House of Cards* (2013–18), in which this contemporary mode of communication has become an important medium for dramatic dialogue. A little before the previously discussed title shot, we see Hae-joo on the train from Incheon to Seoul sending a text message (fig. 17). In the upper right portion of the film screen is a semitransparent enlargement of the cell phone screen through which the passengers on the train can be seen. We see Hae-joo typing on the left, using only her left thumb at a rapid clip, while the letters appear on the extradiegetic representation of the phone screen to her right. A repeated trope throughout

FIGURE 17. Hae-joo texting her friend on her long commute into Seoul in *Take Care of My Cat* (CJ Entertainment, 2001).

the film, the young women send each other text messages, with the text of the message appearing extradiegetically on the screen, sometimes floating in the air, framed as it is here by a projected cell phone screen. At other points the script appears on diegetic surfaces, like bus windows or buildings.

Second, in the space corresponding to the Mediterranean Sea, we see a sign for the Korea Housing Bank (*Chut'aek ŭnhaeng*). From 1967 (and the Korean Housing Bank Act) until 1997, this was a state-owned bank designed to help Koreans finance homes during a time of economic expansion. In August of 1997, as part of a larger trend toward liberalization begun in the early 1990s, it was privatized into the Housing and Commercial Bank and then merged in 2001 (the year *Take Care of My Cat* was released) with Kookmin Bank (KB),[18] which at the time of this writing is not only one of the largest banks in Korea but also one of the Korean banks with the highest percentage of foreign ownership (as high as 84 percent in 2007).[19] The shot of the Korea Housing Bank in the opening credits thus captures the last moments of this vestige of the developmental state before its transformation into a fully contemporary transnational financial institution and from the somewhat literal point of view of finance capital (i.e., the brokerage across the street).

The Korea Housing Bank also appears later in the film, first in the background when a despairing Hae-joo, after a depressing after-work drinking session with her fellow value-deficit coworkers, beckons Chan-yong, the young man whose interest in her she has ignored throughout the film. Having been frankly reminded about her limited prospects by her coworkers, Hae-joo reluctantly becomes reconciled to the fact that Chan-yong—not the handsome broker at the firm, and certainly not her own professional success—represents her best prospect. As if to cement the point, the camera reverses position, shooting from inside the glassed-in area where the bank's ATM kiosks and some pay phones are located (fig. 18). In a shot that one might be tempted to characterize as *neoliberal indirect discourse*, the film depicts Hae-joo and Chan-yong quite literally from the point of view of a bank, a perspective emphasized by the prominence of the glass surface (here the bank's literal walls) that separates the camera from the actors, a glass partition that repeats the trope from the title sequence. It was not uncommon for Korean filmmakers of the period to use creatively the perspective of an ATM camera. Jang Joon-hwan did so, for example, in his *Save the Green Planet* (*Chigurŭl chik'yŏra*, 2003), in which police use ATM video to chase a lead; and Park Heung-sik used it in *I Wish I Had a Wife* (*Nato anaeka issŏssŭmyŏn choketta*, 2001), in which

FIGURE 18. Shot of Hae-joo and Chan-yong sitting in front of the Korea Housing Bank and a reverse-POV shot from inside the bank in *Take Care of My Cat* (CJ Entertainment, 2001).

characters reveal their most private emotions to CCTV cameras in ATM kiosks. In the present scene the bank's perspective seems to downplay surveillance and instead peers sympathetically and even with a good deal of humanity at a moment of frailty, encouraging us to forget momentarily that we are looking from the literal perspective of a bank, which, in assessing more existential forms of credit, monitors not only our behaviors but our feelings as well.[20]

Third, to the far left, we see coming into focus a view of the Seoul Olympic Stadium, the centerpiece for the 1988 Olympics, which is often regarded as the inaugural moment of rapid modernization and globalization in Korean history.[21] Serving as a monument for modernity in Korea iconography, the stadium also anticipates the infrastructure built for the 2002 World Cup tournament, which was being finalized when *Take Care of My Cat* was released in 2001, including a stadium in Incheon. In this triumvirate of images in the title sequence, the film constellates digital phone technology, finance capital (specifically in relationship to housing mortgages), and Korean global modernity. These are three central concerns in the film.

Digital Analogues

About halfway through, Ji-young and Tae-hee encounter the ghostly figure of an indigent woman while walking on a bridge away from Incheon International Harbor, where they have been handing out fliers for Tae-hee's family's business. The encounter occurs on a bridge that spans a group of train tracks just after a bus passes by on the road. In this milieu, defined by transit (and one that connects transit to transience), Tae-hee talks about their high school group and how they seem to be drifting apart. Across the street the older woman with disheveled hair clutches a clear plastic bag with some sort of garment inside it and rushes to menace them with a wordless glare. Proceeding on their way, they are clearly shaken, not least because the woman serves as a projective mirror of their own preoccupations. After a beat, Ji-young confesses that she is worried that she will turn out like the woman, whom she refers to as a beggar. Tae-hee, in contrast, states that people like the old woman pique her curiosity: idealizing their freedom, she wonders where they wander all day.

Despite their disagreement, they agree that the woman embodies their uncertain futures. Although Tae-hee idealizes unmoored itinerancy, her fetishization of travel is motivated by a desire to work. Earlier in the film she had inquired at the Seamen's Center about the possibility of working on a ship, and her plan to leave Korea is inspired by her attraction to jobs available in Australia.[22] One of her complaints about her father is that he does not pay her for her labor. When she cuts her image out of the family portrait just before her departure, she is rejecting not only her father's patriarchal authority but also the practices of an exploitative employer, from whom she takes exactly (and no more than) the amount that she has estimated she has earned. In contrast, Ji-young foregrounds the ghostly woman's vulnerability, a condition that she has already experienced in the short time since graduation from high school. Ji-young thus criticizes Tae-hee's idealism, focusing instead on the danger that is inextricable from what Tae-hee thinks is freedom.

On the one hand, this transit-heavy environment—on a bridge over train tracks, near a harbor, in the shadow of a new airport—reflects the construction of an extraordinarily robust network intended to strengthen the Korean economy as it moves away from the crisis years of the late 1990s. On the other hand, the transient woman suggests that these forms of progress are accompanied by the obsolescence of certain forms of labor, particularly those that were prominent in the 1960s and 1970s. Indeed, the ghostly woman's encased garments invoke the sewing factories that once employed armies of Korean women who helped drive the once thriving Korean textile industry, which played a pivotal role in the rise of this so-called Asian Tiger economy in earlier days.[23] The ghostly woman thus links the individual experiences of the young women to a broader economic history.

It is important not to idealize the developmental state in the ROK, which would be to idealize, as well, its authoritarianism under Park Chung-hee. Jin-kyung Lee's *Service Economies* is particularly useful in this context for its discussion of the deep complicity between the Korean developmental state and US imperial power. She points out that the ROK provided the highest number of troops of any ally in support of the US war in Vietnam (and in the second US war in Iraq as well).[24] In this context Lee argues that the ROK becomes a neocolonial or subimperial nation, which "takes place through the dominated group's internalization of colonizing discourses and governmentality as their own."[25] This transformation involves not just ideological absorption but includes political economic dimensions as well, specifically Korea's fostering of a transnational labor force as labor costs rose in Korea,[26] with militant Korean labor unions gaining a foothold.[27]

The film's nostalgia for gendered labor in a developmental context is thus somewhat ambiguous. A residuum of the sewing factories embodied by the ghostly woman, Ji-young's desire for a textile career tellingly misunderstands contemporary modes of production. Ji-young is interested not in textiles as physical objects but rather more specifically in the patterns reproducible on the fabrics. Somewhat naively, she spends her time making complex drawings on paper, diligently marking up tiny squares one at a time with colored markers. When Tae-hee notices the elaborate designs on the box that Ji-young makes for Hae-joo's birthday gift (a cat), Tae-hee comments, "It's pretty cool. But still it must be boring to paint all this one by one."[28] Invoking the pixels from the global map at the beginning of the film and the similarly rendered old-style letter boxes from the airport terminal displays in the closing credits, Ji-young's textiles belong to the milieu not of the historical Korean factory but of contemporary digital industries. But though Ji-young criticizes her grandmother for mending socks, which she regards as a waste of time in a global economy in which they are cheap, her own labor seems equally old-fashioned, mistaking digital making as manually performed. Anachronistically producing what amount to hand-crafted pixels, Ji-young's would-be textiles are made as if in the old factory, through a painstakingly repetitive process that harks back to the repetitive sweatshop labor of previous generations.[29] The lingering sound of the grandmother's manually powered sewing machine that we hear as Ji-young climbs the stairs to her room to work on her designs thus suggests that Ji-young's labor is much more like her grandmother's than she might admit. Significantly, later in the film, she confesses in a job interview that she does not know how to use a computer. Although she dreams of producing textiles in a digital era, she is scarcely equipped to do so.[30]

The fetishization of handheld communication for these five young women, as if five digits on a single hand, becomes an ironic grasping of the machinery of their own erasure. The representation of texting in the film literalizes this drama: their words gain only fleeting traction on the surfaces around them. As I have begun to explain, this is an explicit visual trope in the film, one that simultaneously performs the tragic ephemerality of digital touching and inscription. We see an example in the scenes in which Tae-hee serves as a typist for a quadriplegic poet who cannot type for himself. When she asks why he refuses to use a computer instead of the old, manual typewriter that he needs Tae-hee to operate, he responds that then he would otherwise have no excuse to see her. Though offered as a joke, his comment and clear fondness for Tae-hee imply that he regards her typing as an intimate act. They work together, after all, in his bedroom. Being left behind, in fact, is the subject of much of his poetry:

> Everyone comes and goes, but I am always waiting.
>
> People move, and I sleep.
>
> In that way I feel as if I am always asleep.

Sleep here is dormancy amid the rapid clip of modernity. Along these lines the poet serves as a figure of predigital technologies. In addition to the typewriter one notices an arrangement of old analog cameras on the shelf by the window.

The most striking element of these scenes in the poet's bedroom, however, is the way in which his words and Tae-hee's typing register extradiegetically, digitally imposed on the surface of the desk where she works (fig. 19). As Tae-hee types, the words (a postproduction insertion) appear, mimicking the analog mechanics of the typewriter, even scrolling upward when she pulls the paper out of the typewriter. Remediation occurs here in different registers—in the relationship between spoken words, typed pages, and digitally imposed script, on one hand, and in the ekphrastic relationship between poetry and film, on the other. Ironically, in this chain of signification in which the poet's spoken words become typed onto a hidden page and digitally revealed to the filmic audience through the aforementioned contrivance, the words are decidedly transient. They flash on the screen as typed writing and vanish just as quickly. The poet's words, which anticipate the people in his life disappearing, seem, indeed, to predict Tae-hee's departure at the end of the film, which as we will see is represented as an act of dematerialization. Tae-hee's typing and its subsequent disappearance also seem to perform the drama of gendered, self-effacing labor, as described in Natalia Cecire's account of Gertrude Stein's invocation of the typist as a figure of automatized women's work in her famously unreadable style: "This identification with the machine and the denial of her

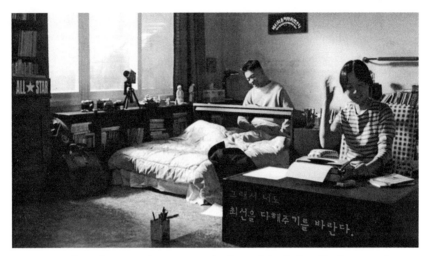

FIGURE 19. Extradiegetic inscriptions on the front of the desk as Tae-hee types in *Take Care of My Cat* (CJ Entertainment, 2001).

work as 'hard labor' renders the typist an apparatus herself, rhythmically and repetitively moving her fingers as she serves as an unmarked conduit for another's words."[31] In her feminist Kittlerian reading of Stein's aesthetic practice,[32] Cecire calls attention to what Tae-hee's typing and the film's general portrayal of underemployed women also shed light on: the tendency of a certain kind of gendered labor to go unacknowledged.[33]

Doubling the oscillating status of gendered labor between visible and invisible registers, the digitally rendered typewritten text in this scene toys with the line between diegetic and extradiegetic representation. On one hand, the words are only visible on the screen by the filmic audience and not by the characters in the film, but on the other hand, this text is printed on a diegetic object in the film, in this case the front of a desk, so that the materiality of the script seems to bind to an object within the frame of the film. This trope repeats throughout: digital words (mostly in the form of electronic text messages) appear on physical surfaces, like the bus window above Tae-hee's head as she texts Ji-young, before disappearing soon after. The digital in this context becomes a way to compensate for the lack of agency for the young women, a way to register their touch, but also implies a resignation to the transience of such compensatory gestures. Shortly after we see Tae-hee on the bus sending Ji-young a text message, for example, there is a shot of Ji-young near the airport failing to receive it. Next to her floating in the air, as if unfixed to any surface, we see an envelope insignia signifying an incoming message. The text message itself then scrolls from the bottom to the top of the screen as the camera turns skyward to capture the underside of a plane taking off. It is as if, along with the airplane, the text message has flown into the sky, missed by its intended addressee. What are presented in the film as moments of expression and communication (of poetry and friendship) almost immediately become moments of erasure. Remediation in the film—turning spoken poetry into typed text, type into digital information, and digital phone messages into film—expresses the pathos of a disappearing technology and mode of production rather than celebrating the emerging one.[34]

In the final shot of the film we see the confluence of digital script and filmic form in the word "Good Bye," which appears in English,[35] superimposed over an airplane that seems to be landing, echoing the scene in which Ji-young seems to miss the text message from Tae-hee. The big difference with the film's final text message, however, is that there is nothing diegetic about it. Though it would be appropriate given their departure from Korea in the previous scene, we do not regard it to be a text message sent from Tae-hee and Ji-young to their friends. Rather, it is a message directed at the audience that takes the place of the classic film announcement "The End" (or "Fin"). We might say that the film texts us.

By extension, we imagine the invitation to a cinematic experience that, like Park Chan-wook's 2011 film *Night Fishing* (*P'aranmanjan*), which was shot entirely with an iPhone 4, reproduces the affective intimacy to which handheld technologies aspire. Offering something like the logic of a handheld film, *Take Care of My Cat* thus imagines a kind of intimacy with a technology in which the forms of emotional proximity that technology allows are confused with and displaced onto the technology itself. The transience that seems to define the general milieu of the film links the construction of the extraordinarily ambitious material infrastructure that attempted to infuse the Korean economy with a new vitality as it moved forward from the IMF Crisis years of the late 1990s with the production of the more tragic forms of obsolescence that inevitably accompany what we might otherwise call progress.

Ghost Ships on the Yellow Sea

In the port town of Incheon in the contemporary moment of financialization, another mode of this fluctuation between material and immaterial modes is manifested in the ghostliness of transnational capital. In nineteenth-century British discourse this characteristic was sometimes figured in an old ghost-ship legend, namely in appropriations of the Flying Dutchman story. Sir Walter Scott, for example, in his long poem *Rokeby*, mentions the "Demon Frigate," and elaborates on the reference in a note:

> This is an allusion to a well-known nautical superstition concerning a fantastic vessel, called by sailors the Flying Dutchman, and supposed to be seen about the latitude of the Cape of Good Hope. . . . The cause of her wandering is not altogether certain; but the general account is, that she was originally a vessel loaded with great wealth, on board of which some horrid act of murder and piracy had been committed; that the plague broke out among the wicked crew who had perpetrated the crime, and that they sailed in vain from port to port, offering, as the price of shelter, the whole of their ill-gotten wealth; that they were excluded from every harbour, for fear of the contagion which was devouring them; and that, as a punishment of their crimes, the apparition of the ship still continues to haunt those seas in which the catastrophe took place, and is considered by the mariners as the worst of all possible omens.[36]

The story has been read as bespeaking the curse of empire.[37] The horrid acts of murder and piracy here are the inevitable consequences of an enterprise that seeks its fortune far from home. As Giovanni Arrighi has described, Britain's economic hegemony was an *extroverted* economy based on the strength of its trade networks (as opposed to the more at least initially *autocentric* American model, which privileged vertical integration).[38] Imported to the British context, the Flying Dutchman represents the nightmare of this model—money that remains caught drifting in the interstitial space between metropole and colony that cannot be converted into the goods, services, or, as it were, relief. Here, capital unable to come ashore is useless money, wealth that cannot buy anything.

But in the context of the reforms demanded by the IMF bailout and its liberalization of monetary policy, floating capital (one might call it liquidity) is an ideal rather than cursed condition. Jin-Ho Jang has argued that one of the dramatic changes that resulted from the financial reforms of the bailout package was a shift in orientation (though perhaps one more perceived than real)[39] to a stock market–centered financial system that foregrounded shareholder value and encouraged speculation, moving away from a model that favored manufacturing, exporting, and "greenfield" investment, which focuses on building business infrastructure from the ground up.[40] In financialized economies money aspires to become deterritorialized, unmoored in the mode of the historic ghost ship.

Through the buying and selling of such instruments as derivatives and credit default swaps, capital no longer seems to require material objects in the form of commodities in order to facilitate accumulation. In a gloss of Arrighi, Fredric Jameson has described contemporary finance in quasi-gothic terms that synthesize our historic ghost ships with Derridean hauntology:

> Now this free-floating capital, on its frantic search for more profitable investments . . . will begin to live its life in a new context; no longer in the factories and the spaces of extraction and production, but on the floor of the stock market, jostling for more intense profitability, but not as one industry competing with another branch, nor even one productive technology against another more advanced one in the same line of manufacturing, but rather in the form of speculation itself: spectres of value, as Derrida might put it, vying against each other in a vast world-wide disembodied phantasmagoria.[41]

The movement of capital in the contemporary financialized present literalizes the phantasmagoric ghost ship of legend, but the free-floating state of ghostly capital that once signified its tragic position outside of economic circulation now describes its flow through these circuits. It's not that the ghost ship cannot come to port; it no longer wants to.

Not coincidentally, floating in *Take Care of My Cat* becomes an ideal rather than cursed condition. Tae-hee's fantasies about travel, in this context, seem expressions of desire to be like money: deterritorialized, unmoored from strictures, and free to pursue opportunity as it arises. Lying on a boat that serves as a piece of furniture in the twins' house, Tae-hee muses about this freedom as the mise-en-scène shifts counterfactually to an imagined, tranquil river where Tae-hee floats on a boat with her eyes closed. Her subsequent voice-over inverts the Flying Dutchman legend: "I just want to keep wandering around. The thought of just living in one place suffocates me. On an endlessly sailing boat, living like flowing water, never stopping, like nomads, lying like this on a boat, watching the clouds go by and reading a book." Instead of understanding the nomadic condition in relation to a new kind of labor as, for example, in the work of Boltanski and Chiapello,[42] Tae-hee idealizes it, not exactly as floating on a ghost ship but (with a good deal of slippage from vessel to dynamic force) as "flowing" as in water. In wanting to flow freely throughout the world, Tae-hee, in response to her abject position in contemporary Korean society, cathects not to the position of a specific traveler (her vision is scarcely embodied) but, more radically, to something like the condition of money. To be clear: she does not want to *have* money; she wants to *be* money.[43] Accordingly, like money in Jameson's theoretical excursion, Tae-hee (with Ji-young and her parent's money in tow) takes flight at the end of the film into its surface, as we will see shortly, becoming a literal, dematerialized embodiment of floating capital.

Just before the film's final farewell text message, we see Ji-young and Tae-hee looking at the departure screens at the airport, deciding where to go (they have decided to leave Korea in search of work). Reversing the clichéd ending of the classic American western, the characters do not move away from the position of the viewer, disappearing into the sunset on the horizon, but rather walk *toward* the viewer and vanish instead into the foreground, into the space of the screen (fig. 20). Like the digitally superimposed words that appear on various surfaces in the course of the film, the tenuous existence of the young woman *in* the film is represented as a tenuous existence *on* its surface, as if to ask, To what extent is the new economy touchable and inhabitable? Although the ending of the story for the two young women reads as an escape from an environment that affords them few opportunities,[44] it leaves unanswered the question of their destination and fate. If the destination is indeed Australia, as implied earlier in the film, we know that they will be entering an equally fraught situation that abounds with exploitation, including a robust sex-trafficking network that preys on precisely the situation in which Ji-young and Tae-hee find themselves. The film makes only a subtle nod to this context when Tae-hee mentions the idea of a *working holiday* in her pitch to Ji-young about leaving Korea. This

FIGURE 20. Closing sequence of *Take Care of My Cat* (CJ Entertainment, 2001).

is perhaps a reference to the Australian visa of the same name used by women and traffickers to enter the country for this purpose.[45] These possibilities are left unnamed and ignored by the rendering of vanishing as the abstract site of possibility, giving the ending the feeling of relief rather than despair. Their departure in search of more opportunity is thus represented not as the traversal of space but as a kind of transubstantiation; they become immaterial.[46] Perhaps, then, we might imagine Tae-hee's boat as a financialized revision of the Flying Dutchman.

Living in Incheon, Tae-hee need only look around her to find inspiration for this vision: on the one hand, at the abundant evidence of flowing capital responsible for the massive infrastructural buildup in the region (a prominent backdrop in the film), and on the other, at the absence of wealth among the residents of the area, especially her friends and neighbors. She seems surrounded by wealth, but no one seems wealthy. The setting for the film's final moments, the Incheon International Airport, both embodies and facilitates this dream of freely flowing capital in deterritorialized space.[47] The airport is part of the Incheon Free Economic Zone (IFEZ), which provides tax incentives designed to promote foreign investment and exchange (most visibly for travelers in the form of duty-free shopping). Built on land reclaimed from the Yellow Sea and architecturally designed to evoke the cargo ships in Incheon Harbor, the Incheon Airport in this manner, in this modest capacity, functions as a neo–ghost ship, providing a place for nomadic capital to flow unrestrained.

Airports have been frequently represented in film and literature as immaterial and interstitial: the nonplace of transit. An undifferentiated space, the airport is where the unnamed narrator (Edward Norton) of David Fincher's *Fight Club* (1999) first invents his alter ego. In Jonathan Lethem's *Dissident Gardens* (2013) the protagonist, on entering the airport where he will remain delayed in the novel's final pages, imagines the airport's ungrounded ontology: "your mind prepared, by beginning to levitate off the surface of the planet in advance."[48] Even more so with heightened security after 9/11, airports have become marked in Western representations as a new kind of extraterritorial, denationalized space in between nations, where state sovereignty becomes vulnerable. Both based on the true story of Merhan Nasseri, for example, who lived for eight years at Charles DeGaulle Airport because his travel papers had been stolen while he was en route to England, Philippe Lioret's *Tombés du ciel* (1993) and Steven Spielberg's *The Terminal* (2004) represent the airport as a state of exception outside of national jurisdiction. As Matthew Hart suggests, the purgatorial space of the airport threshold is defined by "the operations of an extraterritorial space that remains only partly visible, the power of which lies in its very inscrutability, its ability to remain just the other side of what we know."[49] In *Take Care of My Cat* this immaterial, interstitial quality of airports becomes a way of giving final form to its abiding anxiety about obsolescence. Despite the fact that the Incheon International Airport signaled an optimism in 2001 for a new economy, the young women remain disconnected from the network it opens, just as they vanish from the world that emerges.

Farther south in Incheon there is even fuller realization of the neo–ghost ship. Built on mudflats reclaimed from the Yellow Sea and one of three so-called smart cities planned for the Incheon Free Economic Zone, the Songdo International Business District, at the cost of $40 billion, is the first phase of this ambitious venture (fig. 21). It promised to be a technologically advanced, supremely wired, networked community (designed in partnership with the American firm Cisco Systems) that is international in orientation and conception and thus the perfect home for international finance. According to its website, the city, about the size of downtown Boston and built from scratch by the American firm Gale International, "boasts the wide boulevards of Paris, a 100-acre Central Park reminiscent

FIGURE 21. View of the Northeast Trade Tower and Central Park in Songdo. Photo taken by author.

of New York City, a system of pocket parks similar to those in Savannah, a modern canal system inspired by Venice and convention center architecture redolent of the famed Sydney Opera House."[50] Perhaps most significantly, transnational corporations in these cities were meant to enjoy generous tax incentives put in place in order to stimulate international business. Although there are residences planned for the areas and people will, indeed, live there, the most important inhabitant of the city is capital. Also an island like the land on which Incheon Airport sits, Songdo is eerily reminiscent of CEO Carl A. Gerstacher's notorious wish for the Dow Chemical Company:

> I have long dreamed to buy an island owned by no nation . . . and by establishing the World Headquarters of the Dow Company on the truly neutral ground of such an island, beholden to no nation or society. If we were located on such truly neutral ground we could then really operate in the United States as U.S. citizens, in Japan as Japanese citizens, and in Brazil as Brazilians rather than being governed in prime by the laws of the United States. . . . We could even pay any natives handsomely to move elsewhere.[51]

Like Gerstacher's dream island, Songdo would in theory be the kind of deregulated neutral ground that makes an ideal habitat for global finance.[52] Songdo thus reconjures Tae-hee's imaginary dinghy, in which the Flying Dutchman is reimagined as an ideal rather than tragic condition. Unmoored and unrestrained, these ghost ships on the Yellow Sea are vessels for wealth that no longer require that it be brought onshore. In 2001, when *Take Care of My Cat* was released, work had just begun on the Songdo project, but its planning had already been the subject of a good deal of publicity. The fleeting sense of digital intimacy represented in the film registers a bit differently in the shadows of Songdo. If the final part of Gerstacher's dream is that the natives will leave, then *Take Care of My Cat* imagines that not even payment is necessary, because they will simply disappear into obsolescence.

In the summer of 2014 I was first able to visit Songdo, staying in a hotel right next to the Northeast Trade Tower and the Songdo Convention Center, the two centerpieces of the urban landscape, and I returned in subsequent years to check up on the city's progress. Although the city officially opened in 2009, it was still effectively empty in 2014 and only incrementally more populated in following years. While there were a fair number of businesses, mostly service and retail, and some residential life, it certainly lacked the bustle of a global financial hub. What seemed most absent was foreign business activity. Although there have been a few important wins for Songdo—most notably the relocation of the Green Climate Fund to the city, the establishment of the Korea office for the World Bank, and perhaps most visibly as a filming location for Psy's "Gangnam Style" video[53]—the area seemed bereft of the very forms of commerce and trade that occasioned it in the first place. Songdo already felt like a ghost town.[54]

Sofia Shwayri recounts the contradictions and failures that have characterized Songdo's development since the late 1990s, when the idea was first hatched. For starters, it is an "eco city" whose development began by the destruction of precious wetlands and some of the rare species that inhabited them.[55] More pertinent, the failure of politicians and developers to attract foreign corporations has led to a change in strategy, such that the vision of the city as an engine for a new economy gives way to the reality of just another Korean city, what Shwayri calls the "Koreanization" of its originally international vision.[56] Songdo may well develop into a thriving neighborhood in years to come and shed the feeling of the ghost town—the parks, urban layout, and infrastructure are quite appealing in many ways—but to do so may require an abandonment of the initial dream of a deterritorialized finance zone. Such is the fate of development that meets no demand.

Another important contradiction implied by Shwayri is the ambiguous vision of global power implicit in Songdo's development plan at the current moment of transition between US and Chinese global economic regimes. The ROK occupies a tenuous position in between, still reliant on the United States for security but increasingly dependent on (and, of course, geographically more proximate to) Chinese markets for its economic prosperity. Physically modeled on Western urban aesthetics (New York, Venice, etc.) and marketed primarily to Western corporations, Songdo's strategic plan seems to repress the shifting locations of global economic power, especially China, despite its location in Incheon as a historic site of inter-Asian commerce. As an emerging ghost town, Songdo thus mirrors another historical neighborhood in Incheon that might be regarded as Songdo's predecessor: the famous Chinatown where Bi-ryu and On-ju live. The history of this Chinatown, the only one of its kind in Korea and famously the birthplace of *chajangmyŏn* (Chinese-Korean noodles with black bean sauce), has to do with Incheon's development as a naval port, which was originally hastened because of the establishment of trade routes with China in the late nineteenth century. This trade and the Incheon Chinatown flourished until the late 1940s, when the Korean government began to place unfavorable restrictions on Chinese merchants, and the Chinese government severely limited foreign travel for its citizens. Until it was revived as a tourist location in 2002, the Incheon Chinatown, cut off from the transnational flows of trade that gave rise to it in the first place, suffered a long period of decline, and most of the Chinese residents, like the twins' mother who resides in Japan, left. Even after it was redeveloped for tourists, according to Norimitsu Onishi writing for the *New York Times*, it became a Chinatown that lacks only the Chinese.[57]

In *Take Care of My Cat*, shots of the Incheon Chinatown show empty streets, the only evidence of commerce being Bi-ryu and On-ju's trinket stand, selling cheap knickknacks to skeptical young children who try to barter down their already low prices. The rejected package for which their Mandarin-speaking grandparents refuse to open the door, and which bears the markings of the German-based international shipping company that delivered it (DHL), reenacts in miniature the cessation of trade that ensured the obsolescence of Incheon's Chinatown in the first place. The Chinatown here is a place where the logistics break down; shipments do not arrive. Resigned, the twins leave the package at the doorstep and leave without seeing their grandparents.

Though originally conceived earlier, Songdo is ultimately a legacy of the IMF Crisis, in part a radical attempt to build an economic paradise that might make Incheon a vital global hub of international finance on the level of Singapore and Hong Kong, cities that, according to the Heritage Foundation Index of Economic Freedom, are the most "business friendly" in the entire world. But even putting aside the considerable differences in history and culture, Songdo is scarcely like Hong Kong or Singapore, not least because Korea has pulled back from full commitment to the Special Economic Zone model. In 2013 Korea was only thirty-fourth on the Heritage Foundation Index World Rankings, well behind countries like Japan, Norway, the Czech Republic, and the United States.[58] If we appeal to the historical chart of Korea's relative so-called economic freedom, we see a spike immediately during the IMF Crisis, which can be accounted for by the terms of the IMF bailout package, and then a significant pullback before a more recent escalation.[59] This data ultimately reflects the ebb and flow in Korean economic policy toward deregulation and then back toward more protectionist stances since the late 1990s. Burdened by contradictory logics, Songdo is caught in indecision between a free-trade ethos that wants to deregulate as much as possible and a countering force that remembers that the post-IMF period saw huge increases of foreign ownership in large Korean companies, approaching 50 percent in some cases.[60] To turn Songdo into Singapore, Korea would have to provide much more significant incentives than they are at present, but the fear is that these changes would be throwing good money after bad.

As an urban text, and itself a figure of economic remediation, Songdo is therefore a manifestation of a late-1990s macroeconomic diagnosis that saw a need to accommodate the rising tide of global corporate finance, originating in US and Western European financial centers, but one balanced out by a fear that such accommodations may become tantamount to an abdication of national sovereignty, especially over the remaining value in the manufacturing and export sector. A contradiction covered over by an aspirational discourse about futurity and progress, Songdo is infrastructure born out of hope but legislated more pragmatically. As in the ostensibly happy ending of *Take Care of My Cat*, Songdo produces optimism only by banishing the ghosts that hide in plain sight, as they do in the film just outside the window at Hae-joo's workplace. Both the film and Songdo engage, then, in an economic diagnosis not to come to terms with asymmetrical global financial structures and bleak prospects but, on the contrary, to ameliorate the pains of decline and obsolescence. Rather than oppose these structures, the film and the city wish to reimagine them as inhabitable, to touch their surfaces.

In this way Songdo resembles the more recent ghost ships of Hanjin, as they were so named in an article that appeared in *Bloomberg* on September 6, 2016.[61] The previous week, Hanjin, one of the world's largest shipping companies, had filed for bankruptcy, leaving the eighty-five ships that happened to be at sea and $14 billion in cargo in limbo, prompting *Bloomberg* to reprise the old trope of the Flying Dutchman.[62] Unlike the legendary ghost ship that was flush with wealth, Hanjin was unable to pay even the docking and unloading fees demanded by ports that left Hanjin's ships to drift in open waters until the matter of payment could be resolved. If the Flying Dutchman could not come ashore because of some moral atrocity committed by the crew, even with the benefit of its ill-gotten wealth, Hanjin's great sin was bankruptcy. Although there were plenty of riches on board, including $38 million worth of Samsung phones, and plenty more in the coffers of Hanjin's subsidiaries, the ships remained effectively decapitalized.[63] The breakdown of the global shipping industry came as little surprise to some observers who noted that the industry's recent boom had come under ideal conditions and overly optimistic trade forecasts before China's recent downturn.[64] More recently, profits in the industry had plummeted and many companies were what one commentator termed "zombie carriers," companies hemorrhaging money but propped up by banks that were keeping them afloat.[65] The free trade cities discussed in this chapter and piles of unused cargo ships and containers in the wake of the Hanjin bankruptcy,[66] none of them very old, seem now obsolete nearly from the moment of their inception, now wistful for an imaginary abundance so recently, and fleetingly, taken for granted.

In representing Tae-hee and Ji-young as disappearing into an ambiguously digital space (with the two meanings of the word *digital*, technological and somatic, placed in tension), the film's ending seems to realize these figures as ghostly women, figures that come to echo the original ghostly woman in the film, whose space of haunting is defined ultimately by transition.[67] Begun during the IMF Crisis and maturing with the Hanjin failure, a primary symptom of this transition is the privileging of circulation over production, a desperate fantasy of circulation without content, in which it does not matter that the containers are empty and the workers have vanished.[68] We might think of Hanjin's ghost fleet and Songdo's ghost town as figures that remind us that remediation may be most fundamentally a matter of political economy rather than one of aesthetic form, more material than epistemological. Becoming immaterial in the transition to digital forms at the end of the film, Tae-hee and Ji-young suffer an incomplete remediation and a failed transition, and their immaterial fate signals a larger world economic transition in which new economy infrastructures are nearly obsolete on arrival.

In this context an odd detail, specifically the strange presence of camera smudges on the screen, lingers through the final shots of the film, the scene of Tae-hee and Ji-young at the airport walking into the space of the screen, continuing through the bleed to the shot of the airplane landing, and carrying over all the way through to the end of the film (fig. 22). Barthesian *puncta* that become noticeable as the screens in the background blur and more pronounced in the transition to the next shot,[69] these smudges materially connect these already thematically related scenes and anticipate the film's final text message to the audience, as material traces left on the camera lens (likely watermarks), emphasizing the space of the screen as a site of possible inscription. They are also present in the previous airport scene in which the text message flies up into the sky (presumably, all of the airport scenes were shot together).

But rather than marking the space with contemporary digital data, these small, round smudge marks seem traces perhaps of another, older kind of digital data—that is, fingerprints. This is a particularly fitting visual feature for a film preoccupied with handheld devices. Not likely the simple result of sloppiness, they seem part of a larger ethos of digital touching that the film presents as part of an attempt

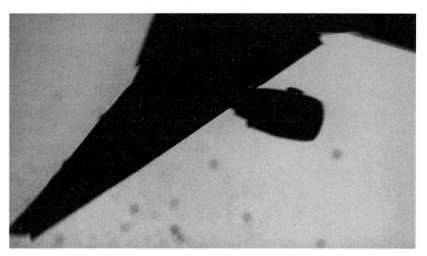

FIGURE 22. Smudges on the screen in the final sequence of *Take Care of My Cat* (CJ Entertainment, 2001).

to redress the immaterial fate that otherwise threatens the existence of the film's protagonists in the hope that a happier form of digital intimacy may be possible, as if touching this handheld film might compensate for an economy in which these young women become immaterial. One might say that the smudges are ghostly fingerprints marking the otherwise pristine surfaces of finance, an older form of digital information vanishing into the apparatus of another. Addressing Heidegger and manual eggbeaters, Mark Goble suggests that "The apprehension of an object's obsolescence . . . seems finally to reveal that we are constantly failing to pay attention to the things we use until the moment when their brokenness throws us into an existential awareness of them, an awareness that we know, at some level, we should have had already in the past."[70] The faint fingerprints in the film function similarly to Goble's eggbeaters. Both are figures of obsolescence that preserve historical awareness, perhaps an awareness of what we should have already known, amid sweeping amnesiac waves. This digital data does not so much represent the ghostly return of the analog repressed, faint inscriptions of the wrongly remediated and dispossessed, but instead offers traces of a moment in which the careful caresses of fingers grasping handheld devices, in unwitting acts of remediation, evince a desire not to recompense or revenge but to touch lovingly once more the technologies that hastened their oblivion.

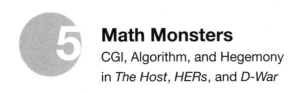

Math Monsters

CGI, Algorithm, and Hegemony
in *The Host*, *HERs*, and *D-War*

For anthropologists Edward LiPuma and Benjamin Lee, a compensatory virtue of the 2008 global credit crisis was the extent to which it made visible the otherwise unseen flows of contemporary finance, specifically the rapid emergence of derivatives trading. Trading in derivatives, once a much smaller-scale mechanism for hedging in a production-based economy, was by the early 2000s a primary mode of accumulation in a global environment thoroughly committed to circulatory capital. In 2004 LiPuma and Lee had expressed frustration: "How does one know about, or demonstrate against, an unlisted, virtual, offshore corporation that operates in an unregulated electronic space using a secret proprietary trading strategy to buy and sell arcane financial instruments?"[1] But by 2012 the fog apparently had lifted, the crisis having "laid bare the underlying and underappreciated foundations of the financial field."[2] An important part of curing the ills of contemporary finance, it seems, perhaps more fundamental than its enormous scale and power, is seeing them at all.[3] At stake is the invisibility of digital apparatuses that constitute networked transactional spaces, calculate financial instruments using complex differential equations, and even enumerate capital itself, digital apparatuses that are so central to this modality of circulation that it becomes difficult to separate medium from message. Indeed, LiPuma and Lee's diagnosis of contemporary financialization might also be read as a warning about the power of today's technologies, a power that inheres not only in vast capacities for rapid calculation but also in their ability to remain invisible. "Mathematical technology," they suggest, "seems so powerful that it absorbs the reality to which it refers."[4]

I have explored the profound effect of IMF restructuring on the Republic of Korea within the context of a transitional world system characterized by fading US dominance, foregrounding in the previous two chapters the demographic reach of such changes beyond the preoccupation with the salaryman that prevailed in public discourse. Moving now from an emphasis on social reorganization prompted by the crisis to focus on the systemic dynamics underlying it, I will address here more directly the logic of US hegemony and its infrastructures. The present chapter will focus specifically on this absorptive ability of mathematical technology as it is manifested in contemporary film, most visibly as CGI (computer-generated imagery). This manifestation indexes a much broader primacy accorded to complex computational strategies in contemporary life, materially linking aesthetics to militarization and financialization. IMF restructuring reached to the core of the Korean political economy, rebuilding its foundations and rewiring its fundamental operations as part of an effort by a declining empire to consolidate its power. In this infrastructural and managerial mode, US hegemony at this moment late in the American century reveals both its autopoietic fantasies and the reality of its weakening global position. If hegemony in Arrighi's account hinges on the ability to provide "the motor force of a general expansion" or align with a broader set of global interests,[5] then this late empire manifestation is far less salutary and far more desperate, something like hegemony without dominance, to reverse Ranajit Guha's formulation,[6] or a hegemony that is no more.

Although it is not art that yields visibility for LiPuma and Lee, their characterization of mathematics matches the work of visual theorists and practitioners more interested in the broader role of digital technologies in culture. Lev Manovich, for example, points out that computers, as part of their primary function, disguise their mechanical operation in order to promote efficiency and maximize power; and Wendy Hui Kyong Chun argues that software is often designed to render "the visible (such as the machine) invisible."[7] In visual art the digital apparatus has been variously defamiliarized: in the Wachowskis' *The Matrix* (1999), falling numeric/symbolic fields signify the operations of both the computers that drive the matrix within the film's diegesis and those that were used to make the film itself. And in similar terms, Joshua Portway and Lise Autogena's remarkable art installation *Black Shoals Stock Market Planetarium* (2004) projects onto the dome-shaped ceiling of a darkened room a computer display that tracks in real time actual stock trades from around the world, revealing ecologies of what the artists refer to as forms of "artificial life," which are figured by glowing blips of light whose brightness accords with trading intensity. Even these cases, however, move from machine to metaphor: they are supplementary representations that only gesture toward hidden machinic operations, supplanting the actual code behind computer animations and global digital networks without actually showing those operations at work.

In these pieces the mathematical apparatus of digital art is never offered up or exposed in the way that, for example, a stroboscopic flicker calls attention to the mechanics of projection or a freeze frame indexes film's material relation to photography in traditional cinema. In a certain (highly debated) strand of cinematic apparatus theory of previous eras, to see apparatus was to see ideology; vision was critique. As Jean-Louis Baudry famously suggested in a 1970 article: "Concealment of the technical base will also bring about a specific ideological effect. Its inscription, its manifestation as such, on the other hand, would produce a knowledge effect, as actualization of the work process, as denunciation of ideology."[8] In contrast to traditional cinematic forms, views of the machinery of digital forms either are unintelligible before transcoding or are gestured toward in more notional forms, which present mathematical abstractions in more familiar or concrete terms. This remediation is a function of the digital image itself, which, as D. N. Rodowick has pointed out, is "no image at all, but information."[9]

One consequence of such an environment is the emergence of what LiPuma and Lee call the *abstract symbolic violence* of geopolitical speculative capital, which is "not accomplished physically by means of military force or colonialism" but rather appears in the provisions of World Bank loans and IMF adjustment policies.[10] As with the invisible digital networks that govern this system, the economic power of speculative capital "damages and endangers the welfare and political freedoms of those in its path, and does so without ever revealing itself."[11] Although they emphasize transnational corporations, they invoke here another late capitalist invisible power, namely, US hegemonic empire and, more specifically, the particular form it takes from the early 1970s to the early 2000s. Then, according to David Harvey, the United States—after having emerged in the postwar period as a kind of "Empire Lite," which used superior military power to protect "client regimes" that supported US economic interests—employed economic measures to hold on to its power.[12] This regime occurred in the context of Arrighi's *signal crisis*, the moment when hegemonic economies begin their decline and turn toward finance capital, which Fredric Jameson calls "free-floating" forms of value that, divested from the very economic theaters that initially produced national strength, reemerge as "spectres of value . . . vying against each other in a vast world-wide disembodied phantasmagoria."[13] In this context the United States preferred, as Bruce Cumings puts it, "the virtues of a multilateral economism to the vices of direct coercion and intervention," opting for what he elsewhere describes as "a light hold on the jugular."[14]

Harvey's account in this broad context reminds us that symbolic abstract violence requires the participation of less inchoate agents, what Chalmers Johnson describes as the "empire of bases" of US global militarism, which needs only to display its power *en potentia*.[15] Thus, the violence of speculative capital is not just the by-product of a new mode of systemic accumulation but also a de facto form of weaponry as hegemony shifts into more subtle registers. But given that the systemic operations here—US hegemony and global financialization—are also self-eliding, the problem of making the invisible visible returns in expanded scope. More to the point, how can forms of aesthetic representation work to make the conjuncture of finance capital and digital technology visible?

From Grendel to Frankenstein's monster to Godzilla, one strategy that literature and cinema have often returned to is the monster that figures an everyday or ordinary social problem in terms that are distinctly out of the ordinary. A more refined figure for the present context is the CGI monster of contemporary action cinema, which not only represents the anxieties surrounding today's massive capital flows and seismic geopolitical shifts but also speaks to questions of digital materiality, not least because it is itself a digital product. I turn to three films released in the long wake of Korea's IMF Crisis—Bong Joon-ho's *The Host* (*Koemul*, 2006), Kim Jeong-joong's *HERs* (*Hŏsŭ*, 2007), and Shim Hyung-rae's *D-War* (*Tiwŏ*, 2007). *The Host* and *D-War* are big-budget CGI monster movies that foreground their own digital apparatus in relation to the history of US hegemony in the Republic of Korea (ROK) and its latest financial iteration in the IMF Crisis, whereas *HERs* seems to intuit uncannily the CGI logic and truth of algorithmic apparatus in relation to the specific history of these systemic problems. All three films offer allegories of American-Korean relations at this late juncture—relations of late capitalism, of late empire, and of late (and now strained) partnership in a massive cycle of accumulation—through the optic of digital production. As I have stated throughout, the IMF Crisis in the Republic of Korea is an important case study for thinking about this moment of global economic hegemony because it lays bare the asymmetric power relations that had undergirded the US-ROK partnership since its inception. The subject of a good deal of public anger, IMF restructuring accelerated already nascent economic restructuring in Korea, encouraged a turn to financialization, further eroding what was left of the protectionist developmental state, and established conditions that were extremely favorable for Western investment capital at the expense of Korean middle- and lower-class workers.[16]

In pointed contrast to finance's fantasies of immaterial formlessness, which would correspond to the evaporation of capital's impediments within deregulated markets, popular film in this period reflects on its innate proximity to finance, specifically on the proximity between its own material apparatus as film becomes increasingly a digital medium and the economic apparatus that the IMF Crisis inserted into the center of Korean public discourse. These reflections are often self-reflexively allegorical in the sense that they foreground their rhetorical orientation and frustrated relationship to their supposed referents. Paul de Man famously called attention to this aspect of allegory: in his account allegory rejects the nostalgia for reference in symbolism and repeatedly gestures toward, while simultaneously eliding, "an unreachable anteriority."[17] As opposed to the symbol, allegory always calls attention to itself as a linguistic operation.

At a time when computing technology claims the capacity to solve problems of indeterminacy, algorithmic recursion in these films reveals itself as a further flattened, instrumentalized version of allegorical repetition, and visualizing these processes offers insight into the emerging conflict between human practices and machinic apparatuses that defines our moment. Insofar as deconstruction has taught us to valorize the critical capacities that repetition entails, allegory in these films calls attention to their own tautological repetitions.[18] Compelled by the discursive fallout of economic crisis, these films attempt to make visible not only the apparatus that drives cinematic representation today but also the radical complicities and genealogies of digital representation that cinema shares with contemporary military and financial technologies. Thus, part of the art of seeing the invisible digital is to recognize the surprising imbrications of artistic media of the present with current technologies of control and power, all of which mobilize digital logics to mitigate and master worlds full of contingency, complexity, and risk. Allegorical CGI monsters in these films thus function as a point of contact and collusion between the inhuman, machinic apparatus that pervades today's control technologies and human life. As I will argue, these CGI monsters help to make visible the invisible forces that work behind the scenes of everyday life in an age of financialization.

War and (CGI) Cinema

Conceived well before the emergence of digital cinema but just after Ronald Reagan's proposed Strategic Defense Initiative (a.k.a. Star Wars), Paul Virilio's *War and Cinema* (1984) posits a deep interconnection between its titular terms.

More than simply justifying war as propaganda, cinema for Virilio is materially connected to war in an age defined by the "growing derealization of military engagement."[19] Virilio points out that in a period of advanced radar systems, satellite imagery, and smart missiles, vision itself becomes the essence of weaponry. Perfecting the optical turn in warfare, which escalates from binoculars and flare guns to simulators and guidance systems to remotely operated drones, the *sight machines* of present-day military technology adhere to the motto that "winning is keeping the target in constant sight."[20] As the military theater of operations becomes increasingly complex, it is the cinematic mode alone that is capable of seeing the totality of war.[21]

One consequence of this transformation is that military and cinematic technologies become radically intertwined, especially as the battlefield becomes increasingly electronic. Virilio offers a host of examples that carry on the legacy of nitrocellulose, which was used in both film stock and explosives: the Dykstraflex camera, created for the film *Star Wars*, was based on a pilot-training system; the "Red Flag" military practice range used cinematic special effects in place of actual exposure to the Soviet defense system; and remote-piloted Scout aircraft employed television cameras to perform surveillance and targeting operations.[22] In a later book, *Desert Screen* (1991), published after the first US invasion of Iraq, Virilio updates his vision, insisting that the new "weapons of communication" allow for a new "purely technical imperialism" in which "the conquest of the market is henceforth confused with that of a military supremacy."[23]

Computer-generated monsters are also significant in this context for their multivalent intimacy with the military. Having many current military applications, CGI was originally derived from military weapons technology—first adapted from analog, antiaircraft computers—and developed through military-funded research and defense contracts. As Tom Sito puts it in his history of computer animation, "Despite a hagiography of counter culture and social freedom, CGI is as much a result of government funding as scratch-resistant lenses or Mylar," and "without the incentives and open-ended funding from the feds, the kind of computer graphics we now take for granted would not have been possible."[24] Fueled by massive government funding of private-sector research and development during and after the Cold War, the rise of CGI and related technologies is part of a still-emerging trend in which, according to Timothy Lenoir and Henry Lowood, "the military-industrial complex has become the military-entertainment complex" and, as such, "the training ground for what we might call post-human warfare."[25]

The uncanny tribute in *D-War* to CGI's genesis in war-making becomes obvious in this context, particularly in the depiction of sublimely large military legions, a trope that has become commonplace in digital filmmaking while avoiding the infamous *Ben-Hur* (1959) logistical nightmare. In the film's first large-scale CGI battle scene, the armies of darkness mercilessly rout a small village in an exercise of absurd proportions: the residents of the village defend themselves with martial arts against the might of preternatural forces equipped with some kind of advanced missile technology, ironically freighted to lumbering prehistoric creatures. Because a tiny fraction of such an army would have been sufficient, the scene seems motivated not by any drive toward narrative or realism but rather by the simple aesthetic desire to demonstrate the visual capacities of CGI, which correspond precisely to military capacities. The battle itself is *fait accompli*; the real interest here is instead in watching the machinery run.

Hosting Hegemony

The Host might be understood as a sensitive treatment of this relation between the Korean cinema and US military might. The film narrates the story of a monster that is the product of American military negligence and the havoc the creature wreaks on the city of Seoul, from the point of view of a family whose daughter the monster abducts. One way of conceiving Bong's much-heralded genre bending is to read the machinic operations of CGI monsters in *The Host* as speaking to the impositions of US hegemony.[26] The monster of *The Host* indeed offers a complex allegory of the intricacies of US hegemony in Korea. Since its formation in 1948, the Republic of Korea has been a US ally in an asymmetric partnership, serving as an anticommunist bulwark for the United States in the global Cold War in exchange for economic and military support. The United States has thus been understood paradoxically both as a central ally to the ROK and as a threat to Korean sovereignty. Since its inception, US military occupation of Korea has generally not controlled the local population by force but has instead allowed its client regime to emerge and grow, while grounding any sense of futurity in a Cold War logic in which an anticommunist ideological position would flow seamlessly into an unchallenged commitment to capitalist expansion in terms favorable to US interests, providing at the same time models and opportunities for fostering the ROK's own subimperial ambitions.[27]

There are several different and, in a sense, conflicting evocations of America's presence in the film. The release of "Agent Yellow" to destroy the monster echoes not only the biochemical genesis of the monster but also the infamous use of

Agent Orange by US forces in Vietnam; confusion about the existence of the virus turns out to be the result of American military and medical incompetence. Perhaps most significant, the film as a whole was inspired by the controversial decision in 2000 of US Army mortician Albert McFarland to dump dangerous chemicals into the drains at the Yongsan Army Base in Seoul, and thus into the Han River, against vehement protests by environmentalists.

Of course, the key allegorical figure in the film is the monster itself, of which we get a clear view early on. Some unholy combination of fish, amphibian, and reptile, *The Host*'s monster is aggressively multiple: it swims, runs, jumps, grabs its prey with tentacle-like appendages, and even swings acrobatically beneath bridges with its long tail (fig. 23).[28] Although it feeds on human flesh, it is oddly gentle, even parental, with the two children it saves for a later meal. Furthermore, and amazingly for a film about a large genetic mutation terrorizing the residents of Seoul, the monster is not even the central preoccupation of the governmental agencies and military officials that dictate crisis response. The film's real danger is rather a virus for which the monster is a presumed host, a shift that is doubled in the change from the film's original Korean title, *Koemul* (meaning monster), to its English version.[29] The monster thus seems designed to evoke something like the same complex mix of positive and negative feelings that the United States has generated over its long alliance with the Republic of Korea.

To further complicate the already complex semiotics of the allegory, we learn from the bonus features on the DVD version of the film that the monster was,

FIGURE 23. The monster in *The Host* (Showbox Entertainment, 2006).

in fact, the product of a US special effects company, a now defunct San Fran-cisco–based firm called The Orphanage.[30] In part an American product, both in the film's diegesis and its production, the monster in *The Host* calls atten-tion to a larger problem of Korean sovereignty vis-à-vis US authority within its own national boundaries.[31] The American figures interspersed throughout the film—from the serviceman who first fights the monster alongside Gang-du (Song Kang-ho) to the doctor who drills into Gang-du's brain—assert their authority over their Korean counterparts, just as unnamed higher US authorities working in conjunction with the World Health Organization and the Centers for Disease Control in Atlanta intervene and decide to use Agent Yellow on the monster toward the end of the film, a decision, when announced in a television news broadcast, that is accompanied by stock footage of on-duty American soldiers, primarily in the Persian Gulf.

Perhaps in this context it makes sense that the monster both allegorizes and occasions US military force: US military mismanagement is the monster's literal origin, but recognition of this irony leads not to correction but to an even more irresponsible American decision. Under the cover of cooperation, the brutish disregard of the US military for Korean interests causes the conditions in which further US intervention becomes necessary, thus echoing the clichéd tautology often seen in monster films in which one form of military technology (tanks, planes, missiles) faces off against another (CGI images) in a strangely mirrored conflict, one that uncannily invokes the ironic situations in Afghanistan and other places where the United States had previously armed insurgents against other enemies and later had to face its own weaponry.[32]

But if US hegemony appears as a general subject, the deeper focus of *The Host* is arguably the Korean experience of the IMF Crisis. In the third preamble sequence of the film, a businessman, just after catching a glimpse of the monster in the river below, jumps to his death off a bridge, evoking the phenomenon of IMF suicides, which became pervasive after the crisis. As Hsuan Hsu points out, given that the monster feeds on human flesh, and "since Bong notes that such suicides in the Han River happen 'almost every day,' the monster's growth may be directly correlated to the conditions affecting the Korean economy and those whose livelihood depends on it."[33] So the scene represents a double desecration: the businessman is first driven to suicidal despair by financial hardship, and the subsequent defilement of his corpse literalizes the metaphoric language that describes the IMF's actions as *vulture capitalism*. As Hsu points out: the film "turns out to be an allegory not just of U.S. military occupation but also of neoliberal market reforms."[34]

Indeed, the military's strategy in the film, to double down on a certain kind of force when that force has been shown not to work, offers an ironic repetition of an economic strategy that had compounded the Korean debt crisis. After early attempts to scapegoat "crony capitalism" for the 1997–98 Asian financial crises, particularly in Korea, economists and historians have argued that it was rather a liquidity crisis caused in large part by neoliberal policy, made possible by what Laura Hyun Yi Kang calls "an unprecedented availability of credit and transactional mobility of speculative capital."[35] So if the cause of the liquidity crisis had much to do with the financial liberalization of the early 1990s, which was, in Harvey's words, "Clinton's price for supporting Korea's incorporation into the OECD," then the IMF restructuring, in pushing greater degrees of financialization, doubles down rather than reverses course.[36] If the solution to the US military intervention in *The Host* is more US military intervention, then the solution to neoliberal reforms in the IMF Crisis is more neoliberal reforms.

One of the most brilliant suggestions of *The Host*, however, is the radical overlap of the two allegories, reflecting an awareness of the history of US hegemony in which neoliberal market economics complements rather than opposes neoconservative military aggression. Though in recent times considered mutually exclusive options—as different as Bill Clinton's foreign policy was from that of George W. Bush's—they have become increasingly viewed as related modalities of US hegemony. Nathan Hensley, for example, describes the "brute physicality" of the latter as emerging "with almost mechanical inevitability in conditions of material downturn."[37] In other words, where we might want to see the film simply as an allegory for the brute fact of US military might, that might appears itself as the figure for a different but no less determinate form of US power: the economic power it exerts via its various financial instruments. So if we are tempted to see *The Host* simply as an allegory, I suggest that it is—like the monster itself—something more complicated: an allegory of an allegory.

The Host thus exposes the complexities of the US-ROK relationship in the long wake of the IMF Crisis—a period in which neoconservative military escalation in the Middle East, designed to secure US economic advantages (alluded to in the film), becomes visible in relation to the imposition of US economic hegemony that had been going on for decades. It is not surprising, then, that one quintessential allegory for neoliberal financialization, understood no longer in opposition to neoconservative hawkishness, becomes the US military itself, for which the CGI monsters are ritual repetitions. So, while neoliberal reform was more relevant to the shape of US hegemony in the Korean context, their stakes after the IMF Crisis become clearer in relation to the neoconservative spectacle in the Middle East, to which the Republic of Korea contributed military support. *The Host*'s monster, an allegory of an allegory that brings together a range of political and economic effects, emerges as a potent figure for the historical complexities of this moment.

From Allegory to Algorithm

There is, though, more to the work that the CGI monster does in *The Host*. More than simply an allegory (or even an allegory of an allegory), *The Host* works in material ways to make the invisible operations of US hegemony in the Republic of Korea visible. A realization of practical mathematics, CGI uses software that performs geometric calculations to synthesize digitally captured and manipulated images with images filmed in live shots. As Rodowick explains, the goal is "to constitute a space that is mathematically definable and manipulable. It is as if the algorithmic construction of space seeks, in its definition of realism, to correspond to a world defined only by Cartesian coordinates and their algebraic manipulation of geometric shapes."[38] An emphatically geometric form and the image-product of algorithms that effect three-dimensional representation, the monster calls attention to the spatial logics it demands as the anchor of any scene in which it appears (belatedly, of course, in postproduction), as well as the broader ideological geometries that constitute US hegemony. Both more and less than an allegory, *The Host*'s CGI monster is not only a figure for the operations of US hegemony and global finance; insofar as CGI is code, it not only represents but *is* the logic that underwrites financialization and a late hegemony that financialization in turn underwrites.

Like much of the software that stands behind contemporary finance, the development of advanced CGI depended on algorithmic calculations that only became possible with powerful computers. Many of these algorithms are recursive, breaking down a large task or problem into smaller incremental versions and requiring massive numbers of mechanically processed progressive repetitions. Significantly, some of the reality effects of the highly refined CGI of the last two decades, and the recursive algorithms that make them possible, compute random variables and probability, falling under the rubric of *stochastic* systems, which combine deterministic and random elements. Such mathematics has had a profound effect on the contemporary world.[39] In the late 1940s Stanislaw Ulam, working as part of a team that developed the scientific basis for nuclear weaponry at Los Alamos, developed his Monte Carlo Method, which relied on repeated random sampling to obtain numerical data and was so named to invoke casino gambling. Wondering about how to calculate win-probability in solitaire, Ulam reasoned that it would be more efficient to play repeated games with a computer; with enough repetitions and data sorting, the results would cease to seem random.[40] Stochastic volatility models have been used in derivative pricing to modify and account for deficiencies in the classic Black-Scholes formula and the Gaussian copula formula developed by David X. Li in the early 2000s (dubbed "the Formula that killed Wall Street" for its role in spurring the derivative boom and the 2008 financial crisis), both of which allowed the modeling of hugely complex risk. Algorithms here implicitly claim to overcome indeterminacy; recursion mitigates chance in stochastic systems, thus giving way to more predictable outcomes. The transformation of simple geometric forms into those that appear real in CGI (textured, idiosyncratic, and so on) also hangs on calculations of random variables based on chance, processed so that they behave as if they were not.

As moving three-dimensional images have become increasingly detailed and complex, stochastic modeling and sampling have become important in computer graphics, especially as the size of these images as files have posed a challenge for computing capacity.[41] But as this mathematics and the algorithmic procedures that execute it become more prominent, even in aspects of filmmaking that most explicitly involve the manipulation of digital forms (like CGI), the artist does not engage so much with the mechanical apparatus of the machine as with an abstracted version in the form of interfaces, which distance the user from the mathematics. Digital filmmakers work increasingly at the level of image with the help of software and less at that of code. Fundamentally a technology of mediation, then, the computer interface, and in particular software, according to Alexander Galloway, "is not merely a vehicle for ideology"; it is an allegory for it. That is, "the complexities and contradictions of ideology . . . are modeled and simulated out of the formal structure of software itself."[42] Software is thus allegorical in de Man's sense, self-reflexively referring to the power relations that inhere in acts of representation themselves.

That ideology is so thoroughly embedded in the machine constitutes the central insight of Galloway's book, whose title names the critique: *The Interface Effect*. "A medium that does not mediate," the interface is the control-society technology par excellence because it sublimates poststructuralism's anxieties about presence and truth into the open-source logic of media systems: "What was once an intellectual intervention is now part of the mechanical infrastructure."[43] On one hand, the fate of allegory holds form: once a rhetorical mode that, *pace* de Man, confronted the "painful knowledge" of "distance in relation to its own origin" and renounced the implicit nostalgic desire for identification that inhered in the symbol, allegory now names the simulation of rhetorical form that incorporates deconstructive critical capacities into machinic operations.[44] But this absorption, on the other hand, is also ameliorative: because the interface for Galloway is not primarily a thing—a screen, keyboard, mouse—but rather a "general technique of mediation evident at all levels," the interface as allegorical device offers the opportunity to "gain some perspective on culture in the age of information."[45] So although his control-society focus compels him to foreground how technologies repurpose and thus enfeeble deconstructive critique, he seems to apply the very critical capacities of allegory proposed by de Man in order to read the ideological valances of interfaces by emphasizing their procedural characteristics. Given that the procedures of these interfaces involve algorithms, this machinic form of instrumental repetition seems to preserve the rhetorical function that de Man ascribed to allegory, giving us something like an *allegorithm*.[46]

Algorithmic logics in *The Host* emerge within allegorical structures, as if to reformulate the fundamental mathematical geometries that digital film production both mobilizes and elides, such that the very act of ascertaining form's intimate relation to ideology constitutes its most crucial insight. We see this logic, for example, in the behavior of Gang-du's family as they hunt for and eventually confront the allegorical monster; all of their efforts seem uncannily to reproduce aspects of control-society infrastructure. Comically financed by gangsters whose usurious terms are reminiscent of the IMF's bailout conditions, the family at first seeks the safe return of Gang-du's abducted daughter, Hyun-seo (Go Ah-sung), by randomly and repeatedly tracking through the sewers around the Han River, calling out the young girl's name. Represented in a sequence condensed into a recursive montage, their method frustrates Nam-il (Park Hae-il), Gang-du's brother: when performed by human actors, algorithmic repetition amounts to tedium. Eventually, Nam-il thinks to contact his friend at, significantly, a telecommunications company, where he is able to identify the cell tower that transmitted Hyun-seo's last call in just a few moments, crucially, by using the company's computer.

Amid the concrete pillars that support the Wonhyo Bridge, in a scene seemingly both defined by infrastructure and belying the film's preoccupation with infrastructural aesthetics, the finale also suggests an algorithmic logic in which the monstrous problem must be addressed by a sequence of smaller efforts. There is a strangely episodic quality to the fight, consisting of a series of individual struggles in which the characters' personal histories allegorically inform the fighting. These individual efforts form a network of cooperation that succeeds in progressively weakening the monster before it finally dies. Harking back to his university days spent as a student protestor, Nam-il launches a series of Molotov cocktails. Already reeling from the effects of the Agent Yellow, the monster frantically retreats, but when the homeless man who has joined Nam-il pours gasoline down the throat of the monster from the underside of the bridge above, Nam-il fails to capitalize on this attack and drops his final projectile. Stepping into the fray at this precise moment, Nam-ju (Bae Doona) ignites one of her arrows and hits the monster on her first shot, redressing an earlier moment in the film when she had failed in a televised archery competition. These otherwise allegorical struggles become sequenced in a kind of networked aesthetics in which a succession of coordinated efforts gradually produces a desired outcome.[47]

Gang-du's role in finishing off the monster culminates in a moment that most indexes the digital infrastructure of CGI. Rather than solving the problem of Korean sovereignty thematized in the film (the Agent Yellow is actually very helpful), the death of the monster points instead to the greater truth of digitality over hegemony. Set ablaze by Nam-ju's arrow, the monster makes a beeline for the river, but Gang-du intervenes, driving a metal pole deep into the monster's throat. As it slowly expires, we see some of its blood trickling down the pole toward the digits on Gang-du's left hand, which is halfway up the pole. He releases his left hand, and the camera pans to his right, which has been palm up, bracing the end of the pole. As he releases this right hand, we see that the end of the pole has left a circular imprint on his palm (fig. 24). As the physical imprint left behind by an otherwise immaterial digital monster, the circle on Gang-du's palm and the straight pole he has appropriated as a weapon (itself a kind of interface) together become material traces of the binary digits—the zeroes and ones—that fundamentally constitute the monster's computer-generated existence. The film visually echoes this binary thematics throughout, for example, in the archery competition with its arrows and targets; in the bridge suicide that contrasts the circular ripples caused by the monster in the river with the linear architectural

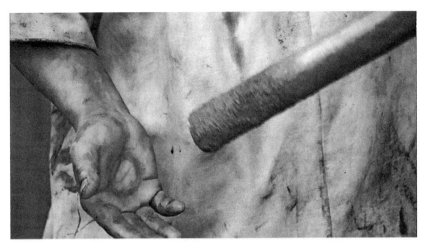

FIGURE 24. Gang-du's hand in *The Host* (Showbox Entertainment, 2006).

forms in the distant cityscape; and in the mourning scene in which we see from above the bodies of the family members lying prostrate in grief on the gymnasium floor, framed by what seems to be a basketball free-throw circle. It is not until the finale, however, that these visual thematics emerge in direct relation to the CGI object. As figures, the columns, arrows, and poles in relation to the final zero on Gang-du's hand function like Barthesian *puncta*, which lay bare CGI's artifice: the digital monster is revealed as the monstrous digital, reminding us that more fundamental than the blood that courses through its veins and flows down Gang-du's pole to the monster's informatic (and not organic) existence are the zeros and ones that constitute its digital materiality.

The Gina Algorithm

Although it is far from a CGI monster film, *HERs* seems to intuit the critical capacity of recursion as a linchpin that connects military, financial, and aesthetic forms in its retooling of allegory as algorithm. A series of loosely related shorts about the difficult lives of three Korean American women, all of whom are named Gina, the film narrates their preoccupations, hopes, and frustrations as they seek solace and redress within what seem hopeless environments. A kind of CGI determinacy lingers subtly in the film in the way it arranges its central figures. Reminiscent of Galloway's *polytych*, which he describes as "the distributed network as an aesthetic construction," the film's triptych structure presents successive vignettes about the different Ginas, each played by a different actor.[48] They are not likely the same person, yet we are meant to understand them as part of a continuum. Though loosely organized to follow the trajectory of a sex worker's decline, the film stages a series of repetitions that resist cohering into an overall narrative. A kind of typology, character here is, to borrow Aaron Kunin's formulation, "a formal device that collects every example of a kind of person."[49] But rather than offering a single character standing in for a typology, the film offers a kind of recursive taxonomy that lends itself to systemic reading; discrete subjectivities become legible only within larger socioeconomic frames. Bundled together, these otherwise separate narratives begin to display predictable patterns, a kind of Gina algorithm.

This algorithmic structure also mimics the tautological atavisms of US hegemony in the Republic of Korea. Although there is no action-packed military conflict in the film, the specter of Korea's military horizons reemerges with respect to the film's interest in prostitution, a watershed issue in modern Korean history that is inextricable from US military presence. The film's displaced preoccupation with this issue returns most obviously in the final section of the film, when, in a military vehicle, Tim (Chris Devlin), the on-duty US Army corporal, picks up the hitchhiking Alaska Gina (Susie Park), who is on her way to see the Aurora Borealis. Later in the film Tim responds to Alaska Gina's advertisement card. Though presented as a pair of chance encounters between strangers, their meetings evoke, on American soil, the history of military prostitution in Korea that has occurred under US military supervision and in partnership with the Korean government since the end of a similar system under Japanese colonial rule.[50] The film also indexes the concomitant history of Korean complicity, of locals who benefited from the shadow economy, represented in the film by Lucas (Will Yun Lee), the LA policeman who earns money on the side by doing favors for a pimp, and K (Karl Yune), the guide who brings a Japanese sex tourist to a Korean-owned brothel in Las Vegas. In contextualizing the Gina stories in relation to US military prostitution, the film links these contemporary narratives of global vagrancy to the subgenre of Korean camp-town narratives and their anti-American, antihegemonic associations.[51]

Implicitly linking patterns of recursion to hegemonic tautologies, each section of the triptych proceeds similarly without being the same, relating bleak stories about women in horrible situations, struggling with rape, loveless relationships, clinical depression, alcoholism, and death. Under the generic rubric of what Lauren Berlant describes as a cinema of *precarity*, these stories explore not just individual examples of desperation and dependency but also what she calls, in systemic terms that echo the earlier discussion of tautology, a "neoliberal feedback loop" that functions to distribute and shape experiences of insecurity with great efficiency in contemporary life.[52] Indeed, depicted as the objects of violence, abuse, exploitation, and brutality, the Ginas are very much at-risk figures; their daily lives are filled with victimization, not only at the hands of men ambivalent to their well-being but also from global economic forces that are invisible except in aggregate.

Spatializing this systemic precarity, the film calls attention to particularly inhospitable landscapes that seem bounded by rigid horizons that function not as sites of futurity and progress but as locations for highly bounded acts of wandering, like the tunnel that LA Gina (Kim Hye-na) scampers through at the beginning of the film. At the end of each section, the Ginas walk off into a long landscape shot until each meets the horizon, into which the respective protagonists seem nearly, but not entirely, to disappear. Though all located in the American West, these are not the landscapes of the classic western that Jane Tompkins describes as providing opportunities to control or dominate one's surroundings.[53] Instead, viewed through a stationary camera, each Gina moves from foreground to background, almost but not quite disappearing, moving in more or less straight lines to the vanishing point, guided by a road or railroad tracks, as if to emphasize the geometries they inhabit and the gridlines that define their spatial relations (fig. 25). Although the Ginas are not CGI figures, their movements in these scenes reveal in spatial terms their bounded geometric position as defined by the economy in which they circulate.

The lightly adumbrated story of a fourth Gina in the film, which frames the other three more developed narratives, subtly locates this economy in the wake of the IMF Crisis. The opening scene of the film depicts a preimmigration Korea Gina being spoken to by an unidentified man about her impending travel. Sensing her reticence, the man tells her, "It's not like once you leave you can't come back. You're going for good reasons. It might be hard for two, three years, but afterward you'll be better off." Although their conversation is elliptical, one infers that she is going abroad to become a sex worker, a nightmare of flexible labor and one that became more prominent in the wake of the Korean credit card crisis, an epiphenomenon of the IMF Crisis caused in large part by government incentives that encouraged consumer spending. Although these measures helped produce what looked like an economic recovery in the narrow sense, it came at the cost of a dramatic increase in personal debt and credit card delinquency, as well as a sharp decline in

FIGURE 25. Landscape shots at the end of each section in *HERs* (Bada Entertainment, 2007).

household savings. Faced with debt and limited prospects in a nation that regarded women's employment as a low priority in the wake of the financial crisis, women like Gina had few employment alternatives, and after the crackdown on domestic prostitution in 2004 in Korea, many were openly recruited for sex work abroad, as a potentially lucrative recession-era job opportunity.[54] In a 2006 special report in the *San Francisco Chronicle* that told the story of a trafficked Korean sex worker who was desperate to find a way out of massive debt, Meredith May reported that the Republic of Korea is one of the world's leading importers and exporters of the sex trade, despite the general wealth of the nation.

The recursive logics of *HERs* thus uncannily mimic the patterns of contemporary financialization and recast the drama of one shadow economy, that of camp-town prostitution, within the context of the new economies of risk, a shift that echoes the way in which IMF restructuring gave rise to what Jin-Ho Jang calls an "Anglo-American economic system" focused on investment culture.[55]

As by-products of financialization and US economic intervention in the post-IMF context—in occupying distinctively North American landscapes in a series that ends with an encounter between a Gina and an American GI (from whom one is tempted to say her name originates)—the Ginas evoke what is sometimes angrily regarded as a history of US culpability, resituating this history within the context of IMF vulture capitalism. The camp-town economy is reimagined as a risk economy populated by free agents attending to their precarity.

The Gina algorithm, however, bridges the military camp-town economy to those of late capitalist finance not only as two historically related modalities but also as recursive figures in a vicious circuit. They are not just the products of a financialized economy; they also help perpetuate its violence. Interestingly, in this context of at-risk figures, the film seems ironically to valorize chance and risk in other forms. The homeless LA Gina wanders into a Korean church where Lucas happens to be the usher; she later fights her own fear and returns with him to his tiny home in a storage unit. Although Las Vegas Gina (Elizabeth Weisbaum) can't bring herself to introduce herself to K at any of the meetings he arranges, they finally meet when K happens to call her service, not realizing that the woman who arrives is the same one whom he has been courting online. As mentioned previously, Alaska Gina coincidentally meets US Army corporal Tim when she is hitchhiking and then later as a client. In all three cases, prompted by a chance encounter, each Gina takes a risk (or at least contemplates one) within a romantic context. In addition, the film thematizes risk in the form of gambling in literal and figurative forms: LA Gina ventures into uncertainty in fleeing her pimp; the entire milieu of Las Vegas Gina is defined by the casinos on the strip, which is her stomping ground; and Alaska Gina risks her very life in pursuing her spiritual quest.

Given the film's ambivalence regarding risk, at once the object of fear and the fetishized site of possibility, perhaps it is not too strange that, in the otherwise dystopian scenarios that *HERs* comprises, the endings of each section contain hopeful moments—with each Gina musing wistfully about palm trees or ice cream, or else shielding herself within a protective fantasy. Similarly, each section inserts a set piece that represents a moment of idealization when a crisply edited vision of happiness interrupts the otherwise bleak mise-en-scène. Los Angeles Gina plays out giddy domesticity in Lucas's spartan digs; Las Vegas Gina imagines herself in a bath filled with vibrant flowers; and Alaska Gina fantasizes about a chance encounter with a moose on a desolate road. Echoed by the affective reprieve at the end of each section, these fantasies function not only to elide each Gina's participation in the shadow economy but, more importantly, to sustain fictions of freedom that mitigate harsh material conditions. Although they are clearly the victims of these bleak risk economies, they seem nevertheless to enter them not as sites of inevitable despair but of possibility. Perversely calling attention to the material components of the brutal feedback loop of contemporary finance that transforms the debt of the insecure into securities, *HERs* thus not only gives form to the ironies and limits of late capitalism's bounded freedom; it also demonstrates the many layers of complicity through which its subjects augment their geometries. This is a freedom made possible only by the concealment of the material apparatus and history that animates the economies in which they circulate. The point is to shed light on these concealments.

And Liberty for All

One important insight of the Gina algorithm is that precarity scales from individual to aggregate. Gina is a person, a type, and a figure for a larger body politic. This widening gyre (or vicious circuit) returns us to LiPuma and Lee's *abstract symbolic violence* and its implied connection between military and economic forms of aggression as manifested in their description of the derivative as "a real economic weapon."[56] In the book's final pages, after accounting for the weapon's power, they designate the vulnerability of individual states. Even relatively large and stable economies are no match for it, they suggest, because their central banks have little control over the value of their own currency in the current regime of global derivatives; the strength of their domestic production economies cannot protect currency valuations; and radical fluctuations of currency have become so much the norm that it is impossible to avoid this form of finance.[57]

It is not surprising in this context that derivatives trading ramped up in Korea during the 1990s. Official derivatives trading began in the ROK in 1996, the year before the crisis, with the opening of the national derivatives market, expanding and diversifying after the IMF Crisis as part of the wave of financialization of the period. From 2001 to 2003 the volume of equity index derivative trading exploded and has continued since.[58] Even companies involved in Korea's robust production/export economy turned more of their assets and attentions to derivative trading (most notoriously in KIKO, or "knock-in knock-out" options, a currency derivative), at first as a hedge against market fluctuations but gradually in pursuit of profits that could outweigh those of the company's traditional operations.[59]

Some economists have even argued that derivatives speculation in the form of derivative-based, credit-swap contracts were a significant cause of the 1997–98 crisis itself. J. A. Kregel, for example, suggests that over-the-counter structured derivatives packages in the mid-1990s, which concealed risk and circumvented regulatory measures, composed more than half of the total lending in the Republic of Korea just before the economy collapsed.[60] Precarity for both the Ginas in *HERs* and nonhegemonic economies like Korea's is a function of a forced absorption into a larger system that, crucially, is *both* enabling and oppressive. As the material form of spectral value, a kind of nonintrinsic secondary value, the derivative bespeaks a specific anxiety in late US hegemony from a Korean perspective, the fear not only that one cannot disentangle oneself from the hegemonic structure but also that one abets its tautological reproduction.

A far less subtle figure of imbrication is the serpentine monster at the end of *D-War*, the Imoogi that aspires to be a dragon, which wraps itself around the iconic US Bank building in downtown Los Angeles (fig. 26). Remarkably, the police in the film erroneously refer to it as the "Liberty" building, echoing (surely intentionally) George W. Bush's famous mistake in his 2006 State of the Union Address when speaking about a counterterrorism success in thwarting an Al Qaeda plot to destroy the Los Angeles building, which had apparently been a target for the attacks on 9/11/2001 and again in 2002. Ironies abound, not least in the way the mistake connects neoconservative rhetoric in which Islamic terrorists threaten American liberties to the global machinations of the, here bluntly allegorized, US banking industry as part of the IMF-Wall Street-Treasury complex in the name of financial freedoms. In the present

FIGURE 26. Imoogi wrapped around the "Liberty" building in *D-War* (Showbox Entertainment, 2007).

context, Bush's thesis statement in that speech, that "America remains at risk," obtains an unintended implication: America remains at the mercy not only of terrorists who take advantage of lax defense measures but also of bankers who prey on insufficiently regulated financial markets. *D-War* thus stages yet another tautology: we witness not just monster versus humanity but also monster versus monster (as in the *Godzilla vs . . .* films), as if the monstrous allegory of US hegemonic financialization in *The Host* had come back to life as an edifice, sans artifice, to challenge this literalized version of the Korean economy. Allegory in the basest of forms, it is the US Bank building versus a (would-be) Asian Dragon. Amazingly, the latter as return of the repressed in redressing the ills of vulture capitalism finds strange alignment, in the context of Bush's speech, with the Islamic militants that seek revenge for American hegemonic aggressions in the Middle East.

But while this scene is unmistakably one of antagonism, the monster's relation to the US Bank building also registers as an embrace. Hostile antipathy notwithstanding, the monster figures the problem of disarticulation within the structure of derivation, as well as a broad anxiety about paired fates and complicity. This tautological image is also, then, a picture of the radical imbrication of two countries. In this respect it is reminiscent of Derrida's reading of horizons in Husserl's *Origin of Geometry*, in which he argues that Husserl tautologically "makes the a priori and the teleological coincide."[61] For Husserl, grappling with the thorny question of objectivity's origin, the horizon is notionally crucial to the invention of geometry because it bridges the subjective experience of space to universal objective knowledge through what he terms a shareable *we-horizon*.[62] Extrapolating in these terms, US hegemony operated by determining Korean horizons, initially allowing the South Korean state to emerge and grounding any sense of futurity in a cold war, anticommunist position that would pair favorably with an unquestioned commitment to capitalist expansion. This Asian Dragon becomes in turn exemplary both of American beneficence and of the capacity of Western capitalism to flower in Asia. Extraction from such imbrication becomes tricky business. In previous geopolitical modes we might use the word *decolonization* and label the discourse *postcolonial*, but because the partnership between the United States and Korea begins with liberation, it becomes difficult to imagine what it means to liberate oneself from the condition of liberty itself. Indeed, relative to Japanese colonialism, US hegemony in Korea *is* a postcolonial discourse.

In this respect, this scene in *D-War* anticipates the so-called candlelight protests that exploded in Seoul during the summer of 2008 in response to the decision in the Korea-US Free Trade Agreement of 2007 that reversed the ban on American beef imports imposed in the wake of the Mad Cow scare in the period. Although there was a great deal of anger directed at the shift in trade policy and the prospect of diseased meat entering the Korean market, the protests were also an occasion to vent a good deal of anti-American sentiment and frustration with Washington Consensus economic policies, without necessarily making the cause explicit.[63] In comparison to the previous generation's prodemocracy protests or even the anti–Park Geun-hye demonstrations in 2016–17, the candlelight protests were more diffuse and less focused by a central group of organizers. Indeed, while concerns specifically about the quality of beef that would be shipped to Korea were justifiable, the scale of the protests surprised the Lee Myung-bak administration, which saw itself as simply following the course of the FTA signed under the previous Roh administration. The massive release of public anger and rage—upwards of seven hundred thousand people filled the streets of downtown Seoul at the height of the protests—seemed disproportionate to the specific issue that occasioned the event. These were, in a sense, geometric protests about the tautological horizons that formed the coordinates of American hegemony for generations, which were beginning to shift. Seeking an answer to the question of what decolonization might look like in a geopolitical context in which hegemony elides itself as such, these protests expressed a desire that had been nascent since the 1980s and flared up further after the IMF Crisis, but the impulse for disarticulation became complicated for the upstart whose own strength is modeled on the power it would depose.

Imbrication in *D-War*'s finale thus describes a hegemonic relation as a technological one. At the level of digital apparatus, the Imoogi's embrace of the building also figures the material connection among CGI monster, military technology, and contemporary financialization. The scene denies abstract symbolic violence its subtlety. In terms that overlap with Virilio's, military and financial forms of aggression become one and the same in this theater of digital representation. In a world in which the economy "is not only driven by software . . . in many cases the economy is software," Galloway has recently suggested "that one cannot be neutral on the question of math's ability to discourse about reality, precisely because in the era of computerized capitalism math itself, as algorithm, has become a historical actor."[64] In short, "*After software has entered history, math cannot and should not be understood ahistorically.*"[65] The tautological formations in these films, both unwittingly and self-consciously, indicate these relations. By recursively indexing the machinic structures of algorithm-driven digital production within allegorical figures, math monsters in these films personify an apparatus that seems otherwise invisible and ahistorical.

The fact that hegemonic imbrication occurs not just as ideology, but more fundamentally through infrastructural coding, complicates the question of extraction even further. These films suggest that the hegemony of US influence late in the American century inheres not merely in false consciousness or unwitting complicity but also in a systemic infrastructure of deeply intertwined interests reflected in the very codes that govern social relations at the heart of hegemonic domination. Furthermore, when such material interests diverge late in the cycle of empire, systems become imposed instead of springing forth naturally from overlapping motivations. In Luhmannian terms, US hegemony in this late iteration dreams for itself an *autopoietic* social system; the tautologies that we have seen prevail throughout these films are rhetorical forms that express the desire for such self-replication.[66] Indeed, Luhmann's description of the autopoietic system as a "powerful mechanism to guarantee its continuity in the face of a lack of understanding and even in the face of open rejection" helps explain the odd combination of antagonism and embrace in the *D-War* finale. But these films also suggest that fantasies of autopoeisis are just fantasies, ultimately expressing the desperation under which such measures become necessary as much as they do the logistical facts of the operation. The mathematic logics that run through the films discussed in this chapter are ultimately functionalist strategies of organization that impose systemic principles precisely at the point when the systems fail to run on their own accord.

6 Wire Aesthetics

Tube Entertainment's Flops and Hegemonic Protocols

What I will call the *wire shot* is a common trope in contemporary film and video, peaking in the first decade or so of the twenty-first century, in which human perspectives are imagined to occupy the physical space inside of a fiber-optic cable. Most commonly emphasizing the point of view of the person traveling through the wire, the shot cuts abruptly between disparate settings or conditions (real to virtual, flesh to code), underscoring transmission as wonder. Often employed as a quick transition between scenes, it has become a clichéd mark of slick editing that viewers often miss entirely. We might think of it as a further reification of *cyberspace*, which Wendy Hui Kyong Chun describes as an ultimately fantastical attempt to make sense of the form of publicity that internet infrastructure makes possible.[1] But if the internet user in Chun's critique is "*created* by 'using' in a similar manner to the way drug users are created by the drugs they (ab) use,"[2] the ideal subject of the wire shot is unaware of such ironies. The shot has become so pervasive that any comprehensive catalog would take too much time, but a quick list of illustrative examples might include the 2010 Disney production *Tron Legacy*, at the moment when Sam Flynn enters the computer world built by his father in the original 1982 film; the 2011 Marvel Production *Thor*, in which Thor and his companions travel via portal to the distant land of Jotunheim to confront the Frost Giants; the 2014 Luc Besson film *Lucy*, in which the title character comes to experience human history as a searchable database; and the 2011 Autotrader.com commercial, in which cars race though a cybernetic course in the mind of a potential buyer (fig. 27).

The previous chapter focused on the way in which declining US hegemony reached for a mathematical infrastructure in hopes of building a self-replicating system that would preserve US economic advantages well past their expiration date, while obscuring the force necessary to put such a system into place. The wire shots discussed in the present chapter echo the fantasies of economic mastery that

FIGURE 27. Clockwise from the upper left: wire shots from *Tron Legacy* (Disney, 2010), *Thor* (Marvel, 2011), *Lucy* (EuropaCorp, 2014), and a 2011 Autotrader.com commercial.

we have seen through the middle part of this book—that of the *segyehwa* punk or of digital intimacy—but they also make explicit the largely unacknowledged material frames that circumscribe such fantasies. Though clearly ideological, the wire shot fundamentally links its view to the apparatus that makes it possible; thus, it invites an account of the reproduction of such fantasies beyond false consciousness. This chapter will thus center the notion of *protocol* as a bridge term that connects the infrastructure to its reification.

Visually speaking, wire shots tend to depict tightly bounded landscapes that reach toward a vanishing point on the horizon, something in the mode of Henry Moore's WWII paintings of Londoners sheltering in the tubes of the Underground. Owing debts to sci-fi depictions of interstellar travel,[3] the wire shot imagines traversal instead through interior expanses, something like the feeling of being shot through a tube, imagining the inhuman space of network connectivity as inhabitable and bathing the experience in speed-of-light exhilaration. As such, the wire shot follows the lineage of cinematic phenomena like the early twentieth-century Hale's Tours amusement park attraction, in which viewers could view films inside of a converted train car that were shot from the perspective of a moving train.[4] A slightly later version of the kind of predigital, virtual entertainment (like panorama and diorama) that Anne Friedberg describes as replicating the flâneur's "mobilized virtual gaze,"[5] these amusement park films worked to incorporate into the purview of human experience the feeling of machinic speed, what later becomes with the advent of the automobile, in Enda Duffy's account, an "adrenaline aesthetics."[6] The wire shot also follows in the fantastical spirit of nineteenth-century misunderstandings of telegraph technology as a physical space, through which, for example, a mother might attempt to send her faraway son a dish of sauerkraut.[7] These misunderstandings were somewhat justifiable given that pneumatic delivery tubes were invented not before but as a consequence of telegraphic communications systems, specifically as a way to manage large numbers of stock exchange communications at busy hours, when it became more efficient to bundle them physically and send bulk via tubes rather than as individual telegraphic messages.[8] And though these pneumatic tubes were in fact an extension of telegraphy infrastructure, they also offered a physical manifestation and a way to understand, like our wire shot, more mysterious technological operations.

The more contemporary examples mentioned above of the wire shot seem qualitatively different from, say, Krzysztof Kieślowski's 1994 film *Trois couleurs: Rouge*, which depicts wired connection as disorienting and mechanical, in tracing the route of an electric telephone signal through copper and through undersea channels and subterranean tunnels. Kieślowski employed a fish-eye effect that flattens wire space instead of providing inhabitable depth (fig. 28). It is the sort of sensory dissembling that David Bell in Don DeLillo's first novel, *Americana* (1971), feels on "being sucked into the telephone," a feeling in which the telephone's "tunneling lure" mediates human desire by channeling it through a communications network.[9] In more recent iterations, in contrast, we identify this experience as a welcome dematerialization of our newly informatic bodies, as Tao Lin's protagonist does in *Taipei* (2013), imagining himself "traveling alone in the vacuum-sealed tube of his own life—he'd be suctioned and from which he'd exit, as a successful

FIGURE 28. Wire shot presented with fish-eye effect in *Trois couleurs: Rouge* (MK2 Productions, 1994).

delivery to some unimaginable recipient."[10] Lin's account evokes the similarly glee-
ful entubed traversal of Felix the Cat in the 1924 cartoon "Doubles for Darwin"
(fig. 29).[11] Although it is a transatlantic telegraph cable that Felix travels through,
his usage seems anachronistic: physically traveling to Capetown, South Africa, via
wire in order to learn whether or not human beings descended from monkeys,
Felix uses the global cable network to perform what amounts to a Google search.
In the present fiber-optic era,[12] in which it has become possible to think of the
networks of routers, servers, and subterranean/undersea wires that constitute the
global internet as a social space, the wire shot represents in similar affective terms
the experience of information transported through a conduit.

  Chun's critique of cyberspace points out that the common view of internet
spaces, of which the wire shot is an extreme (if banal) rendering, promotes a
false sense of privacy and user-agency in what have become privatized, user-
exploiting technologies that produce a marketplace rather than a commons. This
is also to say that the fiction of the individual user-agent is an effect designed
precisely for the sake of control within the bounds of specific protocols. Focusing
on three films produced by the production firm Tube Entertainment, in which
wire shots abound, this chapter examines this dynamic as encompassing not

FIGURE 29. Felix the Cat traveling through an undersea telegraph cable to Capetown,
South Africa in "Doubles for Darwin" (1923).

just the individual's imaginary relationship to network infrastructure but also transnational economic relations within the context of US financial imperialism, and it explores the wire shot's fantastical encoding of mechanical relations in the manner of data connectivity and also of hegemonic protocols in the manner of empire. The proto–wire shots discussed above anticipate more contemporary encodings of information and capital, encodings that ultimately preserve the very material histories that they seem to leave behind. In this context it is important to recognize that the moment of US financial imperialism with respect to the Republic of Korea in the 1990s, beginning with the negotiations for the latter's entrance into the OECD in 1993 and the IMF bailout discussions in 1997–98, coincides almost precisely with the deregulation of the communications industry in the United States and the concomitant US-led buildup of global network infrastructure as well. Although it is important to appreciate the different specific contexts for these events, they are also materially bounded as part of the broader construction of hegemonic financial protocols throughout the period,[13] not least because the triumphal euphoria around the new economy (later relabeled as *irrational exuberance*) provides the confidence and justification that underlie the so-called Wall Street-Treasury-IMF Complex's push for liberalization. The wire shot figures not only the false consciousness of the user in relation to an only partially visible infrastructural apparatus but, more importantly, the material protocols of a financialized economy committed to the very infrastructure that seeks to exact tribute from protected assets.

Protocols of Compression

For a precursor, albeit an unlikely one, we might look to Ezra Pound's 1913 poem "In a Station of the Metro," which points subtly to the historical appropriation of rail infrastructure as a logical site for the laying of wires. There is the well-known story about Pound exiting the train at La Concorde station in Paris, seeing a series of beautiful faces, and experiencing a sudden emotion that he tries to capture first in a thirty-line poem and then, six months later, one of half that length. With the Japanese *hokku* in mind a year later, he produces the final version, in which human emotion obtains the quality of data. Despite his slow download problem, Pound later described his compositional arc in uncannily mechanical terms. The point became "to record the precise instant when a thing outward and objective transforms itself, or darts into a thing inward and subjective."[14] In equating the data of faces at the metro station to the floral image, the poem not only preserves

and condenses the original emotion;[15] it also indexes the precise instant of conver-
sion itself, the darting movement of which mimics the subterranean trains whose
infrastructure originally occasioned Pound's project. La Concorde station thus
looms large in the poem, not just as a generalized site of modern technological
novelty but, more specifically, as a figure of innovative traversal. Accordingly, in
the smallest file possible, what he called an imagist poem, Pound foregrounds
the logic of data transfer.[16] Combining brevity with emotional expansiveness, we
might describe "In a Station of the Metro" as a poem about compression, and
imagism as an aesthetics that attempts to minimize what a data engineer would
call *lossyness*. The best evidence of the poem's success is that any self-respecting
student of Pound can reproduce it automatically a century later.

Pound's poem thus becomes an episode in what Jonathan Sterne describes
as a general history of compression that includes older media phenomena like
radio-signal compression, half-tone printing, code books for optical and electric
telegraphy, and even codexes (in relation to the more unwieldy scrolls they replaced). Sterne's account of this history, in fact, is strongly reminiscent of Pound's
vision of imagist aesthetics: not aspiring to verisimilitude "the general history
of compression instead asks how media manage and enact relations shaped by
one or more conditions of finitude."[17] Like imagism, compression minimizes
redundancy and textural depth in order to facilitate more efficient communication. Radical finitude in Pound's most iconic imagist poem yields a similar effect
to compression in Sterne's account: "Limited definition can produce particularly
intense modes of experience."[18] Occasioned by the apparatus of transportation,
Pound's poem opens onto communications infrastructure, a dyad that we will
see frequently reproduced in the wire shot. We might even read the idiosyncratic
spacing in the original 1913 publication of the poem in *Poetry*, not in the literary manner of caesura but rather as reminiscent of telegraph messages in the
informatic manner of data.[19]

To dart quickly toward a moment on the technological boundary of today's
digital milieu, a second antecedent might be the Wachowskis' 1999 film *The
Matrix*, which connects to Pound more than one might imagine, its climactic
scene, indeed, occurring *in a station of the metro*, an abandoned subway station
where Agent Smith attempts to thwart Neo's connection at a telephone booth.
Featuring a mise-en-scène that, like Pound's poem, seems to intuit the history
of laying subterranean communication cables in subway passages, the film is
full of tunnels, sewers, and dark hallways that robustly thematize infrastructural

networks. In addition, the film is famous for its appropriation of what is sometimes called *wire fu*, the use of hidden wires in Hong Kong cinema to film kung
fu scenes, in which we mistake the hidden labor of production staffers pulling
cable through pulleys and harnesses for the star's supernatural fighting abilities,
as is the case in this climactic scene in *The Matrix*.

But in comparison to mid-1990s technology films like *Hacker* (1995) and
Johnny Mnemonic (1995), which promiscuously represented the space inside
computers and virtual networks in a series of delightfully guileless, graphic subli-
mations, *The Matrix* is relatively restrained. There are only three wire shots proper
in the film, which surprisingly do not occur when characters enter the matrix.
Instead, they frame the film, beginning in two cases with the camera zooming
into a precise point on a computer screen—in the first case the center of a zero
in a field of green numbers and, in the second, the space between the M and the
F in the phrase "SYSTEM FAILURE"—before moving through digital corridors
(fig. 30). Both of these shots—we are invited to think of them as digital rabbit
holes—also conclude by returning from this virtual space back into the diegesis
of the film, fixing onto a physical object (a flashlight and a telephone mouthpiece
respectively) to mark the endpoint of the wire's virtual transmission.

Despite its proclamation in contemporary discourse for heralding a moment
of technological emergence, *The Matrix* is revealed in these scenes as oddly old-
fashioned. Though imaginatively representing new modes of connectivity, it is
also about their frustrations.[20] Dependent on landlines as nodal points, characters
are constantly running in search of grounded telephones and are rerouted when
access is blocked. Mirroring Neo's ascension from clumsy neophyte to deft messiah, the connection itself is magical once achieved, but the experience leading
up to it is protracted and vexing. Connection is no easy feat. In this respect the
film seems to document the way in which technological apparatuses layer their
infrastructures on top of older ones, in a process that Tung-Hui Hu describes
as *grafting*.[21] Just as telegraph and telephone cables took advantage of railway

FIGURE 30. Wire shots in *The Matrix* (Warner Bros., 1999).

right-of-ways, newer fiber-optic networks combined with existing copper systems rather than replacing them entirely. Grafting means, then, that these physical networks, despite their claims of making older systems obsolete, actually preserve the histories they seem to replace. We might think of *The Matrix*, released in 1999 in the earliest days of broadband, not as announcing the newest technological subregime but as a swan song for an older one. It is, undeniably, the greatest film ever made about the dial-up internet connection.

If the wire shot offers a view of the plumbing, it is not necessarily one that offers critical purchase. Rather, it functions as a reification in a manner that echoes Jonathan Crary's articulation of late capitalism's aggressive infringements on human sleep, in which individuals must "invent a self-understanding that optimizes or facilitates their participation in digital milieus and speeds" and enact a "fantasmatic compatibility" with fundamentally unlivable conditions. This act of impersonation attempts to literalize the human entrance into an electronic mirage, under the pressure "for individuals to reimagine and refigure themselves as being of the same consistency and values as the dematerialized commodities and social connections in which they are immersed so exten-sively."[22] Wire aesthetics meets these criteria, shaping human experience accord-ing to what Katherine Hayles characterizes as the unacknowledged "biological, social, technological systems in which we are embedded" and which reproduce "nonconscious" forms of cognition.[23]

While wire aesthetics casts light on these inhuman cognitive systems, however, it does so in fantasmatic form, participating in the reification it only seems to expose. It not only transmutes informatic networks to human scale; it also sub-mits to the pressures that define contemporary forms of commerce and finance. We travel through global conduits with fiber-optic glee, but elided are the asym-metric relations that inhere in today's unbalanced, material infrastructure, for which various interests have spent enormous resources to magnify rather than repair. Indeed, the early dream of cyberpunk egalitarianism has been significantly chastened, not least by the full embrace of digital technologies by financial agents. We know, for example, by the late 2000s, more than 70 percent of activity in con-temporary financial markets was conducted by automated trading algorithms.[24] The average holding period for stocks went from four years at the end of World War II to eight months by 2000 to two months in 2008 to twenty-two seconds in 2011.[25] The Spread Networks cable completed in 2010, which cost $300 million and involved tons of dynamite in the Allegheny Mountains, was built to shave a mere three milliseconds off transmission times between Chicago and New York markets. Because the cable formed a much straighter line than the traditional routes for communications cables following the restricted geography of railroad tracks, and because there were only twenty available slots, Spread Networks' speed advantage—imperceptible by humans but an eternity for lightning-fast machines—became available only to firms with significant means.[26]

The wire shot thus indexes the incongruities of a transitional moment facilitated in part by decreasing US corporate profitability after 1973, a general period of postindustrial stagnation in Western economies that pressured successive waves of corporate rationalization and mergers-and-acquisitions activity and, later, the 1996 US Telecommunications Act, which allowed for considerable vertical integration in the US communications industry. We might even think of the wire shot more narrowly under this rubric as the self-reflexive imprimatur of the increasing consolidation between motion picture companies and telecommunications businesses in the period, notably in the case of Time Warner Communications, which brought under the same corporate umbrella (among other enterprises) the making of movies and the management of internet cable networks. There is much to say about this complicated story, which includes the notorious merger with AOL in 2001 and the largest annual corporate loss in history ($98.8 billion), but the most salient part for the present context is that the storied motion picture company, with the development of the high-speed cable modem, found itself at the millennium with an unexpectedly profitable division, which had originally been part of a vertically integrated distribution strategy. Time Warner had previously aspired to distribute its own content directly to consumers, cutting out middlemen (theaters, video stores, etc.), but when delivery systems like interactive television proved unreliable and unprofitable, the company leveraged its already-in-place cable-television network for the internet service providing business, finding a new revenue stream.[27]

In this multifaceted context the wire shot indicates a massive nonhuman infrastructure that connects the individual consumer to the world not just virtually but physically through miles of subterranean and undersea cables,[28] while obliquely pointing to the tensions and ambivalences within the history of the global internet, which was originally developed by US military agents and privatized in the mid-1990s, thereafter becoming understood as the contemporary period's public discursive space and marketplace *par excellence*.[29] An important aspect of that which we may read in wires, then, is a history of US hegemonic infrastructure. To be very clear, I do not mean to suggest crudely that the global internet simply *is* the mode of contemporary US hegemony in an era of financialization, though some version of that claim is plausible.[30] Rather, I want to make a case for thinking about its design and history as a kind of *heterotopia* that indexes what is distinct about US hegemonic modalities, specifically at the moment of empire's declension.[31]

In this vein Alexander Galloway and Eugene Thacker have pointed out that "networked power today is based on a dialectic between two opposing tendencies: one radically distributes control into autonomous locales; the other focuses control into rigidly defined hierarchies." Furthermore, the exceptionality of the current American regime is its ability to take advantage of these conditions as it aims "to establish sovereignty in a new political structure that is antithetical to traditional modes of sovereignty."[32] This regime accomplishes this strategy by asserting not *power* but *control* (associated with modulation, distribution, and flexibility) and, more specifically, "protocological control," which determines the terms and conditions in which the various actors in a network can interact. Protocol, as Galloway writes elsewhere, "does not produce or casually effect objects, but rather is a structuring agent that appears as the result of a set of object dispositions."[33] As such, it is "both an apparatus that facilitates networks and a logic that governs how things are done within that apparatus."[34]

This technological account of network infrastructure happens to correspond with recent political economic descriptions of late US empire, after its financial turn in the 1970s, as modeled less on colonial occupation (though one cannot ignore the US military's historically unprecedented size and reach) and more on an asymmetrical infrastructure of free trade. Washington Consensus global economic policy indeed contained many elements of a logistics business. In this respect today's global fiber-optic networks follow the legacy of British submarine telegraph cables, which famously adhered to an "All Red" logic, connecting the many territories of the British Empire, most significantly London to India, without touching foreign soil. Developed at a moment of increasing dissent, it was designed as a defensive technology to assist military and governmental entities in managing empire at a moment when that task was becoming more difficult. Armand Mattelart goes so far as to suggest that the "undersea cable was one of the clearest illustrations of Victorian hegemony."[35] An early version of the internet designed as a military communications channel in the 1960s, the US's ARPAnet was conceived in similar terms. Both were networks of wires meant to facilitate the management of global hegemonic regimes that were becoming harder to manage, and—though to be sure, both grew beyond these original intentions—their histories bespeak the moments from which they emerged. In this context we might think of the wire shot as a site at which the protocols of transnational art and the protocols of military-financial hegemonic tactics converge.

In a number of different critical works, Galloway has championed Gilles Deleuze's short essay "Postscript on the Societies of Control" to suggest that digital technologies usher in the epistemological shift that Deleuze briefly outlines in his essay, from the kind of *disciplinary societies* that Michel Foucault famously detailed to *control societies*, which are characterized by flexibility, openness, and network logics.[36] But while this account has been useful to our understanding of the dramatic impact of rapid technological change, critics have suggested that the pendulum has swung too far toward self-fulfilling prophecy. Chun cautions that Deleuze's analysis "unintentionally fulfills the aims of control by imaginatively ascribing to control powers it does not yet have and by erasing its failures."[37] In a fuller polemic Tung-Hui Hu considers the *longue durée* of cloud technology to demonstrate how seemingly distributed networks often function in a more "centripetal" fashion, arguing that there is often a disparity between digital infrastructural networks as popularly conceived and their actual functioning. Most important, Hu refuses the notion that digital networks make traditional sovereign power obsolete and that "the cloud may actually effect a return to sovereignty," most significantly through what he calls, the "sovereignty of data." Achieved by grafting "control onto older structures of sovereign power, much as fiber-optic networks are layered or grafted onto older networks," the sovereignty of data inheres in how "the cloud veils hard power with the look and feel of soft power."[38]

Galloway's account is perhaps more dialectical than Hu gives credit for, in its weighing of horizontal distributive forces against the production of "rigidly defined hierarchies,"[39] but its perpetuation of Deleuze's epistemological conceits invites this treatment by threatening to subordinate useful observations about digital infrastructure to more inchoate claims about the historical transformation of "society." While we need not quibble the merits of documenting the dramatic impact of digital technologies, recent criticism in media studies, like that of Chun and Hu, have followed in the tradition of Siegfried Zielinski's media archaeology,[40] in employing broader technological rubrics to demonstrate the many historical continuities that accompany what seem to be epistemic ruptures. We also learn that the epistemic view often elides the messy array of alternative possibilities that seemed feasible before they did not. Hu's focus on the layered idiosyncratic history of fiber-optic networks as a history of grafting allows us to see in the wire shot the emergence of a dialectical relationship between the fantasy of network infrastructure and its material reality. For Hu, "the network is always more than its digital or physical infrastructure. The network is primarily a systemic belief that 'everything is connected.'" And because "reality can never match up to the system of belief . . . the network exists primarily as a state of *desire*."[41] Similarly, Chun suggests that the notion of cyberspace, although largely mistaken as an accurate descriptor of network functioning, was nevertheless generative, providing corporations a model for constructing user spaces that blinded "users to their own . . . vulnerability" and "screened issues of power and discrimination," as the internet transformed "from a U.S. military- and academic research–based 'network of networks' to an extra spatial consumerist international."[42]

This last bit of periodizing is crucial. The tendency to imagine the world pre- and postdigital networks can also obscure the transformation of the internet itself during the 1990s, when it changed from something many users believed was "truly public" into an entity resembling a shopping mall—"a privately owned, publicly accessible space" with a profoundly different backbone because internet service providers (ISPs) "closed their cables to competing traffic."[43] In a series of essays written between the mid-1990s and the early 2000s (collected in *Dark Fiber*), Geert Lovink tracks the trends, ruptures, and continuities during this period of rapid transformation when the future of the internet seemed rife with possibilities, as embodied, for example, by the makeshift network established in war-torn Albania in 1997 to assist Kosovar refugees, even as the forces of privatization, what Lovink encapsulates as "the hegemonic Californian cyberculture," sought to foreclose them.[44] Describing these latter forces as ushering in "an age of implementation, not innovation," Lovink links his assessment of new-economy business models—based on "software, infrastructure and access, not with content"—to a broader political economy: "a mix of neoliberal state politics and entrepreneurial myths" aimed at achieving a "high productivity, low inflation economy."[45] The cocktail of governmental and corporate actions that Lovink cites here (cost flexibility, open financial markets, entrepreneurial culture, telecom and labor deregulation, etc.) reads almost identically to the market liberalization policies imposed by the IMF bailout.

No uncanny doubling, both the privatization of the internet and the Korean IMF bailout package were backed by the same US corporate interests and involved strategies of value extraction from formerly public infrastructures, offering increased scale and efficiency as justification. A 1995 US State Department memorandum, entitled "U.S. Global Audiovisual Strategy," bridges these two contexts. A list of strategic protocols designed to open foreign media markets, like Korea, that were guarded by protectionist quota systems, the memo's final directive laid bare its general orientation: "Improve the conditions of investment for U.S. firms by liberalizing existing regulations."[46] Such a directive indicates not just an analogy between the expansion of the US telecommunications industry in the 1990s and the simultaneous push to liberalize Korean markets by US agents but a material relation as well. As I mentioned in my introduction, Robert Wade and Frank Veneroso suggest that IMF restructuring produced fire sale conditions for Western firms, one likely to "precipitate the biggest peacetime transfer of assets from domestic to foreign owners in the past fifty years anywhere in the world."[47] One key site for this transfer was Korean telecommunications, and this targeting involved a further push to restructure the industry itself once Western firms gained increased stakes in the companies.[48] It is no surprise, then, that new economy firms tend to devalue content and elide the labor that produces material infrastructure because network flexibility depends on radical cost-cutting so that capital can flow primarily to the agents who control the infrastructure.

Although the technological revolution appears to usher in a new epistemological regime, it does not seem to offer a significantly different political economy, despite the zeal with which the "new" economy was heralded in the 1990s and continues to be today, both in the US and in Korea. The rise of network infrastructure might instead be viewed in the context of US financial practices in the wake of deindustrialization. One of Google's axiomatic strategies, for example, is "Monetize the Traffic, Not the Content,"[49] following the legacy of what Arrighi (borrowing from Alfred Chandler) describes as the "economy of speed." In this account, US corporations gain advantages from vertical-integration strategies pioneered by railway companies and then revolutionized by "the rise of mass marketers (the mass retailer, the advertising agency, the mail order house, the chain store)," who were able to internalize "a whole sequence of subprocesses of production and exchange" and thus to minimize "the costs, risks, and uncertainties involved in moving goods through that sequence to the economizing logic of administrative and long-term corporate planning."[50] In radically minimizing production and prioritizing distribution infrastructure, the new internet corporate giants may seem to depart from the traditional operations of vertical integration that Arrighi had in mind, but their emphasis on logistics, risk management, and, indeed, infrastructure constitutes a fuller realization of this speed economy model. Given that it employs a fraction of its midcentury industrial counterparts and that it destroys old economy sectors in replacing them (e.g., Amazon and the so-called *retail apocalypse*), the ability of this new economy to buoy the US economy as a whole, and not merely leverage its logistical advantages to extract value from existing sites of production for the sake of a relatively small number of venture capitalists, remains dubious.

Even so, the businesses of new media giants have increasingly focused on infrastructural investment, not just in the construction of massive data centers but also in the routing of network traffic. The largest internet companies are physically present at the world's most heavily trafficked internet exchanges (Palo Alto, Ashburn, London, Amsterdam, etc.) in the form of routers that are plugged directly into the exchanges and peered onsite to other large routers of high-traffic web firms, with servers often placed in spaces rented in parasitic facilities near these exchanges that cater to the needs of large firms who want servers in physical proximity to access points.[51] An important characteristic of internet network distribution as currently constituted inheres in the distribution of traffic not just between nodal points across geographical expanses but also *at* the nodal points themselves, where routers of the largest firms are directly and asymmetrically interconnected, with the largest of them occupying the most central, privileged positions.[52] Corporate location trumps geography in these arrangements: traffic between Amazon and Google need not travel the miles between, say, Seattle and Palo Alto but only the feet between their routers. An even more dramatic example (and perhaps the clearest confirmation of the new economy's reliance on rentier strategies) is Google's purchase of 111 Eighth Avenue in Manhattan in 2010 for the tidy sum of $1.9 billion, making it the single most expensive real estate transaction that year in a city known for pricey real estate. Adhering to the proverbial adage, location was indeed crucial, but it was specifically the building's advantageous position in relation to the city's fiber-optic infrastructure that made it so valuable. Google could rent prime space in the major exchanges, but here in the center of global finance, as Andrew Blum suggests, it would have its own exchange.[53]

Keeping in mind the historical continuity between the new internet logistics models and those of older speed economics, I want to blend Hu's account of the network as a state of desire to the expansive sense of infrastructure in Galloway's rendering of protocol in order to consider the way fantasies about the internet, like the wire shot, may be as much constitutive of the infrastructure as the infrastruc-ture is constitutive of the fantasy. Leaving aside network epistemologies, we might instead focus on the way in which many internet firms and hegemonic agents alike, understanding their business as logistical in nature, explicitly employed protocol control as material strategy for expanding their purviews, not just at the level of machines and hard wiring but also at the more inchoate levels of platform and terrains of network sociality. As Mattelart argues, the "eschatological belief in the 'information society' hides the fact that, as the ideal of the universalism of values promoted by the great social utopias drifted into the corporate techno-utopia of globalization, the emancipatory dream of a project of world integration, characterized by the desire to abolish inequalities and injustices in the name of . . . social solidarity, was swept away by the cult of a project-less modernity that has submitted to a technological determinism in the guise of refounding the social bond."[54] Because the assumption is that markets, information, and people all want to be free, protocol becomes not just the ideology of the infrastructure but also the material basis that constitutes it. If protocol control determines the terms and conditions under which actors in a network interact, then one of the effects of this mode of control is the production of protocological feedback loops. Technofinancial protocols become the reason and occasion for the reorganiza-tion of Korean economic strategy after the IMF-imposed structural adjustments in a similar manner. Protocol is presented not as one out of a range of possible ideological positions but rather as the fundamental condition of the infrastructure that governs all interactions. It is not neutral but reproduces itself as if it were. Through protocol hegemony aspires to become material.

Down the Tubes

In considering the protocols of late-empire US hegemony, I will examine a group of what we might call highly *derivative* Korean films from the post-IMF period, all of which were produced by Tube Entertainment, a Korean motion picture company founded in 1999 by Kim Seung-bum after a successful tenure at Ilshin Investments, in hopes of capitalizing on the new popularity of Korean-made blockbuster films.[55] Tube Entertainment's attempt to exploit this new market de-mand involved a simple strategy: plug Korean actors and sensibilities into tried-and-true Hollywood formulas. Though production values were certainly higher than the quota quickies of the 1970s, these more recent films were similarly opportunistic in reaching for easy profits. Formulaic plots notwithstanding, Kim became a pioneer in the new financial modes of Korean film production, which changed after the IMF Crisis into a more speculative venture.[56] In this newly risk-tolerant context, Tube Entertainment became known for its flops.[57] *Natural City* (*Naechurŏl sit'i*, 2003), *Resurrection of the Little Match Girl* (*Songnyangp'ali sonyoui chaerim*, 2002), and the self-reflexively titled *Tube* (*T'yubŭ*, 2003) all failed at the box office despite large production budgets. Jinhee Choi, in fact, directly faults some of these films for the temporary halt of blockbuster production in the middle of the decade.[58] Indeed, *Resurrection of the Little Match Girl* did so poorly at the box office that it bankrupted its investors[59] and ended the career of Jang Sun-woo, who had been an extremely important director since the mid-1980s. While the pejorative sense of *derivative* is appropriate in each of these cases, my point is less aesthetic dismissal than consideration of the way filmic derivations reflect their protocols. Taken together, these films offer a useful vision of a series of aesthetic practices that offer a collective picture of a business model, which in turn indexes the economic history from which it emerges. More specifically, these films place what Hu calls "network desire" in more social, less abstract contexts and call attention to the way in which protocols function to mitigate and obscure the various costs of realizing this desire. All of these films address the individual's relationship to a larger system. Under this rubric the wire shots that abound in Tube Entertainment films, along with related depictions of tubes, tunnels, and corridors, serve both as a self-reflexive brand insignia and also as an index of the material protocols that underlie the company's practices.

Natural City is not just a mechanically derivative film; it is a film about mechanical derivation. Concerned with the problem of how to reproduce a cyborg consciousness identically in another body, as well as with the nightmare of endless replication, the film embodies art in the age of biopolitical reproduction by serving as a self-reflexive meditation on unimaginatively derivative practices. Cyborgs in the film are part of the fabric of daily life, helping authorities control a stratified population without dissent. The bulk of the narrative takes place in one of two telling locales: the first being the general rain-soaked, postapocalyptic noir mise-en-scène that is lifted, along with a number of iconic shots, straight out of Ridley Scott's 1982 classic *Blade Runner*. The second is NEUCOM, the control center for the massive interconnected network that is Mega City, which not only borrows its name from the city in *The Matrix* but, like its namesake in the Wachowskis' film, imagines itself to be a computer. Liberally borrowing plot elements as well from *Blade Runner*, *Natural City* tells the story of a police officer who has fallen in love with his cyborg girlfriend and takes extreme measures to extend her limited life, abducting a prostitute whose body might serve as a host for his girlfriend's computerized brain. Their relationship is a clear appropriation of the one between Deckard and Rachael in Scott's 1982 film.

Wire shots in the film reflect this derivative strategy. In a scene that reaches deep into the bag of cheap cinematography tricks, for example, the cop, R (Yoo Ji-tae), and his cyborg doll, Ria (Seo Lin), ride through the city streets on a motorcycle, and the various effects—fish-eye lenses, slow motion, time-lapse photography, deliberate blurring, etc.—conspire to refashion the cityscape as if it were an enclosed tube. Shot primarily from the point of view of the riders, the sequence transports the viewer through the city's streets and tunnels with a kind of ease, accompanied by a cloying, soft-jazz soundtrack. As the city disappears into an indistinguishable haze inside the tube created by the motorcycle's speed, we remain inside an anesthetic bubble, a space that echoes the opening scene in the film in which R and Ria pay to relax obliviously in a computer-generated oasis in the middle of an otherwise bustling airport. Crosscut with views of Ria affectionately clutching R as the rear passenger on the motorcycle, the first-person shots represent the feeling of connectivity as the ability to traverse space effortlessly in relation to the emotional bond between man and machine, both the cyborg on his back and the vehicle between his legs.

What the film implies in its various deployments of wire aesthetics is explicitly thematized in one of its central plot devices, namely that of *neural transfer*. Strikingly, both the film's protagonist, R, and the antagonist cyborg, Cyon (Lee Jae-eun), have the same goal: to implant a cyborg's brain inside a human body so that the former can continue living. Despite their antagonism, both hero and villain fight to reproduce (and not contest) the primacy of the cybernetic. One might say here that being hopelessly in love with an expiring robot is precisely the feeling of making a hopelessly derivative genre film. Both the film's protagonist and Tube Entertainment in general seem deeply compelled not to challenge the hegemonic dominance of NEUCOM and Hollywood respectively but to replicate their forms.

The figure of hegemony is even more explicit in Jang Sun-woo's 2002 film *Resurrection of the Little Match Girl*. Plainly named "The System" and voiced by an English-speaking figurehead projected, *Wizard of Oz*–like, onto a large screen, the film's central authority is Western, military, and corporate; it also has the radical capacity to manufacture worlds akin to the reality-shaping powers of machines in *The Matrix*. As the organizing force behind the game in the film, the System explicitly manages the ambitions of Ju (Kim Hyun-sung), the Chinese-food delivery boy who plays the Neo role in the film. Ju remains deeply committed to the System's infrastructure, even as he suffers under it. As his ability increases, he feels more connected to and empowered within the network, but he never reflects on the way in which his opposition to the System functions ironically as validation. The task is to master the System's system, not to unplug.

The film is self-consciously derivative, taking its title and loose premise from a Hans Christian Andersen story, "The Little Match Girl." More important, it also bluntly announces its indebtedness to the narrative and visual logics from millennial Western films that explore video-game aesthetics, like David Cronenberg's *eXistenZ* (1999) and, most significantly of course, *The Matrix*, using Korea's emerging professional video-game culture as an occasion to refashion the American subgenre for a new national context. The film's derivations are plainly visible, for example, in its many citations of the Wachowskis' visual effects, not just bullet time in general but, more specifically, the slow-motion, bullet-avoidance acrobatics from the source text's most iconic moment. These citations, however, seem less like postmodern appropriations in acts of performative mimicry and more like efforts to reproduce protocols. The film seems less invested in genre-bending or in claiming artistic autonomy and more interested in affirming the global networked environment through which these transnational citations become possible. Furthering their definition beyond "the rules that make sure the connections actually work," Galloway and Thacker describe protocol as a layer of the global internet between that of material infrastructure (wires) and application (programs) that "regulates flow, directs netspace, codes relationships, and connects life-forms."[60] In this context the film, by the director of the self-consciously titled *Bad Movie* (1997), seems intentionally derivative, revealing an oddly informatic relation to its predecessor, which it doesn't reproduce in the manner of homage but rather transfers in the manner of data. The film's emphasis on protocol reveals its debt to the 2009 Neveldine and Taylor film *Gamer*, which asks us, according to Steven Shaviro, "to pay attention to *how it works* instead of *what it means*."[61]

Befitting the characteristics of what J. D. Connor has described as a "chaos film," a genre that enacts an "endless quest to conquer risk,"[62] *Resurrection*, with its alternate endings and nonsensical plot elements, presents itself in such terms. Accordingly, Ju spends a lot of time in the film trying to figure out not how to win the game but how to play it. Because the game's interface is a lot more unwieldy than in *The Matrix*—there is a much more fluid relationship in *Resurrection* between what is inside the game and what is outside—the protocols are far more complex for Ju than they are for Neo, who has an innate ability into which he must tap. It is worth mentioning here the scale of the film's flop. An attempt on the part of a director with art-house credentials to reach a mass audience, the film was sometimes met with extreme anger because of its byzantine plot. One viewer complained that the many millions spent on the film's production might have been better spent to help flood victims,[63] a charge applicable of course to any big-budget film but one that is normally reserved for only the biggest failures. Because of this emphasis on protocol, *Resurrection* spends a fair amount of time developing its own metadiscourse in which Ju and the designer of the system discuss the weird, arbitrary rules of the game; at one point, for example, Ju is instructed quite randomly to catch a mackerel with no bait. In some ways plot becomes indistinguishable from protocol: though he originally struggles with its rules, Ju eventually masters the game. But unlike Neo, who is a messiah figure, Ju reaches instead for technical proficiency within a technocratic milieu.

In contrast to the elegant wire shots that frame *The Matrix*, there are too many to count in Jang's film, which collectively represent networks in cluttered disarray. The labyrinthine network in the film is tangled instead of streamlined; and by making a mess out of the matrix, the film seems to restore what the wire shot elides, that is, the fact of social complexity (fig. 31). Radical connectivity, we learn, is chaotic

FIGURE 31. Some of the numerous wire shots in *Resurrection of the Little Match Girl* (Tube Entertainment, 2002).

because so is sociality. In this context it is important to remember that *Resurrection of the Little Match Girl* is much more of a class story than *The Matrix*.[64] As a Chinese-food delivery boy, Ju occupies an abject position within Korea's burgeoning technofinancial economic ecology, and his love interest, Hee-mi (Lim Eun-kyung), the little match girl in the game's diegesis and a mythic figure of precarity, works as a clerk in a shabby video-game parlor. In the film's dénouement, however, we learn that the System, which seems to have abided its own apparent destruction in the film's climax, has "wired" a good deal of money to Ju, now ensconced in hard-earned domestic bliss with Hee-mi and their new child.[65] The System's game thus functions as a vehicle for class elevation, and the most significant entity that ultimately comes through wires in the film is money.

The messy network of wires in the film, however, refuses the fantasy of the internet as a rational network; the film returns us to the irreducible muddle of sociality that vanishes in understandings of social relations in market terms. Significantly, this is an insight on which the film seems to stumble while moving in the opposite direction. It wants to reproduce the elegance of the matrix and to master its protocols, but the irredeemable gumminess of social relations is an intractable morass that undoes the fiber-optic pleasure of systemic traversal. Particularly characteristic of Jang's many wire shots, then, is his peculiar use of variable speeds to interrupt, prolong, and otherwise complicate the rushing enervation of the shot. Rehearsing bullet time in many more varieties, these pauses serve in part to accentuate what we might identify as moments of *acceleration*, invoking what Stephen Shaviro has termed *acceleration aesthetics*, which captures "the extent to which capitalism generates its own form of dissolution."[66] In this mode *Resurrection* does not model political resistance in its aesthetic forms (on some level, it very much wants to be *The Matrix*); rather, it confirms the unsustainability of any attempt to organize the messy social infrastructures that networks attempt to codify. If *Natural City* is a film about making derivative films, *Resurrection of the Little Match Girl* might be understood as a film about the difficulty of such an endeavor. Making a derivative Hollywood movie, it turns out, is harder than it looks.

Smooth derivation, in contrast, is not a problem in the eponymously titled *Tube* (2003), a slick remake of the 1974 Palomar/Palladium production *The Taking of Pelham One Two Three*, with elements of the Keanu Reeves vehicle *Speed* (1999) thrown in for good measure. Forming a transpacific feedback loop, the concept was reborn in 2009 Hollywood as a Tony Scott–directed extravaganza. But even though Scott's film reprised the original 1974 title, it seems to owe more to the Korean remake. *Tube* might be described as a *bailout film*, a subgenre that might be understood as a subset of disaster narratives and characterized by the effort to diffuse a sudden crisis, the solution to which becomes inextricable from confronting the flaws in the system tasked to deal with the situation. Central to the bailout film, we might say, is systems analysis.

A story about disaster prompting institutional introspection, *Tube* centers on Kang Gi-taek (Park Sang-min), a disillusioned former elite covert-ops agent turned terrorist, who hijacks a subway train in Seoul to avenge the surreptitious dealings of the corrupt government official who had originally assembled Kang's elite squad and then eliminated each of its members along with their families in cover-up. Taking place largely in the remarkable Seoul subway system, for which the film serves as loving hagiography, *Tube* focuses on the relationship between infrastructural networks and human kinship, by using an ensemble cast to develop a complex social field with disparate and conflicting interests, which decision makers must ultimately weigh in a cost-benefit analysis. Although the infrastructure of the Seoul subway system begins as a metaphor for more complex networks of human relations that constitute society in general, this analogical relationship eventually serves as cover for the subsumption of social concerns within broader and more abstract demands for systemic integrity, which privilege capital accumulation over human flourishing.

Though neither is explicitly cited, a pair of related historical phenomena seem to inform this interest: on the one hand, the ongoing intense railway labor unrest in the post–IMF Crisis period as pressures to privatize the largely state-run enterprise mounted and, on the other hand, the fully realized privatization of Korea Telecom during the same period.[67] In 2003, Seoul's subway system was controlled by three state-owned agencies working in concert, including the Seoul Metropolitan Rapid Transit Corporation (the organization in *Tube*). Overlapping with the controversial discussion about also privatizing KORAIL (Korea's national railway), strikes, strike threats, large-scale protests, and tense negotiations were common in the period when crisis conditions pressured state-run ventures to perform more efficiently. Part of a larger program of financial liberalization, the drive toward privatization in South Korea that began in the 1990s was intensified by the specific demands of the IMF bailout. These restructuring measures were explicitly resisted by labor unions, which pushed back against rising irregular employment as a strategy for dealing with corporate and public debt.[68] In this antagonistic schema the transformation of Korea Telecom, for advocates, was a success that provided a blueprint for struggling Korean rail agencies. But while the net benefits of the transformation of Korea Telecom are arguable, complicated by the dramatic growth of the industry in general during the period, the costs could be somewhat disconcerting. As government regulations eased in the privatization process, foreign ownership increased, fanning anxieties about Korean sovereignty over its vital infrastructure and its largest corporations.[69] It should be noted in this context that Korean telecommunications companies were among those most heavily targeted by Western capital, which led not only to direct foreign investment in the companies but also to a subsequent push to transform industry policy according to "United States–originated, neoliberal regulatory norms."[70] And in the years following the release of *Tube,* Korean telecom firms began to enter the media content production industry, including film.[71]

Trains and the people who run them are an obvious concern of *Tube*, but cell phones are also featured with special prominence, allowing for alternative channels of communication outside of the official state network, and their use in the film represents a victory for privatizing logics, under the rubric of the film's perverse celebration of irregular labor. When forced to follow orders, employees fall in line with blinkered institutional protocols or serve the interests of corrupt politicians. When they act on their own initiative, they efficiently arrive at innovative solutions. This is certainly the case for the maverick cop Jang Do-joon (Kim Suk-hoon), and for Officer Kwon (Son Byung-Ho), who continues to try to save the passengers on the train after he is relieved of his duties for taking a principled stance. Even the terrorist Kang is an expression of suppressed individual interest, a rejoinder to a high-placed government agent corruptly overstepping his authority. In a film that is ultimately about a workplace, the best kind of work is free to follow creative modes of action.

The film thus defends privatization more generally as a social value than as a specific policy objective for Korean rail. No longer mere labor, work exists in an alternative arena of principled behavior in terms that echo Boltanski and Chiapello: "the distinction between private life and professional life tends to diminish."[72] Precisely by blurring this distinction, the workers in the film succeed against mismanagement by misguided authorities. The film is a love letter to the literal infrastructure it depicts, but it is deeply antagonistic to what it regards as outmoded state-run apparatuses. Although the film contains almost no explicit allusions to American power, it embraces one of the primary protocols established by the IMF as part of an American hegemonic infrastructure that demands strategically asymmetric, but seemingly equitable, global marketplaces that ultimately make state assets available to Western capital.

There are, of course, many perspectival shots of trains rushing through tunnels that are structurally similar, but we only get a wire shot proper just past the halfway point in the film. Following a failed SWAT attack, Detective Jang jumps into an open train car before it speeds off. After a tracking shot from outside the train, we see from Jang's perspective as he rushes toward Kang. At this point comes the wire shot: the camera reverses to face Jang and then rapidly retreats through a series of four or five subway cars (fig. 32), accompanied by the familiar wire-shot whooshing sound. The camera moves implausibly through the windows of the closed doors that separate the cars until finally taking a position behind Kang's right shoulder as he waits for his adversary. The shot has a *mise-en-abyme* quality: encased, as it were, in the tube of the train inside the tube of the train tunnel that is reimagined as the space inside of a cable, the wire shot here represents this diegetic space as fantasmatically traversable at inhuman speeds and in which it becomes possible to pass through closed doors without breaking them. We can also see the grafting in the sense Hu describes: if the rush of the wire forces erasure, blurring together the discrete elements of the scene, then it ironically seems to preserve their histories as well, namely the material connection between histories of mass transportation and mass communication. The ensuing exchange of gunfire continues in the scene's impossible mode; Jang and Kang take turns shooting at each other from approximately five cars away through closed doors. The bullets fly past the bodies of each, somehow passing through the unshattered windows of the doors separating them, leaving streaks in

FIGURE 32. Wire shot on the subway train as Jang and Kang prepare to fight in *Tube* (Tube Entertainment, 2003).

the air reminiscent of laser guns in science fiction movies. For some inexplicable reason, each disposes of his gun long before Jang reaches the car in which Kang waits, where they engage in hand-to-hand combat. In any number of ways the sequence makes no sense.

Although it fails to adhere to the laws of physics (or reason), the scene does remain devoted to the fantasy of connectivity. Putting aside logistical impossibilities, the wire shot in this scene functions singularly to put Kang and Jang face-to-face, despite the fact that they originally occupy different cars. Furthermore, the scene transforms the space of public infrastructure into one of private conflict, a showdown between a pair of antagonists with a long personal history. The failure of gunplay, however nonsensical, makes the more intimate hand-to-hand combat necessary. Collapsing the two historical infrastructural purposes of underground train tunnels, then, the train here functions as something like a cell phone, a mode of public transportation morphing into a means of private communication. With the camera rushing backward through interior space, this depiction of the train-as-wire radically collapses distance, transforming the subway into a network site. Insofar as the post-IMF histories of these industries in Korea have been understood as exemplifying the benefits of opposite strategies vis-à-vis privatization, this imaginative transformation in *Tube*, from public infrastructure to private network, makes clear which side of the argument it takes.

At the end of the film's long climax, after the villain Kang has been deposed, Jang decides to remain inside the front subway car, which contains the bomb, because the train can now only be operated manually. The other passengers remain aboard the second car, which they manage to detach, and watch Jang as he speeds away, sacrificing himself for the other passengers and the many residents of Seoul who would have been the victims of Kang's plot. It is, in effect, a suicide mission, and, in this context, it is worthwhile to note that a number of the action sequences in *Tube* would have been impossible had the film been produced just a few years later because of the subsequent construction of the now ubiquitous suicide barriers in Seoul subway stations. Like the bridges over the Han River, subway platforms in the post-IMF period became identified as sites of suicide for recently unemployed workers, and the characters in the film leaping onto the tracks as trains pull into the station would have been legible in this context. Jang's suicide mission metonymically invokes these other deaths.

In a final melodramatic sequence, as Jang pulls away from the now safe passengers as their car slows to a halt, Kay (Bae Doona), a pickpocket with a crush on the policeman, tearfully watches. When he becomes too distant to see, she grabs the video camera of a passenger standing next to her and zooms in on Jang's face, making him visible through the camera's display screen before he becomes too distant once again. Soon, his train car explodes, and the tunnel goes dark. In essence here, framed by the subway tunnel, Kay makes a wire shot (fig. 33). The camera's zoom function rapidly bridges the otherwise increasing distance in the subway tube between the two cars. The shot is reminiscent of Alfred Hitchcock's famous vertigo shot (or *dolly zoom*), achieved by simultaneously tracking backward and zooming forward, on a horizontally constructed set that resembled a tunnel more than the tower at Mission San Juan Bautista. Kay is not literally tracking backward, but the disparity in speeds between the two subway cars produces a similar effect. Her hastily made wire shot, however, does not produce disorientation as in Hitchcock but rather a fleeting sense of connectivity between Kay and Jang, whom her technological intervention makes proximate, if only for an extra moment. In this manner trains in the film are repeatedly reimagined as if they were cellular phones—not modes of transportation but of communication.

After we see Jang's train car explode, the film cuts to Officer Kwon, who reprises his painfully earnest mantra: "sometimes, there's a train that nobody can stop."[73] Kwon is an apt voice for this sentiment because he epitomizes Tube Entertainment's depiction of workers—be it in the form of the rogue cop, pro gamer, pickpocket, or subway-system manager. It turns out that these are all films about work, filled with figures of flexible labor that chafe against narrow institutional boundaries while at the same time embracing those varied trains that nobody can stop, whether it is biological replication in *Natural City*, hegemonic systems in *Resurrection of the Little Match Girl*, or privatization in *Tube*. In all three cases these figures of flexible labor combine unruliness before authority with ideological compliance, but they do so less as a matter of false consciousness than as commitment to protocol.

FIGURE 33. Kay (Bae Doona) makes a wire shot in *Tube* (Tube Entertainment, 2003).

Natural Protocols

A very obvious rejoinder to Officer Kwon's mantra is that there need not be any such trains, but such a rejoinder never comes. The film's final commitment to Kwon's belief lays bare the work of protocol in Tube Entertainment products, explicitly to reimagine the results of very specific institutional operations and political decisions as irrefutable natural facts, and implicitly to privilege functionalist views of economic processes that subordinate the needs of individuals to systemic imperatives. Protocol naturalizes such conceits and the vision of social stability that they guarantee and reproduce. The sublimation of mass transportation into mass communication reflects the desire to reform older practices in line with newer imperatives, relaxing localized barriers to allow for optimal network performance. In privileging the health of the network over that of individuals, social stability becomes supplanted by more abstract logics of equilibrium. Nevertheless, the strength of the system is understood to be in no way inimical to individual freedom; labor flexibility becomes indistinguishable from freedom writ large. This is ultimately a monetarist impulse keyed toward financial imperatives that recasts social equilibrium as market stability, prescribing the clearing of impediments to allow markets to follow their supposedly natural inclination.

In this context Kay's handmade wire shot at the end of *Tube* captures the potentially problematic image of Jang moving slowly away in his suicide mission—an Angelus Novus smoking his last cigarette, facing away from his imminent death. We have seen this heroic death before, many times in fact, perhaps most vividly at the end of the Touchstone Pictures production *Armageddon* (1998)—a bailout film if there ever was one. Thinking of his daughter back home, Harry Stamper (Bruce Willis) dramatically takes the place of his would-be future son-in-law as the short straw with the dubious honor of staying behind to detonate the bomb that would destroy the asteroid on a crash course with Earth. Jang, like Stamper (who is a kind of high-tech miner), is a figure of labor's irreducibility that must be sacrificed for the greater good. Despite our advances in technology and logistics, and despite the fact that there always seems to be a far easier solution that is willfully ignored, someone always has to stay behind because the damn detonator always fails. This ritual killing is a common trope in contemporary American and Korean cinema, a drama that relegates flexible labor in logistics economies to its logical conclusion, disposable labor.

Like all ritual killings, this one must be repeated. As the last image at the end of the final tunnel in *Tube*, the explosion of the train car and Jang's body within it (along with the labor theory of value) seems to suggest that all obstacles have finally been cleared. If the cost of network desire is the rather inflexible form of labor that inheres in the body of Jang, then *Tube* is all too happy to pay. But we know that the costs spiral: from Stamper to Jang, this figure has become a trope precisely because there is no sacrifice sufficient to the continual demands of capital. In such protraction, it becomes clear that the goal of such hegemonic protocols is not social stability but the reproduction of a supposedly autopoietic system primed for unrestrained accumulation in a globally deindustrializing environment in which the exploitation of labor in production can no longer allay the pressures of declining profits. As in *Sympathy for Mr. Vengeance*, value extraction becomes more attractive in the absence of value production, as partnerships between capital and labor break down and profits must be sought in increasingly brutal appropriations.

With a more holistic sense of social stability falling by the wayside in late-capitalist economies that are increasingly comfortable with bubbles and crises, hegemonic protocols function to naturalize monetarists conceptions of equilibrium, which require a devaluation of labor. To this end, Tube Entertainment films valorize the monetarist underpinnings of the IMF bailout, which was orchestrated by the US Treasury Department under Larry Summers following in the tradition of Robert Rubin, for whom the crisis posed an opportunity, according to Wade and Veneroso, to force "Asian governments to reshape their domestic economies in line with Western models" to such a significant degree that even Henry Kissinger expressed the need for restraint.[74] Under such guidance, the IMF ignored other viable, and arguably less costly, options because of its reformist imperatives.

Such imperatives were deeply rooted by the late 1990s, and IMF restructuring reshaped the Korean economy not only according to Western economic models but also their histories. In 1977 the United States Congress added monetary oversight (in the form of price stability and long-term interest rates) to the original mandate of the Federal Reserve Bank, which had been geared toward full employment, inaugurating what is referred to as the Fed's "dual mandate," and inflation control became an explicit priority for the Fed when Paul Volcker took over as chair in 1979. A primary variable in discussions of inflation targeting in turn became labor flexibility, a priority that represented a departure from the original orientation toward full employment.

This was the context in which the macroeconomic theoretical concept, the NAIRU (non-accelerating inflationary rate of unemployment) rose to prominence. An equilibrium concept most commonly understood as the rate of unemployment at which inflation is constant, NAIRU understands labor and inflation to be in a relationship of tension. Although these key elements of the dual mandate were not originally thought to be in conflict, NAIRU proposed that they were indeed so. In his famous 1968 essay "The Role of Monetary Policy," Milton Friedman laid the groundwork for this thinking in what he called the *natural rate of unemployment*. Ideal monetary policy for Friedman operates on an equilibrium principle geared toward stable currency valuation. A refinement of the Phillips Curve and most fully realized in the NAIRU, the idea is that too low unemployment, which crosses the NAIRU line, would bring about increasingly perilous monetary conditions and return us to previous eras of stagflation (increasing inflation with decreasing growth). Characterizing Keynesian maneuvers toward full employment as unwittingly reckless, NAIRU both justifies labor flexibility and perhaps even more significantly insulates its insight from other variables. Like Jang and Stamper, labor must be sacrificed for the greater good.

As an instrument designed to balance employment against inflation and to cast the former as the controllable variable, it gradually became a key macroeconomic protocol, first in the West and then through the Washington Consensus apparatus in OECD countries, like the Republic of Korea. Among others, Anwar Shaikh has demonstrated that the premise is deeply flawed in empirical terms, pointing out that such concepts fail to account for the correspondence between rising inflation and rising unemployment in the 1970s and the 1980s and conversely the more recent steady and falling rates of inflation in OECD countries and the US respectively.[75] Despite much scholarship that debunked the premises on which it stands,[76] the rise of NAIRU as a financial optic in the late twentieth century as part of a broader monetarist turn nevertheless remained crucial for an increasingly influential global protocol that privileged capital mobility and price stability, indexed toward monetary rather than social relations.[77] Unemployment becomes "a structural phenomenon that fiscal and monetary policy could do nothing about,"[78] a stance that Washington Consensus models have perpetuated, according to William Mitchell and Joan Muysken, by remaining "content to adopt *ad hoc* responses to theoretical and/or empirical anomaly in order to retain the basic desired property of the model."[79] By defining financial stability as price stability, NAIRU defends the value of credit-money and creates conditions in which private profits can be gained in bubbles while socializing the losses.[80] Following this logic, the IMF's strenuous insistence on low inflationary targets as part of the bailout conditions was never up for serious debate because it constituted a constitutive protocol rather than an adjustable variable. Wade and Veneroso suggest that the "inflation route" to dealing with the massive debts of Korea firms and economic recovery, though not without its social costs, would have been far preferable to the draconian restructuring that the IMF ultimately demanded.[81]

Tube Entertainment films are not explicitly about NAIRU. However, these films do respond to the exigencies that such policy instruments put in place, subscribing to a set of economic principles and the systems that reproduce them and lending credence to the kind of technological determinism that Mattelart described above, in which network logics subsume social bonds. Most fundamentally, these films, as does NAIRU, understand monetarist and social interests to be in a relationship of tension. Tube Entertainment's flops thus represent filmmaking in the age of US hegemonic finance, not just because they push for quick profits in derivative modes but, more importantly, because the films themselves encode its basic protocols, which are as much those of Western monetarism as they are of Hollywood clichés. More than ideological figures that bespeak false consciousness, these protocols are key elements of a network infrastructure designed to reproduce its own logics in a closed system forcibly partitioned off from the real economy, as part of a broader effort to prolong hegemonic advantages. Accordingly, Tube Entertainment's catalog rehearses the struggle between monetarist protocols and labor in highly mediated forms that consistently demonstrate the necessity of the former's triumph over the latter. Officer Kwon's unstoppable trains cannot be stopped because individual needs must be subordinated to systemic demands. This form of mediation manifests the protocols that propel the cycle: the IMF's intervention forced Korean economic policy to address hegemonic economic exigencies and in the process hastened the Korean economy's turn to conditions under which further liberalization, in the cascading manner of vicious circuits, came to seem more urgent.

At the same time, we recognize these measures as desperate ones: as much as these protocols bespeak hegemonic orientations, they also reflect the systemic crisis that made them necessary. For the sake of provocation, I will end with the strongest version of the claim: the wire shot is ultimately nothing less than the sublated expression of enthusiasm late in the American century for the explosion of full employment as a worthwhile social goal and its subsumption under the larger and more pressing imperatives of hegemonic monetarism. But the wire shot also preserves in its encoding the hidden desperation of such a fantasy. If networks, as Alan Liu claims, subtract "the need to be conscious of the geography, physicality, temporality, and underlying history of the links between the nodes,"[82] then our remapping of the wire shot recenters what is subtracted in network logics, namely the political economy that gave rise to them. It may be the case that these preserved subtractions remain only in traces, like the material geographies in the body of the ritually sacrificed laborer, which are offered as stubborn (but recursive) remainders. These are geographies that are not explicit but nevertheless remain wired into our protocols.

CODA

Hegemonic Pork

On January 23, 2018, shortly after his inauguration, President Trump formally withdrew the United States from the Trans-Pacific Partnership (TPP) trade agreement, fulfilling a campaign promise that he had shared with his election opponent, Hillary Clinton, who had reversed her earlier support after facing its growing unpopularity with the American public. A version of the agreement was eventually signed by eleven nations on March 9, 2018, without US participation. As much as any moment in recent history, the US withdrawal from an agreement it had done much to shape under the Obama administration marked the end of the Washington Consensus and its vision of a US-centered, liberalized global market. If the American century had already ended as numerous commentators had claimed—with the 9/11 attacks, the second Iraq War, or the 2008 Global Financial Crisis—then the failure of a US-led TPP marked the end of strategies once designed to extend hegemonic influence past the expiration of the US's ability to provide an engine for global economic expansion.

As Perry Anderson's recent book, *The H-Word: The Peripeteia of Hegemony* (2017), has shown, the notion of hegemony has been deployed very differently throughout its rhetorical history, from the interstate version espoused by Arrighi to the class and institutional focus of Antonio Gramsci to the linguistic-turn ideological account of Ernesto Laclau and Chantal Mouffe.[1] I have clearly privileged the determining power of Arrighi's materialism and have regarded more ideological forms of hegemony as post–signal crisis strategies designed to prolong hegemonic advantages past their material justification. Infrastructure and protocol, as described in Chapters 5 and 6, might be thought of as examples of such strategies, which compensate for the lack of material base with logistical solutions at a massive systemic scale.

But this can only go on for so long. As with any crisis, post–IMF Crisis discourse eventually is forced to confront questions of final limitation. How many spatiotemporal fixes can be employed before the machine finally gives out? How much vicious circulation can an economy accommodate before it collapses? Another way to think of Korea's IMF Cinema, then, is not just as marking the end of a period, namely Korea's historical client-state relationship to the United States during the era of American hegemonic power, but also as an early impetus to think through the limits of the US cycle of accumulation and Korea's reliance on it. With all of this talk about endings (of the Washington Consensus, of US hegemony, of the American century), we have reached a moment in very late capitalism at which we are forced to reckon with outer boundaries. As Marx wrote, capitalist reproduction is "not an absolute but only historical mode of production, corresponding to a specific and limited epoch in the development of the material conditions of production."[2]

Twenty years later, many Koreans continue to use the IMF Crisis to mark the historical turning point for the Korean economy. Household debt has skyrocketed, as has income inequality. Economist Lee Je-min has even linked postcrisis stagnation to the low national birthrate,[3] which augurs a catastrophic economic future according to many commentators. Prognostication is tricky business amid such uncertainty, but we might at least say that the recursive effort to double down on the economic policies of the past two decades that continues to dominate contemporary Korean economic discourse (more deregulation, more credit, more privatization, more labor flexibility) along with the latent and staunch commitment to the US-ROK alliance represent both a stubborn unwillingness to acknowledge material realities and an inability to imagine attractive alternatives.

Bong Joon-ho's two most recent films, both produced and distributed in cooperation with US firms, speak directly to current geopolitical conditions as viewed from the Korean periphery. Released the same year that the United States withdrew from the TPP, *Okja* (2017) is particularly relevant to contemporary changes in political economy. To state the obvious, *Okja* is a film about pork distribution. Indeed, the film might be read as a late-capitalist revision of E. B. White's children's classic *Charlotte's Web* (1952), with the farmer Homer Zuckerman now replaced by a multinational food conglomerate, and Wilber by the film's eponymously named "miracle" pig, which offers (according to the corporate spin) a solution for global hunger while modeling sustainable practices by the apparently reformed Mirando Corporation. A thinly veiled play on Monsanto, Mirando intends with this new product to distribute food globally, celebrating its environmental responsibility while hiding the fact of genetic modification. To say that the film is about pork production, however, calls attention to its major aporia, namely the fact that China is completely absent from the film, an important elision considering that China constitutes one-half of the global pork market and has also grown increasingly ambivalent about US distributors precisely because of new anti-GMO requirements for imports. A pork distribution company with a supposedly nongenetically altered miracle pig that does not center China as part of its global strategy is thus as ludicrous as the story about Okja's natural birth.

If the US-supported version of the TPP was an effort late in its hegemonic cycle to maintain US dominance of interstate trade, then the crucial subtext was the rising prominence of China in the global economy as epitomized by the One Belt One Road Initiative, a Chinese development plan that would encompass 40 percent of global GDP and was understood to be a competitor for the TPP.[4] Inattentive to the realities of the actual world market and to China's prominence in it, *Okja* treats pork distribution somewhat nostalgically as a relation of periphery and core, a rural Korean product brought to New York City to serve as part of a neocolonial enterprise. Furthermore, according to Mirando's corporate spin, Korea is not Okja's birthplace; Chile is. Although this claim turns out to be false—Okja was actually the product of a New Jersey genetics lab—the imaginary relation it reflects between Latin America and East Asia acknowledges the parallel histories of two key regions of US hegemony throughout the latter part of the twentieth century. In 1989 Bruce Cumings (quoting Guillermo O'Donnell) crassly noted the striking similarities between the US role in South Korea and Latin America, "coddling the junta or the authoritarians as long as they seem firmly in the saddle, supporting them with military aid, police training, intelligence sharing, CIA 'advisers,' etc. All this is then abruptly forgotten in regime crises—whence the US becomes champion of democracy, inaugurating a 'vain search for "respectable" elements within the authoritarian regime to ally with a democratic centre that the regime has made every effort to erase.'"[5] To this account we need only fill in the subsequent twinned histories of these regions since the 1980s, noting the installation of neoliberal economic regimes by both the carrot (entrance into the OECD) and the stick (IMF bailout packages).

The United States, Chile, and South Korea were also key members of TPP discussions. Although the United States did not originate the TPP, it became the central figure in negotiations when it entered discussions in 2008. Chile was actually part of the original Trans-Pacific Strategic Economic Partnership Agreement (TPSEP or P4) signed in 2005, and South Korea announced its interest as a potential member in the TPP in 2013. With all of its specific understanding of the global marketplace, rendered so clearly in Lucy Mirando's (Tilda Swinton) spunky press conference at the beginning of the film, *Okja* is very much a TPP film. The global pork distribution business that she outlines would have had to navigate the rules and provisions established by the TPP, and the film's elision of China's centrality to the global pork market mirrors the TPP's ambition to create a trading block with enough leverage to extract more favorable conditions from China, which was understandably ambivalent about the invitation to join.

Another relevant feature of the film is Lucy Mirando's transformation of her family's company into something of a media firm. Concerned about the company's image, unlike her austere twin sister, Nancy (also Tilda Swinton), who eventually regains control after Lucy's failure, Lucy devises the global marketing campaign that puts Charlotte's modest web ("some pig") to shame, bringing Okja to Korea as part of an elaborate televised contest to see which nation and farmer can raise the best specimen. These elements of the film remind us that a crucial aspect of the TPP, particularly for US interests, were intellectual property provisions, the global standards for which were to be strengthened significantly in the accord. Such measures culminated the massive transformation of global intellectual property laws and practices in the past few decades that legal historian James Boyle has described as a "Second Enclosure Movement," inviting a direct (if problematic) comparison between contemporary intellectual property consolidation to the enclosure movement in England in the eighteenth and nineteenth centuries, a key transformation in the history of capitalism.[6]

An important change in this movement was the consolidation of TRIPS (Trade-Related Aspects of Intellectual Property Rights). Begun in 1994 during the Uruguay Round (1986–94) of the GATT (Global Agreement on Tariffs and Trade), TRIPS was an important element of the then emergent globalization efforts, particularly for deindustrialized nations like the United States. As Joseph Slaughter has argued, "TRIPS represented an effort of the intellectual property-rich countries of the North to reorganize the global economy of the new world older to consolidate their own trade-related advantage by inventing and securing new streams of revenue." He goes on to point out that, counting patents, "97% of the world's intellectual property is held by the industrialized countries in the North; 80% of the patents registered in the Global South are held by alien residents of industrialized countries, which leaves a total of just 0.6% in the hands of developing nations."[7]

More than an industrial product, Okja becomes important as an intellectual property; thus, it is worth noting that Mirando, the name of the corporation in the film, likely derives not only from Monsanto, the much-maligned multinational food giant, but also Miramax.

Miramax. Monsanto. Mirando.

Though explicitly about global pork distribution, the film is then implicitly about global film distribution. Bong Joon-ho's second project done in conjunction with Hollywood interests—this time with Brad Pitt's Plan B Entertainment—*Okja* was notoriously released simultaneously in theaters and on Netflix, a fact that prompted a loud outcry of booing when the film was screened at Cannes. The subtext for this decision, though mostly unmentioned in the popular press at the time, was the protracted struggle to get Bong's previous US film, *Snowpiercer* (2013), released in the US market, as it was held up by Harvey Weinstein, who wanted to cut significantly from the film before release. The Weinstein Company (formerly Miramax) had acquired the US distribution rights for *Snowpiercer* in 2012, a fact that seems to be recognized in the film's diegesis in the similarity between the logos of train magnate William Gilford and that of the Weinstein Company. Its purported designation as an antimarket economy film by the Korean National Intelligence Service notwithstanding,[8] *Snowpiercer* ultimately reads at least as much like an industry tale about a foreigner trying to make a film under the watchful eye of Hollywood as it does about class conflict and more. The film's version of Weinstein, played by Ed Harris, reprising to some extent his role in *The Truman Show* (1998) as a powerful TV producer, Gilford explicitly refers to Curtis's revolution in the film in Hollywood marketing terms: "a blockbuster production with a devilishly unpredictable plot." One might speculate that Bong's decision to release simultaneously on Netflix was a direct result of his frustrations in working with Weinstein, whose intellectual property claim (i.e., distribution rights) gave him the leverage, as it were, to drive the train. These rights, in fact, seem to be gaining in value with Turner Network Television announcing its intention in 2017 to adapt *Snowpiercer* into a television serial starring the American actor Jennifer Connelly.[9] In this respect Monsanto's brazen attempt in 2005 to patent the "Monsanto Pig" in 160 countries might stand in as a figure for the film's synthesis between industrial product and intellectual property in the figure of Okja. For Lucy Mirando, Okja is a wildly profitable idea worth much more than the weight of her meat.

The dual corporate interests implicit in the name Mirando, giant agribusiness firms like Monsanto and major Hollywood players like Miramax, were major proponents of the TPP. It should surprise no one that former Monsanto lobbyist Islam A. Siddiqui was one of the chief agricultural negotiators for the United States in TPP negotiations.[10] Similarly, the MPAA (Motion Picture Association of America)—the lobbying group that represents the largest producers and distributors of film in Hollywood and has long been an advocate for opening foreign markets for American films (including in both Korea and Latin America)—repeatedly offered its full-throated support of the TPP as it was being negotiated. Members of the United States Senate were furious that the MPAA was given unfettered access to secret documents that senators themselves did not have during the negotiations. The TPP in this context reveals itself to be not so much the signature of a new era of global cooperation as an attempt to preserve the advantages of the world system for powerful corporations in the dying days of US hegemony.

The film's strange preoccupation with translation reflects the challenges and anxieties that attend the task of directing a film in a nonnative language for an English-speaking audience, as well as the problem of a universal hegemonic system that no longer seems universal. Hence, the implicit accord at the climax of *Sympathy for Mr. Vengeance*—"But you know why I have to kill you, you understand?"[11]— dissipates in a scene toward the end of *Okja*. When Jay (Paul Dano), the leader of the Animal Liberation Front, sneaks into Mija's (Ahn Seo-hyun) room to tell her the plan that would save her beloved pig, he has to hold up preprepared placards that describe the plan in simple language with Korean translations below them (fig. 34). Here the ALF are trying to make up for an earlier mistake when an unfaithful translation falsely suggested Mija's agreement to their plan. The

FIGURE 34. Jay (Paul Dano) attempts to communicate the plan to Mija (Ahn Seo-hyun) using translated message cards in *Okja* (Plan B Entertainment/Netflix, 2017).

preoccupation with translation in *Okja*, and in *Snowpiercer* (and in trade agreements in general) as well, turns out to be a preoccupation with the problem of interlinguistic accord, though it becomes clear by the end of the film that Mija's actions, her agreement notwithstanding, are her own.

Unlike the salarymen, *segyehwa* punks, or young women discussed earlier, pigs in *Okja* hold no illusion about their place in the economic imaginary at the end of the American century. This location is made brutally clear in the climax of the film, which takes place at Mirando's massive slaughter-house facility, at which we see a huge pen of pigs somberly waiting to be herded into a machine that will brutally end their lives with a cold mechanical twist and begin their transformation into commodities (fig. 35). Insofar as pigs are genetically modified, abject, and enslaved in the vast, bleak Mirando factory—which not coincidentally is staffed exclusively by immigrant laborers who speak only in Spanish—the film reprises in more literal terms Lisa Lowe's invocation of the twinned traffic in "poison" and "pigs" as the East India Company morphed in the mid-19th century into a governmental entity charged with managing British Empire.[12] Lowe is referring to the pejorative language used to describe, respectively, opium and Chinese *coolies*. In *Okja* this pair of trade commodities become somewhat literalized and compressed into the singular figure of Okja, a genetically modified pig, but the behavior of this fictional American multinational corporation here is no less radical than that of the British Empire. In both cases hegemonic management, which employs poison among it stratagems, relies as well on a surplus population of exploited pigs in literal and figurative senses. Accordingly, unlike many of the films discussed in this study, apparatuses in these recent Bong films are

FIGURE 35. The field of genetically engineered pigs awaiting slaughter in *Okja* (Plan B Entertainment/Netflix, 2017).

not so much explanatory forms that cleverly adumbrate late capitalist procedures with at least some degree of subtlety; rather, they are ruthless manifestations of exploitative practices that no longer require coding. Late in cycles of vicious circulation, the machinations of the system become blunt.

Similarly, the American dark comedy *Colossal* (2016), made by Voltage Pictures, depicts an irresponsible American protagonist in a strikingly literal manner. *Colossal* tells the story of Gloria (Anne Hathaway), an unemployed writer and an alcoholic who is forced to leave New York City and return to her small hometown when her boyfriend, tired of her behavior, kicks her out of their apartment. Unable to quit drinking, Gloria gradually learns that her actions have supernatural, transnational consequences, namely that when she stumbles around a children's playground after a night of drinking, her physical movements correspond exactly to those of a giant monster in downtown Seoul. When she stumbles around in a drunken fit, she terrorizes the residents of the city on the other side of the planet. Rather than teasing through complicated transnational relations, the film is frank: Gloria's drunken behavior is not at all metaphoric or indirect. If she takes a step or waves her arm, the monster in Seoul does the exact same thing. These unconsidered movements in turn directly cause abject terror and massive destruction, with which Gloria eventually must reckon. As in *Colossal*, literalism in *Okja*, in the form of the brutal slaughterhouse, also implies a final recognition of the inequities of the asymmetric system that no longer require metaphors. The vast field of despondent pigs awaiting their slaughter, and that Mija cannot save—even as she rescues Okja along with a baby pig that Okja smuggles in her mouth—makes plain a brutality that can no longer be hidden by clever marketing or other spectacular forms. This is the sort of literalism that emerges at the end of vicious circuits—when all of the artifice has been laid bare and protocols no longer function quite so well. Monstrosity comes only to imply itself.

Notes

Introduction: Revenge Circulates. Empires End.

1. *Sympathy for Mr. Vengeance* (*Poksunŭn Naŭi Kŏt*), dir. Park Chan-wook (2002; Los Angeles: Tartan Video USA, 2005), DVD.

2. For a shortened form I will refer to the Republic of Korea, or South Korea, simply as Korea or the ROK. When differentiating the ROK from the Democratic People's Republic of Korea (DPRK), or North Korea, I will use North and South Korea.

3. *Looking for Bruce Lee* (*Isoryongŭl ch'ajarat!*), dir. Lone Kang (Seoul: Popasia, 2002), DVD.

4. John Seabrook, *The Song Machine: Inside the Hit Factory* (New York: Norton, 2015), 167.

5. See Linda Woodbridge, *English Revenge Drama: Money, Resistance, Equality* (New York: Cambridge University Press, 2014).

6. See John T. Irwin, *Doubling and Incest / Repetition and Revenge: A Speculative Reading of Faulkner* (Baltimore: Johns Hopkins University Press, 1975).

7. See Friedrich Nietzsche, *On the Genealogy of Morality*, ed. Keith Ansell-Pearson, trans. Carol Diethe (New York: Cambridge University Press, 1994), 41–42.

8. See Giovanni Arrighi, *The Long Twentieth Century: Money, Power, and the Origins of Our Times*, 2nd ed. (London: Verso, 2010), 6.

9. See Karl Marx, *Capital*, vol. 1, trans. Ben Fowkes (New York: Penguin, 1976), 247–57.

10. See Karl Marx, *Capital*, vol. 3, trans. David Fernbach (New York: Penguin, 1981), 525–42.

11. Arrighi, *The Long Twentieth Century*, 220–21.

12. Robert Brenner, *The Boom and the Bubble: The US in the World Economy* (London: Verso, 2002), 9, 21.

13. For a compelling empirical study of this transition see Greta R. Krippner, "The Financialization of the American Economy," *Socio-economic Review* 3, no. 2 (2005): 173–208.

14. Joshua Clover, *Riot. Strike. Riot: The New Era of Uprisings* (London: Verso, 2016), 18.

15. Giovanni Arrighi, *Adam Smith in Beijing: Lineages of the Twenty-First Century* (London: Verso, 2007), 185, 209–10. Another likely candidate is the financial crisis beginning in 2007 with the US subprime mortgage debacle. See Annie McClanahan, *Dead*

Pledges: Debt, Crisis, and Twenty-First-Century Culture (Stanford: Stanford University Press, 2016), 13–15.

16. Arrighi, *The Long Twentieth Century*, 314–16.

17. See Robert Wade and Frank Veneroso, "The Asian Crisis: The High Debt Model Versus the Wall Street-Treasury-IMF Complex," *New Left Review* I/228 (1998): 3–23.

18. See Naomi Klein, *The Shock Doctrine: The Rise of Disaster Capitalism* (New York: Metropolitan, 2007), 344.

19. Yoon Min-sik, "South Korea Still Has Top OECD Suicide Rate," *Korea Herald*, Aug. 30, 2015, www.koreaherald.com/view.php?ud=20150830000310; "Suicide Rates by Country," *World Atlas*, Sept. 19, 2016, www.worldatlas.com/articles/countries-with-the-most-suicides-in-the-world.html.

20. Henry Luce, "The American Century," *Life*, Feb. 17, 1941, 61–65.

21. See Arrighi, *Adam Smith in Beijing*, 177–78; and David Harvey, *The New Imperialism* (New York: Oxford University Press, 2010), 14–15. East Asia remained an abiding concern in Luce's vision of a US-led world order, particularly in a cold war context. See Michael H. Hunt, "East Asia in Henry Luce's 'American Century,'" *Diplomatic History* 23, no. 2 (1999): 321–53.

22. See Michael Ignatieff, *Empire Lite: Nation-Building in Bosnia, Kosovo, and Afghanistan* (New York: Penguin, 2003).

23. In Korean, *chaebŏl* can be both singular and plural.

24. Jang-Sup Shin and Ha-Joon Chang, *Restructuring Korea Inc.* (London: Routledge-Curzon, 2003), 69. See also Hyeng-joon Park and Jamie Doucette, "Financialization or Capitalization? Debating Capitalist Power in South Korea in the Context of Neoliberal Globalization," *Capital and Class* 40, no. 3 (2016): 533–54. Although part of the effort of IMF restructuring was to chasten the *chaebŏl* and though there were certainly a number of bankruptcies and consolidation, the power and profits of the remaining firms have only grown since the 1997 crisis.

25. C. S. Eliot Kang, "*Segyehwa* Reform of the South Korean Developmental State," in *Korea's Globalization*, ed. Samuel S. Kim (New York: Cambridge University Press, 2000), 85–86.

26. See Viet Thanh Nguyen, *Nothing Ever Dies* (Cambridge, MA: Harvard University Press, 2016), 137–44.

27. Bruce Cumings, "The Korean Crisis and the End of 'Late' Development," *New Left Review* 231 (1998): 43–72, 46; and Kyung Hyun Kim, *The Remasculinization of Korean Cinema* (Durham, NC: Duke University Press, 2004), 15. For an account of how the Asian "hot" wars of the Cold War helped drive American capital accumulation with a neoimperial framework, see Jodi Kim, *Ends of Empire: Asian American Critique and the Cold War* (Minneapolis: University of Minnesota Press, 2010), 24–27.

28. Arrighi originally looked toward Japan, in fact, to succeed the United States in the world economic order. See Arrighi, *The Long Twentieth Century*, 325–56.

29. The earliest restructuring efforts of this sort date back to the 1980s and the Chun

Doo-hwan government. See Sauk-Hee Park and Mark Wilding, "The Politics of Government Reform in Korea: From Tripartite to Bipartite Politicization," *Administration and Society* 48, no. 9 (2016): 1059–84, 1064–65.

30. See Wonhyuk Lim, "The Emergence of the *Chaebol* and the Origins of the *Chaebol* Problem," in *Economic Crisis and Corporate Restructuring in Korea: Reforming the Chaebol*, ed. Stephen Haggard, Wonhyuk Lim, and Euysung Kim (New York: Cambridge University Press, 2003), 35–52, 48–49. Lim indicates that officials in the Chun Doo-hwan regime had been concerned about a *"chaebol* problem," by which they meant equity and corruption problems that might arise if the government's economic policy relied too heavily on these institutions. Furthermore, they worried that the economic strength of the *chaebŏl* might translate into outsized political power.

31. Paul Krugman, "Asia: What Went Wrong," *Fortune Magazine*, March 2, 1988, http://archive.fortune.com/magazines/fortune/fortune_archive/1998/03/02/238550/index.htm.

32. Keun S. Lee, "Financial Crisis in Korea and IMF: Analysis and Perspectives," Merrill Lynch Center for the Study of Financial Services and Markets, 1998.

33. Ha-Joon Chang, *The East Asian Development Experience: The Miracle, the Crisis and the Future* (London: Zed, 2006), 8.

34. Martin Fackler, "Lessons Learned, South Korea Makes Quick Economic Recovery," *New York Times*, Jan. 6, 2011, www.nytimes.com/2011/01/07/world/asia/07seoul.html.

35. Brenner, *The Boom and the Bubble*, 9.

36. See Jin-Ho Jang, "Neoliberalism in South Korea: The Dynamics of Financialization," in *New Millennium South Korea: Neoliberal Capitalism and Transnational Movements*, ed. Jesook Song (New York: Routledge, 2011), 46–59, 48; Shin and Chang, *Restructuring Korea Inc.*, 56; Martin Hart-Landsberg, Seongjin Jeong, and Richard Westra, introduction to *Marxist Perspectives on South Korea in the Global Economy*, ed. Martin Hart-Landsberg, Seongjin Jeong, and Richard Westra (London: Routledge, 2007), 14; and Seongjin Jeong, "Korean Left Debates on Alternatives to Neoliberalism," in *Economic Transitions to Neoliberalism in Middle-Income Countries*, ed. Alfredo Saad-Filho and Galip L. Yalman (London: Routledge, 2009), 154–65, 155–56. Jin-Ho Jang argues that the IMF restructuring imposed an "Anglo-American economic system" focused on investment culture. Prominent Korea economists Jang-Sup Shin and Ha-Joon Chang have suggested that this new regime is focused on short-term profitability. In contrast, Marxist economists, in rejecting Keynesian nostalgia for the authoritarian developmental state, have cast doubt on the extent of this transition. Seongjin Jeong, for example, characterizes the post-IMF Korean "finance-led regime of accumulation" as not fully realized, pushing back against the call from economists like Chang to return to statist policies.

37. Cf. Hyun Ok Park, *The Capitalist Unconscious: From Korean Unification to Transnational Korea* (New York: Columbia University Press, 2015): "What characterizes the present is the uneven relationship between industrial and financial capital, and not a linear transition from the former to the latter" (18).

38. Cumings, "The Korean Crisis," 52.

39. Quoted in Klein, *The Shock Doctrine*, 339.

40. Ibid., 345.

41. Shin and Chang, *Restructuring Korea Inc.*, 54.

42. Ibid., 56 (my emphasis).

43. Paul Virilio, *Desert Screen: War at the Speed of Light*, trans. Michael Degener (London: Continuum, 2002), 91, 93.

44. Arrighi, *The Long Twentieth Century*, 31.

45. Shin and Chang, *Restructuring Korea Inc.*, 105.

46. See Hart-Landsberg, Jeong, and Westra, introduction to *Marxist Perspectives*, 16.

47. Wade and Veneroso, "The Asian Crisis," 20–21.

48. David Harvey, *The Limits to Capital* (Oxford: Basil Blackwell, 1982), 415.

49. Laura Hyun Yi Kang, "The Uses of Asianization: Figuring Crises, 1997–98 and 2007–?," *American Quarterly* 64, no. 3 (2012): 411–36, 411–14.

50. See A. J. G. Simoes and C. A. Hidalgo, "Where Does South Korea Export To? (2003)," *Observatory of Economic Complexity: An Analytical Tool for Understanding the Dynamics of Economic Development*. Workshops at the Twenty-Fifth AAAI Conference on Artificial Intelligence, 2011, http://atlas.media.mit.edu/en/visualize/tree_map/hs92/export/kor/show/all/2003/.

51. Martin Hart-Landsberg, "The South Korean Economy: Problems and Prospects," in *Marxist Perspectives on South Korea in the Global Economy*, ed. Martin Hart-Landsberg, Seongjin Jeong, and Richard Westra (London: Routledge, 2007), 203–20, 218.

52. Shin and Chang, *Restructuring Korea Inc.*, 41.

53. Harvey, *The New Imperialism*, 115.

54. Joshua Clover, *Riot. Strike. Riot.: The New Era of Uprisings* (London: Verso, 2016), 143.

55. Michael Hardt and Antonio Negri, *Empire* (Cambridge, MA: Harvard University Press, 2000), 362. For critiques of this logic see Joshua Clover, "Value, Theory, Crisis," *PMLA* 127, no. 1 (2012): 107–14; and Annie McLanahan, "Investing in the Future," *Journal of Cultural Economy* 6, no. 1 (2013): 84–87.

56. Marx, *Capital*, 1:266.

57. See Jinhee Choi, *The South Korean Film Renaissance: Local Hitmakers, Global Provocateurs* (Middletown, CT: Wesleyan University Press, 2010), 31.

58. Jeeyoung Shin, "Globalization and the New Korean Cinema," in *New Korean Cinema*, ed. Chi-Yun Shin and Julian Stringer (Edinburgh: Edinburgh University Press, 2005), 51–62, 53.

59. Choi, *The South Korean Film Renaissance*, 19.

60. See Darcy Paquet, *New Korean Cinema: Breaking the Waves* (New York: Wallflower, 2009), 40.

61. Brian Yecies and Aegyung Shim, *The Changing Face of Korean Cinema, 1960–2015* (London: Routledge, 2016), 158. See also Darcy Paquet, *New Korean Cinema*, 62. Paquet

suggests that *chaebŏl* interest in the motion picture business had already begun to decline before the crisis hit.

62. Choi, *The South Korean Film Renaissance*, 19.

63. Ibid.

64. Dal Yong Jin, *New Korean Wave: Transnational Cultural Power in the Age of Social Media* (Urbana: University of Illinois Press, 2016), 28.

65. This is not to say that the phenomena of K-dramas and K-pop postdates Korea's IMF Cinema. Both were popular in Korea and in international markets (particularly regionally) for some time, but the explosive revenues in these subindustries seems to have followed this growth period in film. See Jin, *New Korean Wave*, 71.

66. Yecies and Shim, *The Changing Face of Korean Cinema*, 23.

67. Ibid., 114.

68. Eungjun Min, Jinsook Joo, and Han Ju Kwak, *Korean Film: History, Resistance, and Democratic Imagination* (Westport, CT: Praeger, 2003), 49.

69. See Yecies and Shim, *The Changing Face of Korean Cinema*, 116–17.

70. Lee Kang-ro, "Critical Analysis of Anti-Americanism in Korea," *Korean Journal of International Relations* 44, no. 4 (2004); repr. in *Korea Focus*, http://koreafocus.or.kr/design1/layout/content_print.asp?group_id=143.

71. See Kyung Hyun Kim, *The Remasculinization of Korean Cinema* (Durham, NC: Duke University Press, 2004), 29; Choi, *The South Korean Film Renaissance*, 4–7; and Paquet, *New Korean Cinema*. Their periods overlap, however: Kim's articulation of New Korean Cinema begins in the 1980s and extends through the millennium, whereas Choi's description of the South Korean Film Renaissance focuses more on the so-called 3-8-6 generation of directors (in their 30s, college in the 1980s, born in the 1960s) whose films became prominent slightly later. Paquet combines both subperiods under Kim's rubric.

72. Paquet, *New Korean Cinema*, 110–11.

73. Wonhyuk Lim, Stephen Haggard, and Euysung Kim, "Introduction: The Political Economy of Corporate Restructuring," in *Economic Crisis and Corporate Restructuring in Korea: Reforming the* Chaebol, ed. Stephen Haggard, Wonhyuk Lim, and Euysung Kim (New York: Cambridge University Press, 2003), 1–32, 14–15.

74. Kang-ro, "Critical Analysis of Anti-Americanism in Korea."

75. See Jin-Kyung Lee, *Service Economies: Militarism, Sex Work, and Migrant Labor in South Korea* (Minneapolis: University of Minnesota Press, 2010), 125–83.

76. "Number of U.S. Troops in South Korea," NZ-DPRK Society, https://sites.google.com/site/nzdprksociety/number-of-us-troops-in-rok-by-year.

77. "US Soldiers Charged for Korean Deaths," *BBC News*, July 5, 2002, http://news.bbc.co.uk/2/hi/asia-pacific/2097137.stm.

78. Howard W. French with Don Kirk, "American Policies and Presence Are Under Fire in South Korea, Straining an Alliance," *New York Times*, Dec. 8, 2002, www.nytimes.com/2002/12/08/world/american-policies-presence-are-under-fire-south-korea-straining-alliance.html.

79. See Nicole Risse, "The Evolution in Anti-Americanism in South Korea: From Ideologically Embedded to Socially Constructed," paper delivered at the Korean Studies Association of Australia Conference, 2001, Monash University, Melbourne, Sept. 24, 2001, 88–99, 96–97, http://web.sungshin.ac.kr/~youngho/data/security2/AntiA_NicoleRisse_.pdf.

80. A complementary history might be that of Filipino "Jeepnies," which were originally repurposed US Army jeeps decorated in distinctive, often outrageous, fashion and were used to perform something like a bus/taxicab service. See Harrod Suarez, "Among the Sensuous: Listening to Film, Listening to the Philippines," *Communication and Critical/Cultural Studies* 8, no. 1 (2011): 69–74.

81. Alex Greenbaum, "The Globalization of the Korean Automotive Industry," unpublished manuscript, 2002, 9.

82. Park, *The Capitalist Unconscious*, 57.

83. Chung Ah-young, "Ssangyong Tentatively Agrees to Rehire Dismissed Workers," *Korea Times*, Dec. 14, 2015, www.koreatimes.co.kr/www/news/nation/2015/12/116_193140.html.

84. Park, *The Capitalist Unconscious*, 58–60.

85. Ah-young, "Ssangyong Tentatively Agrees."

86. Ibid.

87. See, e.g., "Layoffs That Sparked Riots Unjustified, South Korean Court Rules," *CTV News*, Feb. 7, 2014, www.ctvnews.ca/business/layoffs-that-sparked-riots-unjustified-south-korean-court-rules-1, no. 1674811.

88. Caroline Gluck, "Seoul Pays Off Its IMF Debts," August 23, 2001, *BBC News*, http://news.bbc.co.uk/2/hi/business/1505131.stm.

89. Park, *The Capitalist Unconscious*, 57.

90. Yang Sung-jin, "Underpaid Production Staff Troubles Film Industry," *Korea Herald*, Oct. 26, 2004, repr. in *Korean Film Biz Zone*, Oct. 27, 2004, www.koreanfilm.or.kr/jsp/news/news.jsp?blbdComCd=601008&seq=122&mode=VIEW.

91. Ibid.

92. Jeremy Valentine, "Rent and Political Economy in Culture Industry Work," *Journal of Cultural Economy* 7, no. 2 (2014): 194–208, 205.

93. David Harvey, "The Art of Rent: Globalization, Monopoly, and the Commodification of Culture," in *Socialist Register 2002: A World of Contradictions*, ed. Leo Panitch and Colin Leys (London: Merlin, 2001), 99. Regarding the Korean government's branding efforts with Hallyu, see Youngmin Choe, *Tourist Distractions: Traveling and Feeling in Transnational Hallyu Cinema* (Durham, NC: Duke University Press, 2016), 9–12.

94. "Films Are the New Stars," *The Economist*, March 17, 2016, www.economist.com/news/business/21695015-ships-and-steel-suffer-entertainment-industry-shines-films-are-new-stars.

95. Ibid.

96. Priya Jaikumar, *Cinema at the End of Empire: A Politics of Transition in Britain and India* (Durham, NC: Duke University Press, 2006), 2.

Chapter 1. Concrete Memories

1. Tzvetan Todorov, *The Poetics of Prose*, trans. Richard Howard (Ithaca, NY: Cornell University Press, 1977), 47.

2. For accounts of literary closure see Frank Kermode, *The Sense of an Ending: Studies in the Theory of Fiction* (London: Oxford University Press, 1967); and D. A. Miller, *Narrative and Its Discontents: Problems of Closure in the Traditional Novel* (Princeton, NJ: Princeton University Press, 1981).

3. Franco Moretti, *Signs Taken for Wonders: On the Sociology of Literary Forms* (New York: Verso, 1983), 145–46.

4. See Arthur Marwick, *The New Nature of History: Knowledge, Evidence, Language* (Basingstoke: Palgrave, 2000); and Hayden White, "Historical Pluralism," *Critical Inquiry* 12, no. 3 (1986): 480–93, 487. See also Alun Munslow, *Deconstructing History* (New York: Routledge, 1997).

5. Michael A. Stanford, *A Companion to the Study of History* (Oxford: Basil Blackwell, 1994), 124.

6. E. H. Carr, *What Is History?* (London: Penguin, 1987), 65.

7. See Ronald R. Thomas, *Detective Fiction and the Rise of Forensic Science* (New York: Cambridge University Press, 1999), 4.

8. See Christina Klein, "Why American Studies Needs to Think About Korean Cinema, or, Transnational Genres in the Films of Bong Joon-ho," *American Quarterly* 60, no. 4 (2008): 871–98: "Slowly the viewer realizes that the true subject of the film is not the serial murders and the detectives' investigation, but rather daily life in the late 1980s—that is, during the darkest years of Korea's military dictatorship. The deep crimes revealed during the course of investigating the surface crime include the corruption and abuse of police power, the casual disregard of civil rights, and the government-stimulated fear of North Korea as a means to keep the civilian population in check" (882).

9. See Patricia Merivale and Susan Elizabeth Sweeney, "The Game's Afoot: On the Trail of the Metaphysical Detective Story," in *Detecting Texts: The Metaphysical Detective Story from Poe to Postmodernism*, ed. Patricia Merivale and Susan Elizabeth Sweeney (Philadelphia: University of Pennsylvania Press, 1998), 2–4.

10. See Kyung Hyun Kim, *The Remasculinization of Korean Cinema* (Durham, NC: Duke University Press, 2004), 22–26.

11. Cf. Klein, "Why American Studies Needs to Think About Korean Cinema," 880; and Darcy Paquet, "Genrebending in Contemporary Korean Cinema," www.koreanfilm.org/genrebending.html.

12. Walter Benjamin, *Illuminations: Essays and Reflections*, ed. Hannah Arendt (New York: Harcourt Brace Jovanovich, 1968), 263.

13. Benedict Anderson, *Imagined Communities: Reflections on the Origin and Spread of Nationalism* (London: Verso, 1983), 24.

14. See Kyung-Hyun Nam, "Hwaseong Killings Still Baffle Police," *Dong-a Ilbo*, April 1, 2006, http://english.donga.com/List/3/all/26/246760/1.

15. Michael Robinson, "Contemporary Cultural Production in South Korea:

Vanishing Meta-narratives of Nation," in *New Korean Cinema*, ed. Chi-Yun Shin and Julian Stringer (Edinburgh: Edinburgh University Press, 2005), 15–31, 15.

16. *Memories of Murder* (*Sarinŭi Ch'uŏk*), dir. Bong Joon-ho (New York: Palm Pictures, 2003), DVD.

17. For a discussion of landscapes in the film see Kyung Hyun Kim, *Virtual Hallyu: Korean Cinema of the Global Era* (Durham, NC: Duke University Press, 2011), 39–41.

18. Cf. Klein, "Why American Studies Needs to Think About Korean Cinema," 880.

19. Fredric Jameson, "The End of Temporality," *Critical Inquiry* 29, no. 4 (2003): 695–718, 699.

20. See Peter Y. Paik, "The Scandal of Bong Joon-ho's *Memories of Murder*," *Let It Read*, Feb. 6, 2013, https://pypaik.wordpress.com/2013/02/06/the-scandal -of-bong-joon-hos-memories-of-murder/.

21. Jacques Derrida, *Archive Fever: A Freudian Impression*, trans. Eric Prenowitz (Chicago: University of Chicago Press, 1995), 91.

22. Rey Chow, "Nostalgia of the New Wave: Structure in Wong Kar-wai's *Happy Together*," *Camera Obscura* 14 (1999): 30–49, 36. See also Fredric Jameson, "Walter Benjamin, or Nostalgia," *Salmagundi* 10/11 (Fall 1969–70): 52–68: "But if nostalgia as a political motivation is most frequently associated with fascism, there is no reason why a nostalgia conscious of itself, a lucid and remorseless dissatisfaction with the present on the grounds of some remembered plentitude, cannot furnish as adequate a revolutionary stimulus as any other" (68).

23. John Kie-chiang Oh, *Korean Politics: The Quest for Democratization and Economic Development* (Ithaca, NY: Cornell University Press, 1999), 91.

24. See Eun Suk Sa, "Development of Press Freedom in South Korea Since Japanese Colonial Rule," *Asian Culture and History* 1, no. 2 (2009): 3–17.

25. Quoted in Oh, *Korean Politics*, 104. These constitutional changes came partially in response to great public demand. See Susan Chira, "Korea's Press Awaits the Promised Freedom," *New York Times*, July 1, 1987, www.nytimes.com/1987/07/01/world/korea -s-press-awaits-the-promised-freedom.html. See also Kyu Ho Youm, *Press Law in South Korea* (Ames: Iowa State University Press, 1996), 58–59.

26. See Darcy Paquet, "The Korean Film Industry: 1992 to the Present," in *New Korean Cinema*, ed. Chi-Yun Shin and Julian Stringer (Edinburgh: Edinburgh University Press, 2005), 32–50, 33.

27. Ibid., 43–45. See also Dal Yong Jin, "Cultural Politics in Korea's Contemporary Films Under Neoliberal Globalization," *Media, Culture, and Society* 28, no. 1 (2006): 5–23; and Doobo Shim, "Hybridity and the Rise of Korean Popular Culture in Asia," *Media, Culture, and Society* 28, no. 1 (2006): 25–44, esp. 31–35.

28. See Mary Ann Doane, *The Emergence of Cinematic Time: Modernity, Contingency, the Archive* (Cambridge, MA: Harvard University Press, 2002), 219.

29. See Lynne Kirby, *Parallel Tracks: The Railroad and Silent Cinema* (Durham, NC: Duke University Press, 1997).

30. Timothy Bewes, *Reification, or The Anxiety of Late Capitalism* (London: Verso, 2002), 32.

31. Stephen Best and Sharon Marcus, "Surface Reading: An Introduction," *Representations* 108, no. 1 (2009): 1–21.

32. Timothy Bewes, "Reading with the Grain: A New World in Literary Criticism," *differences* 21, no. 3 (2010): 1–33, 17.

33. Ibid., 21.

34. Walter Benjamin, "The Work of Art in the Age of Its Technological Reproducibility," *Selected Writings: Volume 3, 1935–1938*, trans. Edmund Jephcott, Howard Eiland, et al.; ed. Howard Eiland and Michael W. Jennings (Cambridge, MA: Harvard University Press, 2002), 108.

35. Miriam Bratu Hansen, *Cinema and Experience: Siegfried Kracauer, Walter Benjamin, and Theodor W. Adorno* (Berkeley: University of California Press, 2012), 88.

36. Ibid., 89.

37. See the account of film's "photogrammatic" characteristics in Garrett Stewart, *Between Film and Screen: Modernism's Photo Synthesis* (Chicago: University of Chicago Press, 1999), 27–39.

38. Derrida, *Archive Fever*, 91.

39. Hansen, *Cinema and Experience*, 156.

40. Doane, *The Emergence of Cinematic Time*, 221–23.

41. Ibid., 228.

42. Walter Benjamin, "The Work of Art in the Age of Mechanical Reproduction," in *Illuminations: Essays and Reflections*, trans. Harry Zohn (New York: Shocken, 1969), 226.

43. Hansen, *Cinema and Experience*, xviii.

44. Alice H. Amsden, *Asia's Next Giant: South Korea and Late Industrialization* (Oxford: Oxford University Press, 1989), 247.

45. See Byung Hwan Oh and S. J. Jeon, "Korea—Concrete Construction Industry—Cement Based Materials and Civil Infrastructure," paper delivered at the CBM-CI International Workshop, Karachi, Pakistan, 2007, 308, http://citeseerx.ist.psu.edu/viewdoc/download?doi=10.1.1.600.7075&rep=rep1&type=pdf; and Sooyong Kim, "The Korean Construction Industry as an Exporter of Services," *World Bank Economic Review* 2, no. 2 (1988): 225–26.

46. John Rennie Short, *Urban Resurgence, Displacement, and the Making of Inequality in Global Cities* (New York: Routledge, 2017), 61.

47. See Young-a Park, *Unexpected Alliances: Independent Filmmakers, the State, and the Film Industry in Postauthoritarian South Korea* (Stanford: Stanford University Press, 2015), 26–28.

Chapter 2. Company Men

1. *Oldboy* (*Olduboi*), dir. Park Chan-wook (2003; Tartan Video, 2005), DVD.

2. Krys Lee, "The Salaryman," in *Drifting House* (New York: Penguin, 2012), 93–112, 93–94.

3. See Chi-Yun Shin, "Two of a Kind: Gender and Friendship in *Friend* and *Take Care of My Cat*," in *New Korean Cinema*, ed. Chi-Yun Shin and Julian Stringer (Edinburgh: Edinburgh University Press, 2005), 123; and Jinhee Choi, *The South Korean Film Renaissance: Local Hitmakers, Global Provocateurs* (Middletown, CT: Wesleyan University Press, 2010), 63. I am bracketing off high school films and comedies (both discussed by Choi) that compose significant subgenres under this larger rubric.

4. The limit of the *kkangp'ae*'s ability to rise marks a dynamic similar to the one Andrew Hoberek discusses in his account of the postwar growth of the middle class in the United States. Against the current nostalgia for the postwar middle class in contemporary American culture, Hoberek demonstrates that such nostalgia misremembers the initial anxiety that inhered in the transition from ownership to salaried labor. In *kkangp'ae* films it is typically the point at which the *kkangp'ae* feels emboldened or entitled to transcend the bounds of wage labor that he experiences violent rebuke. See Andrew Hoberek, *The Twilight of the Middle Class: Post–World War II American Fiction and White-Collar Work* (Princeton, NJ: Princeton University Press, 2005), 9.

5. The film is full of what Keith B. Wagner terms "fragments of labor" or "iconographic elements of the working class or 'salarymen' " that "litter Park's mise-en-scène," including, in the case of the latter, "briefcases, dark-colored business suits, topcoats, and black umbrellas for Seoul's damp climate." See Keith B. Wagner, "Fragments of Labor: Neoliberal Attitudes and Architectures in Contemporary South Korean Cinema," in *Neoliberalism and Global Cinema: Capital, Culture, and Marxist Critique*, ed. Jyostna Kapur and Keith B. Wagner (London: Routledge, 2011), 217–38, 217.

6. Jeon Jong-hwi, "Ministry: More Than Half of Chaebol Workers Are Irregular," *The Hankyoreh*, July 11, 2014, http://english.hani.co.kr/arti/english_edition/e_business /646581.html.

7. For a discussion of *chaebŏl* see Bruce Cumings, *Korea's Place in the Sun: A Modern History* (New York: Norton, 1997), 326–31.

8. Bruce Cumings, "The Korean Crisis and the End of 'Late' Development," *New Left Review* 231 (1998): 43–72, 64.

9. Carter J. Eckert, "The South Korean Bourgeoisie: A Class in Search of Hegemony," in *State and Society in Contemporary Korea*, ed. Hagen Koo (Ithaca, NY: Cornell University Press, 1993), 95–130, 117.

10. See Rob Wilson, "Killer Capitalism on the Pacific Rim: Theorizing Major and Minor Modes of the Korean Global," *boundary 2* 34, no. 1 (2007): 115–33, 127.

11. Hyeng-joon Park and Jamie Doucette, "Financialization or Capitalization? Debating Capitalist Power in South Korea in the Context of Neoliberal Globalization," *Capital and Class* 40, no. 3 (2016): 533–54, 549–51. See also Martin Hart-Landsberg, "The South Korean Economy: Problems and Prospects," in *Marxist Perspectives on South Korea in the Global Economy*, ed. Martin Hart-Landsberg, Seongjin Jeong, and Richard Westra (London: Routledge, 2007).

12. See Roger L. Janelli, *Making Capitalism: The Social and Cultural Construction of a South Korean Conglomerate* (Stanford: Stanford University Press, 1993), 109–15.

13. For an account of the film's treatment of incarceration and torture within a post-9/11 milieu, see Hye Seung Chung and David Scott Diffrient, *Movie Migrations: Transnational Genre Flows and South Korean Cinema* (New Brunswick, NJ: Rutgers University Press, 2015), 188–207.

14. Chan-wook Park, interview, *Neil Young's Film Lounge*, August 22, 2004, www.jigsawlounge.co.uk/film/parkchanwookinterview.html.

15. See Liese Spencer, "Revenger's Tragedy," *Sight and Sound* 14, no. 10 (2004): 18–20. Park Chan-wook is quoted: "Usually when you look at the smart places where rich people live you want to live there too, but here I wanted viewers to feel the opposite" (20). For a compelling reading of Woo-jin's penthouse see Wagner, "Fragments of Labor," 234–35.

16. Su-dol Kang, "Labour Relations in Korea Between Crisis Management and Living Solidarity," *Inter-Asia Cultural Studies* 1, no. 3 (2000): 393–407, 394.

17. See Chang Kyung-sup, *South Korea Under Compressed Modernity: Familial Political Economy in Transition* (London: Routledge, 2010), 5–8.

18. Joseph Jonghyun Jeon, "Residual Selves: Trauma and Forgetting in Park Chan-wook's *Oldboy*," *positions* 17, no. 3 (2009): 713–40, esp. 728–31.

19. See Steve Choe, "Love Your Enemies: Revenge and Forgiveness in Films by Park Chan-wook," *Korean Studies* 33 (2009): 29–51, 40.

20. *A Bittersweet Life* (*Talk'omhan insaeng*), dir. Kim Jee-woon (Seoul: CJ Entertainment, 2005), DVD.

21. Kwang-Yeong Shin, "Economic Crisis, Neoliberal Reforms, and the Rise of Precarious Work in South Korea," *American Behavioral Scientist* 57, no. 3 (2013): 335–53, 336.

22. Hwangbo Yon, "Around One-Quarter of South Koreans Stuck in Low-Wage Work," *The Hankyoreh*, March 5, 2017, http://english.hani.co.kr/arti/english_edition/e_national/785122.html.

23. Hyun-Jeong Kim, "The Shift to the Service Economy: Causes and Effects," *Institute for Monetary and Economic Research, The Bank of Korea*, 7 July 2006, 2.

24. See Kyung Hyun Kim, "'Tell the Kitchen That There's Too Much *Buchu* in the Dumpling': Reading Park Chan-wook's 'Unknowable' *Old Boy*," *Korea Journal* 46, no. 1 (2006): 84–108: "the emergence of Park Chan-wook in recent years is symptomatic of a Korean cinema that has been ushered into a definite kind of post-remembrance and post-political mode" (106).

25. For commentary on *Peppermint Candy* see Kyung Hyun Kim, *The Remasculinization of Korean Cinema* (Durham, NC: Duke University Press, 2004), 19–26; and Todd McGowan, *Out of Time: Desire in Atemporal Cinema* (Minneapolis: University of Minnesota Press, 2011), 181–206. For a theoretical account of trauma and history see Cathy Caruth, *Unclaimed Experience: Trauma, Narrative, and History* (Baltimore: Johns Hopkins University Press, 1996), 10–24.

26. See Friedrich Nietzsche, *The Use and Abuse of History*, trans. Adrian Collins (New York: Liberal Arts Press, 1948): "Then he says, 'I remember . . .' and envies the beast that forgets at once, and sees every moment really die, sink into night and mist, extinguished forever. The beast lives *unhistorically*; for it 'goes into' the present, like a number, without leaving any curious remainder. It cannot dissimulate, it conceals nothing; at every moment it seems what it actually is, and thus can be nothing that is not honest" (13).

27. See McGowan, *Out of Time*, 233.

28. Oh Young-jin, "Chaebol Need Self-Discipline," *Korea Times*, Oct. 26, 2008, www.koreatimes.co.kr/www/news/biz/2008/11/123_31736.html.

29. Ibid.

30. "South Korea Jails Hanwha Head Kim Seung-Youn," *BBC News*, August 16, 2012, www.bbc.com/news/world-asia-19279742.

31. Hong-Bum Kim and Chung H. Lee, "Post-Crisis Financial Reform in Korea: A Critical Appraisal" (2004), working papers 200410, University of Hawaii at Manoa, Department of Economics, 14, www.economics.hawaii.edu/research/workingpapers/WP_04-10.pdf.

32. Ibid., 13.

33. Ibid., 15.

34. Ibid., 13.

35. See Jasper Kim, "Korea's Next Credit Boom—and Bust?" *Wall Street Journal*, Dec. 7, 2009, www.wsj.com/articles/SB10001424052748703558004574580914030704386; and Cho Hyung-jo, "More Borrowers Turn to Credit Card Loans," *Korea JoongAng Daily*, March 7, 2017, http://mengnews.joins.com/view.aspx?aId=3030624.

36. See "Third-Tier Lending," *Korea Herald*, Sept. 26, 2016, www.koreaherald.com/view.php?ud=20160926000978; and Cho Jin-seo, "Japanese Lenders Reap Profits," *Korea Times*, Dec. 1, 2010, www.koreatimes.co.kr/www/news/biz/2016/11/123_77289.html.

37. *Helpless* (*Hwach'a*), dir. Byun Young-joo (Seoul: Filament Pictures, 2012), DVD.

38. See Annie McClanahan, *Dead Pledges: Debt, Crisis, and Twenty-First-Century Culture* (Stanford: Stanford University Press, 2016), 10. See also Joe Deville, *Lived Economies of Default: Consumer Credit, Debt Collection, and the Capture of Affect* (London: Routledge, 2015).

39. Incidentally, both films are rooted in Japanese fiction: *Oldboy* is adapted from a manga series (1996–98) written by Garon Tsuchiya and illustrated by Nobuaki Minegishi; *Helpless* is derived from Miyabe Miyuki's *All She Was Worth* (*Kasha*, 1992). For a comparative analysis of the two *Oldboy* texts see Earl Jackson Jr., "Borrowing Trouble: *Oldboy* as Adaptation and Intervention," *Transnational Cinemas* 3, no. 1 (2012): 53–65.

Chapter 3. *Segyehwa* Punk

1. Jawbreaker, "Boxcar," 1994, on *24 Hour Revenge Therapy*, Tupelo/Communion, mp3.

2. See Brian Edge, ed., *924 Gilman: The Story So Far* (San Francisco: Maximumrocknroll, 2004). The unspoken interlocutor for Schwarzenbach might be best understood as a pair of institutions—the San Francisco punk zine *Maximumrocknroll* and 924 Gilman, the communally run, all-ages punk-rock club in Berkeley, California, which first provided

a venue for bands like Green Day, Rancid, and Offspring, who were also criticized for signing with major labels in the mid-1990s.

3. Stephen Epstein, "Anarchy in the UK, Solidarity in the ROK: Punk Rock Comes to Korea," *Acta Koreana* 3 (2000): 1–34.

4. See Reiichi Miura, "What Kind of Revolution Do You Want? Punk, the Contemporary Left, and Singularity," *Mediations* 25, no. 1 (2010): 61–80; and Lee Konstantinou, *Cool Characters: Irony and American Fiction* (Cambridge, MA: Harvard University Press, 2016). With respect to 1970s British punk, Konstantinou writes, "On the one hand, the emerging punk experienced firsthand the decline of an industrial base in her home country, a welfare state in crisis, and new emerging constellations of labor (service labor, affective labor, immaterial labor). On the other hand, she lived at a moment of countercultural decline, when the Utopian hopes of the sixties seemed to be exhausted. Punk was a means of addressing this situation" (106).

5. The 1993 Sonic Youth documentary *1991: The Year Punk Broke* marks the year in which punk breaks out (in the sense of achieving mainstream success), the year that Nirvana's "Smells Like Teen Spirit" became a surprise hit.

6. Epstein, "Anarchy in the UK," 19–20.

7. See Jesook Song, *South Koreans in the Debt Crisis: The Creation of a Neoliberal Welfare Society* (Durham, NC: Duke University Press, 2009), 49–116. Song's work has been vital in making the experiences of these demographics legible within the larger context of unemployment during the Korean IMF Crisis. Song points out that the state-reported unemployment figures during the period did not even include "women at home and students who wanted and needed to work" (4).

8. Bill Brown, "Global Bodies/Postnationalities: Charles Johnson's Consumer Culture," *Representations* 58 (Spring 1997): 24–48, 37–38.

9. Youngmin Choe, *Tourist Distractions: Traveling and Feeling in Transnational Hallyu Cinema* (Durham, NC: Duke University Press, 2016), 6.

10. For an account of the youth labor outlook after the IMF Crisis see Song, *South Koreans in the Debt Crisis*, 95–116.

11. Yoo Ha's *Once upon a Time in High School* (*Maljukgŏri chanhoksa*, 2004) depicts the popularity of Bruce Lee among Korean high school students in the 1970s.

12. See Vijay Prashad, *Everybody Was Kung Fu Fighting: Afro-Asian Connections and the Myth of Cultural Purity* (Boston: Beacon, 2001), 126–49; and Brown, "Global Bodies/Postnationalities," 36–38.

13. See Jerome Christensen, *America's Corporate Art: The Studio Authorship of Hollywood Motion Pictures* (Stanford: Stanford University Press, 2012), 2–6. Although *Looking for Bruce Lee* is an independent film and free from the specific context that Christensen develops, my account of the film shares with Christensen's account of corporate authorship a sense of being driven by a set of financial exigencies and imperatives that produce a particular mode of filmmaking.

14. Guy Debord, *Society of the Spectacle* (Detroit: Black and Red, 1983), 17.

15. Annie J. McClanahan, "Becoming Non-economic: Human Capital Theory and Wendy Brown's *Undoing the Demos*," *Theory and Event* 20, no. 2 (2017): 509–19, 514.

16. Crying Nut, "Speed Up Loser" (Mal Tallija), 1998, on *Run like a Horse* (Mal Tallija), Drug Records, mp3.

17. *Looking for Bruce Lee (Isoryongŭl ch'ajarat!)*, dir. Lone Kang (Seoul: Popasia, 2002), DVD.

18. See Paul Virilio, *Speed and Politics: An Essay on Dromology*, trans. Mark Polizzotti (Los Angeles: Semiotext[e], 2006): "Western man has appeared superior and dominant, despite inferior demographics, because he appeared *more rapid*. In colonial genocide or ethnocide, he was the survivor because he was in fact *super-quick*" (70).

19. Jean Baudrillard, *The Illusion of the End*, trans. Chris Turner (Cambridge: Polity, 1994), 1.

20. Garrett Stewart, *Between Film and Screen: Modernism's Photo Synthesis* (Chicago: University of Chicago Press, 1999), 9.

21. Ibid., 14. Cf. D. N. Rodowick, *The Virtual Life of Film* (Cambridge, MA: Harvard University Press, 2007): "There is no medium-based ontology that grounds film as an aesthetic medium and serves as an anchor for its claims to exist as a humanistic discipline.... However, the impermanence and mutability of cinema studies as a field should be seen as one of its great strengths" (23–24).

22. Steven Shaviro, *Post-Cinematic Affect* (Winchester, UK: Zero Books, 2010), 33, 51–52. The Korean word Han uses is *isanghada*, which can also be translated as "strange."

23. French and German cinemas (including French New Wave films) were introduced to Koreans in the late 1970s through the establishment of cinema clubs by French and German cultural centers in Seoul. See Nohchool Park, "The New Waves at the Margin: An Historical Overview of South Korean Cinema Movements, 1975–84," *Journal of Japanese and Korean Cinema* 1, no. 1 (2009): 45–63, 54–55.

24. See Katharine H. S. Moon, "Strangers in the Midst of Globalization," in *Korea's Globalization*, ed. Samuel S. Kim (New York: Cambridge University Press, 2000), 147–69, 148–52.

25. See Allen Walker Read, "The Folklore of 'O.K.,'" *American Speech* 39, no. 1 (1964): 5–25.

26. Chris Marker, *Coréennes* [Korean women] (1959; Seoul: Noonbit, 2008).

27. Garrett Stewart, *Between Film and Screen*, 105. See also Catherine Lupton, *Chris Marker: Memories of the Future* (London: Reaktion, 2005), 94.

28. Julia Kristeva, *Possessions*, trans. Barbara Bray (New York: Columbia University Press, 1998). The novel is a murder mystery about a beautiful woman who is found decapitated in her luxurious home.

29. The performance group does not seem to have had a long or highly visible run. They did perform at the Adelaide Fringe Festival in 2000 in Australia. A review of the show praised the cello player but found the dancing, performed by a single female performer, elegant but confusing. See review of "Mongolmongol: My Wonderful Left Hook," March 17, 2000, http://ff.moobaa.com/?p=71.

30. See Michel Feher, "Self-Appreciation; or, The Aspirations of Human Capital," trans. Ivan Ascher, *Public Culture* 21, no. 1 (2009): 21–41, 34.

31. Ibid.

32. See Inkyu Kang, "The Political Economy of Idols: South Korea's Neoliberal Restructuring and Its Impact on the Entertainment Labour Force," in *K-pop: The International Rise of the Korean Music Industry*, ed. JungBong Choi and Roald Maliangkay (London: Routledge, 2015), 51–65, esp. 51–54.

33. See Darcy Paquet, *New Korean Cinema: Breaking the Waves* (London: Wallflower, 2009), 75–76.

34. See Gary S. Becker, *Human Capital: A Theoretical and Empirical Analysis with Special Reference to Education*, 3rd ed. (Chicago: University of Chicago Press, 1993), 15–158; and Theodor W. Schultz, "Reflections on Investment in Man," *Journal of Political Economy* 70, no. 5 (1962): 1–8.

35. An analogous context is the erosion of the Korean middle class. See Cho Kye-wan, "South Korea's Middle Class Is Shrinking, According to Recent Report," *The Hankyoreh*, Feb. 13, 2015, http://english.hani.co.kr/arti/english_edition/e_business/678354.html.

36. Kwang-Yeong Shin, "Globalization and Social Inequality in South Korea," in *New Millennium South Korea: Neoliberal Capitalism and Transnational Movements*, ed. Jesook Song (New York: Routledge, 2011), 11–28, 17–18.

37. There is a certain irony here in appropriating Bruce Lee's iconicity as a figure of one's own process in becoming a brand. The irony deepens in light of Crying Nut's 2012 copyright infringement suit against the Korea pop band CNBLUE. The case was finally decided in favor of Crying Nut in 2016 with a relatively small payment. See Jung Eun-jin, "CNBLUE to Pay Compensation to Crying Nut," *Korea Herald*, Feb. 4, 2016, www.koreaherald.com/view.php?ud=20160204001001.

38. Luc Boltanski and Ève Chiapello, *The New Spirit of Capitalism*, trans. Gregory Elliott (London: Verso, 2005), 18.

39. Ibid., 103. For networks to function properly within the terms of the new capitalism, Boltanski and Chiapello suggest that their incentives need to become naturalized as "self-evident truths." They argue that the notion of the *projective city* functions to meet these needs. Though offered more as an organizational model than a physical place, however, there is an actualization of the projective city in Seoul. Built in 2002, the very same year that *Looking for Bruce Lee* was released, Seoul's Digital Media City was built to house the high-tech businesses of the new economy. A "city" envisioned in direct relation to work, DMC was conceived in 1998, immediately following the IMF Crisis, and opened in time for the 2002 FIFA World Cup tournament, some of the matches of which were played across the street at the World Cup Soccer Stadium. Originally called "New Seoul Town" and then "the Millennial City," it was built on the site of Seoul's former garbage dump, so the metaphoric turn to the new economy as a way to recover out of economic ruin is amplified by the otherwise mute layers of garbage beneath the pavement at DMC. Also apropos of the current context, it is home to the Korean Film Archive, a government-sponsored center for the study and promotion of Korean cinema, and the Korean Film Museum. For an account of Boltanski and Chiapello's "projective city" in relationship to punk and neoliberalism see Konstantinou, *Cool Characters*, 111–13.

40. Jin-Ho Jang, "Neoliberalism in South Korea: The Dynamics of Financialization," in *New Millennium South Korea: Neoliberal Capitalism and Transnational Movements*, ed. Jesook Song (New York: Routledge, 2011), 46–60, 48–49.

41. Woo Seok-hun and Park Gwon-il, [*The 880,000 Wŏn Generation*] (Seoul: Redian Media, 2007).

42. It is important to recognize here that accounts of youth unemployment and underemployment have abounded in the Korean press in recent years. An important subset of this phenomenon is the rise of student loan debt and defaults. See "Number of College Graduates Defaulting on Student Loans Up 8 Times in 3 Years," *Korea Times*, Oct. 31, 2016, www.koreatimesus.com/number-of -college-graduates-defaulting-on-student-loans-up-8-times-in-3-years/.

43. The gloss is taken from an English-language review of the book. Gyeong Su-hyeon, "New Approach to Resolve the Misery of 'Temps Generation,'" a review of *The 880,000 Wŏn Generation*, by Woo Seok-hun and Park Gwon-il, *Korea Focus*, August 8, 2007, www .koreafocus.or.kr/design1/layout/content_print.asp?group_id=101721. For additional commentary on the 880,000 *Wŏn* generation see Kang, "The Political Economy of Idols," 60–61.

44. For accounts of remasculinization in Korean cinema in the 1990s and following see Kyung Hyun Kim, *The Remasculinization of Korean Cinema* (Durham, NC: Duke University Press, 2004), 9–10; and Baek Moonim, "The Beautiful, the Lame, and the Weird: Three Types of Colonial Heroes in Contemporary Korean Films," *Review of Korean Studies* 15, no. 2 (2012): 7–32.

45. For an account of lip-sync acts within K-pop music see Kang, "The Political Economy of Idols," 58–59.

46. See Keith Howard, "Mapping K-pop Past and Present: Shifting Modes of Exchange," *Korea Observer* 45, no. 3 (2014): 389–414, 405–6; and Swee-lin Ho, "Fuel for South Korea's 'Global Dreams Factory': The Desires of Parents Whose Children Dream of Becoming K-pop Stars," *Korea Observer* 43, no. 3 (2012): 471–502, 479–81.

47. John Lie, *K-Pop: Popular Music, Cultural Amnesia, and Economic Innovation in South Korea* (Oakland: University of California Press, 2015), 124–25.

48. Ibid., 126.

49. Jinying Li, "Clowns, Crimes, and Capital: Popular Crime-Comedies in Post-Crisis Korea," *Film International* 7, no. 2 (2009): 20–34, 32.

50. Song, *South Koreans in the Debt Crisis*, 116.

51. See Shin, "Globalization and Social Inequality in South Korea," 16.

52. Alan Liu, *The Laws of Cool: Knowledge Work and the Culture of Information* (Chicago: University of Chicago Press, 2004), 77–78.

53. Sianne Ngai, *Our Aesthetic Categories: Zany, Cute, Interesting* (Cambridge, MA: Harvard University Press, 2012), 202–3.

54. Boltanski and Chiapello, *The New Spirit of Capitalism*, 312. See also Konstantinou, *Cool Characters*: "The punk's solution to her lack of an economic future is complex, but can be identified with the second great punk slogan, the idea that you should, with proper entrepreneurial verve, 'Do It Yourself,' make your own culture, bypass official channels of

recognition, join what we might today call the creative class" (106). See also Michael Sza-lay, "The Incorporation Artist," a review of *Stone Arabia* by Dana Spiotta, *Los Angeles Review of Books*, July 10, 2012, https://lareviewofbooks.org/article/the-incorporation-artist/.

55. See Chanwook Kim, "The Political Subjectivization of Korean Creative Workers: Working and Living as Urban Precariat in Creative City Seoul," *International Journal of Cultural Policy*, August 2017, https://www.tandfonline.com/doi/ref/10.1080/10286632.2017.1361942?scroll=top.

56. Song, *South Koreans in the Debt Crisis*, 19–21.

57. Eve Kosofsky Sedgwick, "Pedagogy of Buddhism," in *Touching Feeling: Affect, Pedagogy, Performativity* (Durham, NC: Duke University Press, 2003), 168–72, 176.

58. Bruno Latour, *Reassembling the Social: An Introduction to Actor-Network-Theory* (New York: Oxford University Press, 2005), 235.

59. See Thich Nhat Hanh, *Old Path, White Clouds: Walking in the Footsteps of the Buddha* (Berkeley, CA: Parallax, 1991), 211–15.

60. See Sanjay Krishnan, "Reading Globalization from the Margin: The Case of Abdullah Munshi," *Representations* 99, no. 1 (2007): 40–73, 41. My account is informed by Krishnan's description of the global as a perspective that "secures for itself the reification of the global as thing." Thus, globalization tautologically reproduces a sense of the global as a "reality effect."

61. On this point my account departs from Feher's, which argues for a resistant politics from within the neoliberal regime (41). Feher seems to understand neoliberalism as epistemic rather than material; he thus can see self-esteem as part of a regime that celebrates new forms of valuation rather than as a compensatory fantasy.

62. Giovanni Arrighi, *The Long Twentieth Century: Money, Power, and the Origins of our Times*, 2nd ed. (London: Verso, 2010), 323–25.

63. Scott W. Fitzgerald, *Corporations and Cultural Industries: Time Warner, Bertelsmann, and News Corporation* (Lanham, MD: Lexington Books, 2012), 195.

64. See Prashad, *Everybody Was Kung Fu Fighting*, 128–29. Prashad also casts Lee as a figure of resistance against the forces of US economic imperialism (131–32).

65. See Leon Hung, *Kung Fu Cult Masters: From Bruce Lee to Crouching Tiger* (London: Wallflower, 2003), 76–98.

66. See Park, "New Waves at the Margin," 50–51.

67. Sangjoon Lee, "Martial Arts Craze in Korea: Cultural Translation of Martial Arts Films and Literature in the 1960s," in *East Asian Cinema and Cultural Heritage: From China, Hong Kong, Taiwan to Japan and South Korea*, ed. Yau Shuk-ting, Kinnia (London: Palgrave Macmillan, 2011), 189–90.

68. See I. M. Destler, *American Trade Politics*, 4th ed. (Washington: Institute for International Economics, 2005), 6–7. See also Arrighi, *The Long Twentieth Century*, 286.

69. See Destler, *American Trade Politics*, 45–52.

70. See Seung-Ook Lee, Sook-Jon Kim, and Joel Wainwright, "Mad Cow Militancy: Neoliberal Hegemony and Social Resistance in South Korea," *Political Geography* 29, no. 7 (2010): 359–69.

71. See Nancy Abelmann, *The Melodrama of Mobility: Women, Talk, and Class in Contemporary South Korea* (Honolulu: University of Hawai'i Press, 2003): "By the millennium one could not but sense the sea change: venture capitalism was everywhere, and *benchŏ* (venture), a veritable household word" (126).

72. Young-a Park, *Unexpected Alliances: Independent Filmmakers, the State, and the Film Industry in Postauthoritarian South Korea* (Stanford: Stanford University Press, 2015), 98–99.

73. Ibid., 94–98.

74. See Nohchool Park, "The Three Faces of People's Cinema: A Critical Review of the South Korean Independent Cinema Movement in the 1980s," *Acta Koreana* 12, no. 2 (2009): 21–53. Park emphasizes the particular significance of *minjung yŏnghwa* in the 1980s, defining it as "cinema that documents the underrepresented aspects of social realities such as grass-roots struggle against socio-political inequalities imposed by the ruling class" (22).

75. Park, *Unexpected Alliances*, 50.

76. A famous example of this communal production ethos is Kim Dong-won's *The Sanggye-dong Olympics* (1988), which documents the hardships of families displaced by construction for the 1988 Seoul Olympics. Kim gave a camera to evictees who were free to record whatever they wished to document. See Nohchool Park, "Gwangju Video and the Tradition of South Korean Independent Documentaries," *Review of Korean Studies* 13, no. 2 (2010): 187–214, 197–98.

77. Park, *Unexpected Alliances*, 48–76. See also Nancy Abelmann and Jung-ah Choi, "'Just Because': Comedy, Melodrama and Youth Violence in *Attack the Gas Station*," in *New Korean Cinema*, ed. Chi-Yun Shin and Julian Stringer (Edinburgh: Edinburgh University Press, 2005), 134.

78. Park, *Unexpected Alliances*, 104.

79. Park, "The Three Faces of People's Cinema," 50.

Chapter 4. The Surface of Finance

1. See Jesook Song, *South Koreans in the Debt Crisis: The Creation of a Neoliberal Welfare Society* (Durham, NC: Duke University Press, 2009), 49–116.

2. A useful comparison is the 2002 Korean film *A.F.R.I.K.A.* (*Ap'ŭrik'a*), which, like *Take Care of My Cat*, features an ensemble cast of young women (including Lee Yo-won) and addresses the various challenges posed to that demographic in the period. But unlike Jeong's film, *A.F.R.I.K.A.* ultimately backs away from social diagnosis in favor of a relatively vapid caper comedy.

3. Song, *South Koreans in the Debt Crisis*, 54–55. As an example of gender inequity within crisis conditions, Song presents the case of the Korean Farmer Association Bank, which laid off 688 women because they were married to men who were also employees of the bank. Song also cites a study by Cho Soon-kyung that states that the real women's unemployment rate at the height of the crisis would have been approximately 20 percent.

See Soon-kyung Cho, *Yôsônghaego ûi silt'ae wa chôngch'aek kwaje* [Women's layoff and suggestions for policy making] (Seoul: Presidential Commission on Women's Affairs, 1999).

4. Raymond Williams, *The Country and the City* (London: Oxford University Press, 1973), 153–54.

5. Song, *South Koreans in the Debt Crisis*: "During the crisis and in its immediate aftermath . . . the feminist discourse on women's independence was severely contested, if not subsumed, by the resurgence of collective activism in the face of the 'national emergency.' Not only did the women's movement recede, but women were reprivatized—forced to retreat to private domains—after having enjoyed a liberalizing social environment during the decades leading up to the crisis" (51).

6. See Jin-kyung Lee, *Service Economies: Militarism, Sex Work, and Migrant Labor in South Korea* (Minneapolis: University of Minnesota Press, 2010): "service labor as a particular kind of labor illustrates to us the most severe contradiction: the fact that the producer (the subject of labor) and the produced (the object of labor) are one and the same being" (12).

7. In 2001 the ROK received a Tier 3 ranking (the lowest possible rank) from the US State Department in its assessment of government efforts to prevent sex trafficking. For commentary and context see June J. H. Lee, "Human Trafficking in East Asia: Current Trends, Data Collection, and Knowledge Gaps," *International Migration* 43, no. 1–2 (2005): 165–201, esp. 188–89. For a report on Korean sex workers in Australia, the implied destination for Tae-hee and Ji-young at the end of the film, see Hyo-sik Lee, "Over 1,000 Korean Women Are Prostitutes in Australia," *Korea Times*, Nov. 14, 2011, www .koreatimes.co.kr/www/news/nation/2011/11/117_98737.html. See also Bronwen Dalton, Haeyoung Jang, Kyungja Jung, and Robyn Johns, "Destination Australia: Working Conditions of Korean Women Working in the Entertainment and Sex Industry," in *Proceedings: The 9th Annual Pacific Employment Relations Association Conference*, Nov. 17–20, 2009, 32–54, 35, https://opus.lib.uts.edu.au/bitstream/10453/16708/1/2009007201.pdf. For an account of the related history of domestic and military prostitution in the ROK see Lee, *Service Economies*, 79–183.

8. Jay David Bolter and Richard Grusin, *Remediation: Understanding New Media* (Cambridge, MA: MIT Press, 1999), 45.

9. Ibid., 5.

10. W. J. T. Mitchell, *Picture Theory* (Chicago: University of Chicago Press, 1994), 151–52.

11. See Mark Goble, "Obsolescence," in *A New Vocabulary for Global Modernism*, ed. Eric Hayot and Rebecca L. Walkowitz (New York: Columbia University Press, 2016), 146–68. The film, indeed, fits under the rubric Goble describes as "the bleeding edge of obsolescence"—that is, "works that increasingly imagine how both technologies and the histories of consumption and production they make real are connected within a global ecology" characterized by "extreme disposability" (162).

12. See Bill Brown, "All Thumbs," *Critical Inquiry* 30, no. 2 (2004): 452–57, 452–53.

13. I wish to make clear that I am not referring to the Autonomist account of immaterial labor but rather to the condition of obsolescence within the kind of workforce that Autonomists idealize in their account of immateriality. See Maurizio Lazzarato, "Immaterial Labor," in *Radical Thought in Italy: A Potential Politics*, ed. Paolo Virno and Michael Hardt (Minneapolis: University of Minnesota Press, 1996), 142–57.

14. For an account of the structural changes in the Korean economy as a result of the IMF Crisis, see Hyeng-joon Park and Jamie Doucette, "Financialization or Capitalization? Debating Capitalist Power in South Korea in the Context of Neoliberal Globalization," *Capital and Class* 40, no. 3 (2016): 533–54.

15. World Bank statistics indicate that in 2001 there were 60.9 cellular subscriptions per one hundred people in the Republic of Korea. In 2010 the number reached 102. In comparison the United States had 45 subscriptions in 2001 per one hundred people and did not cross the one hundred threshold until 2014. In the world as a whole there were only 15.5 subscriptions per one hundred people in 2001, and the number did not cross the one hundred threshold until 2016 (the last available year of data). See "Mobile Cellular Subscriptions (per 100 People)," The World Bank, http://data.worldbank.org /indicator/IT.CEL.SETS.P2. For commentary on the usage of cellular technology by Korean youth see Kyong Yoon, "The Making of Neo-Confucian Cyberkids: Representations of Young Mobile Phone Users in South Korea," *New Media and Society* 8, no. 5 (2006): 753–71.

16. Handheld devices are also one of the most immediate sites of obsolescence in the contemporary technological landscape. This is a planned obsolescence in which the older products are continually replaced by newer models despite the asymptotic trajectory of innovation in the technology. See Mark Goble, "Obsolescence," 162–63. Goble discusses a piece by the Japanese artist Maico Akiba, a functioning iPhone 3 painted to look like it had been salvaged from a landfill a hundred years in the future.

17. See Jukka Jouhki, "*Eomjijok*—The Korean Thumb Tribe—Reflections of Young and Urban Koreans' Mobile Communication," in *Digital Pioneers: Cultural Drivers of Future Media Culture*, ed. Sonja Kangas (Helsinki: Nuorisotutkimusverkosto, 2011), 65–80; and Hyeryoung Ok, "New Media Practices in Korea," *International Journal of Communication* 5 (2011): 320–48, 329–31.

18. See Jeanie Blankenship, "Recent Trends in the Korean Housing Finance Market," *Housing Finance International* 16, no. 3 (2002): 19–25.

19. See Chang Kyung-Sup, *South Korea Under Compressed Modernity: Familial Political Economy in Transition* (London: Routledge, 2010), 109.

20. For an account of the relationship between personhood and credit within the context of financial credit scoring, see Annie McClanahan, "Bad Credit: The Character of Credit Scoring," *Representations* 126, no. 1 (2014): 31–57. See also Lauren Berlant, *Cruel Optimism* (Durham, NC: Duke University Press, 2011), 240–45. Berlant invokes the work of the Surveillance Camera Players of New York, a group of avant-garde performers who "taunt and transgress the operative norms of securitization" by putting on plays in front of surveillance cameras.

21. See Rachael Miyung Joo, *Transnational Sports: Gender, Media, and Global Korea* (Durham, NC: Duke University Press, 2012), 47–50.

22. See Yaeri Kim, "Desiring Displacement: Globalization, Nationalism and Gendered Desires in *Take Care of My Cat*," *Journal of Japanese and Korean Cinema* 7, no. 2 (2015): 149–66, 154.

23. My point here is not to idealize the textile factories as workplaces but rather to point out how they allowed for the inclusion of women's labor into a developmental economy. For insight into the gender/power dynamics of labor in the textile industry, see Ok-Jie Lee, "Gender-Differentiated Employment Practices in the South Korean Textile Industry," *Gender and Society* 7, no. 4 (1993): 507–28. For an account of the semiproletarianization of gendered labor in the industrial context see Chang, *South Korea Under Compressed Modernity*, 74–77.

24. Lee, *Service Economies*, 37.

25. Ibid., 30.

26. Ibid., 185.

27. See Yoonkyung Lee, *Militants or Partisans: Labor Unions and Democratic Politics in Korea and Taiwan* (Stanford: Stanford University Press, 2011), 73–101.

28. *Take Care of My Cat* (*Koyangirŭl Put'akhae*), dir. Jeong Jae-eun (2001; New York: Kino International, 2004), DVD.

29. The film's subtle interest in the Korean textile industry as a historical site of gendered labor points ironically to an absence in the film of any interest in the history of organized labor in Korea, despite its interest in examining Korean work culture. See Hagen Koo, *Korean Workers: The Culture and Politics of Class Formation* (Ithaca, NY: Cornell University Press, 2001), 17. Koo points out that women workers, many of them in the garment and textile industries, were pivotal leaders in the grassroots labor movement in the late 1970s and early 1980s.

30. See Kim, "Desiring Displacement": "this improbable dream helps Ji-young continue to imagine alternative possibilities for herself despite an increasingly hostile reality" (150).

31. Natalia Cecire, "Ways of Not Reading Gertrude Stein," *ELH* 82, no. 1 (2015): 281–312, 297.

32. See Friedrich Kittler, *Gramophone, Film, Typewriter*, trans. by Geoffrey Winthrop-Young and Michael Wutz (Stanford: Stanford University Press, 1999), 194.

33. Cecire, "Ways of Not Reading Gertrude Stein," 301.

34. See D. N. Rodowick, *The Virtual Life of Film* (Cambridge, MA: Harvard University Press, 2007), 19, 22; and Paolo Cherchi Usai, *The Death of Cinema: History, Cultural Memory, and the Digital Dark Age* (London: British Film Institute, 2001). Borrowing from the provocative work of Cherchi Usai, for whom (in Rodowick's gloss) film is inherently an "autodestructive medium" in which every "passage of frames through a projector . . . advances a process of erosion that will eventually reduce the image to nothing," Rodowick argues: "Rather than a haptic object or a stable self-identical form, the film viewer is always in pursuit of an absent, indeed *absenting*, object" (22). The disappearance of Tae-hee and

Ji-young into the surface of the film at the conclusion of *Take Care of My Cat* might be read as an instance of self-consciousness about the dynamic that Rodowick identifies, one that is then grafted onto an economic logic.

35. See Kim, "Desiring Displacement," 152.

36. Sir Walter Scott, *The Poetical Works of Walter Scott, with a Memoir of the Author*, vol. 4 (Boston: Little Brown, 1858), 309.

37. J. Q. Davies, "Melodrama Possessions: *The Flying Dutchman*, South Africa, and the Imperial Stage, ca. 1830," *Opera Quarterly* 21, no. 3 (2006): 496–514, 498.

38. Giovanni Arrighi, *The Long Twentieth Century: Money, Power, and the Origins of our Times*, 2nd ed. (New York: Verso, 2010), 290–91.

39. See Martin Hart-Landsberg, Seongjin Jeong, and Richard Westra, introduction to *Marxist Perspectives on South Korea in the Global Economy*, ed. Martin Hart-Landsberg, Seongjin Jeong, and Richard Westra (New York: Routledge, 2017), 13–15.

40. Jin-Ho Jang, "Neoliberalism in South Korea: The Dynamics of Financialization," in *New Millennium South Korea: Neoliberal Capitalism and Transnational Movements*, ed. Jesook Song (New York: Routledge, 2011), 46–60, esp. 48–51. While this systemic account is valuable, one may overread the turn toward financialization after the IMF Crisis, as it is presented in somewhat overly epistemological terms. For a more nuanced account of the transformation see Park and Doucette, "Financialization or Capitalization?".

41. Fredric Jameson, *The Cultural Turn: Selected Writings on the Postmodern, 1983–1998* (New York: Verso, 1998), 142.

42. See Luc Boltanski and Ève Chiapello, *The New Spirit of Capitalism*, trans. Gregory Elliott (London: Verso, 2005), 470. See also Chi-Yun Shin, "Two of a Kind: Gender and Friendship," in *New Korean Cinema*, ed. Chi-Yun Shin and Julian Stringer (Edinburgh: Edinburgh University Press, 2005), 117–31. Shin reports that Jeong often thought of the idea of a nomad during filming: "I wanted my characters to be girls who possessed nothing permanent and therefore were able to leave. Their relationships change and the girls continue to walk. I believe that if something is not moving, the energy weakens and it needs to be filled with things that are moving" (128).

43. See Walter Benn Michaels, *The Gold Standard and the Logic of Naturalism: American Literature at the Turn of the Century* (Berkeley: University of California Press, 1988): "Money for [Carrie] is never simply a means of getting what you want, it is itself the thing you want, indeed, it is itself your want" (33–34).

44. See Kim, "Desiring Displacement," 157.

45. See Lee, "Over 1,000 Korean Women"; and Dalton et al., "Destination Australia," 35.

46. One might read the scene as a rejoinder to post-Marxist celebration of "immaterial labor" as a site of possibility that might supplant vanishing modes of industrial labor. For theorizations of immaterial labor see Lazzarato, "Immaterial Labor," 132–47; and Michael Hardt and Antonio Negri, *Empire* (Cambridge, MA: Harvard University Press, 2001), 289–94. For critiques of this position see Joshua Clover, "The Problem of Value in Post-Fordist Immaterial Labor," libcom.org, Dec. 1, 2014; and Annie McClanahan, "Investing in the Future," *Journal of Cultural Economy* 6, no. 1 (2013): 78–93.

47. See Matthew Hart, "Threshold to the Kingdom: The Airport Is a Border and the Border Is a Volume," *Criticism* 57, no. 2 (2015): 173–89: "the airport, far from demarking the two-dimensional line between national and international space, becomes a zone of parcelized or disaggregated legal-political geography in which different regimes of rights and obligations apply to different kinds of persons and in which certain aspects of foreign or domestic law may or may not apply, depending on where in the airport you happen to be at one moment" (183).

48. Jonathan Lethem, *Dissident Gardens* (New York: Vintage, 2003), 359.

49. Hart, "Threshold to the Kingdom," 186.

50. Songdo IBD website homepage, www.songdo.com/songdo-international-business-district/why-songdo/a-brand-new-city.aspx (page no longer available); see also http://songdoibd.com.

51. Quoted in Richard J. Barnet and Ronald E. Müller, *Global Reach: The Power of Multinational Corporations* (New York: Simon and Schuster, 1974), 16.

52. See Aihwa Ong, *Neoliberalism as Exception: Mutations in Citizenship and Sovereignty* (Durham, NC: Duke University Press, 2006): "In Asian milieus, the option of exception has allowed states to carve up their own territory so they can better engage and compete in global markets. . . . As the case of China illustrates, zoning technologies encode alternative territorialities for experiments in economic freedom and entrepreneurial activity" (19).

53. It is also frequently used as an outdoor filming location in Korean serial dramas, perhaps because of its relatively untrafficked streets, though in most cases, the audience believes the action to be occurring in Seoul.

54. See Hong Yu, "China's 'Ghost Cities,'" *East Asian Policy* 6, no. 2 (2014): 33–43. While the perceived emptiness of Songdo is very different from what have been called China's ghost cities, the product of excessive speculation and construction, its development nevertheless shares with its Chinese counterparts a kind of blind idealism that was eventually chastened when faced with the lack of real demand.

55. Sofia T. Shwayri, "A Model Korean Ubiquitous Eco-city? The Politics of Making Songdo," *Journal of Urban Technology* 20, no. 1 (2013): 39–55, 53.

56. Ibid., 48–52.

57. Norimitsu Onishi, "South Korea's Main Chinatown Lacks Only the Chinese," *New York Times*, March 2, 2007, sec. A3.

58. Heritage Foundation Index of Economic Freedom, 2013, www.heritage.org/index/pdf/2013/book/index_2013.pdf.

59. Heritage Foundation Index of Economic Freedom, South Korea 1995–2016, www.heritage.org/index/visualize.

60. Jang, "Neoliberalism in South Korea," 52.

61. Sohee Kim and Kyunghee Park, "Hanjin's Ghost Ships Seek Havens with Food and Water Starting to Dwindle," Sept. 6, 2016, www.bloomberg.com/news/articles/2016-09-06/hanjin-s-ghost-ships-seek-havens-as-food-water-start-to-dwindle.

62. Costas Paris and Erica E. Phillips, "Hanjin Shipping's Troubles Leave $14 Billion in Cargo Stranded at Sea," *Wall Street Journal*, Sept. 7, 2016, www.wsj.com/articles/billions-in-cargo-remains-stranded-at-sea-1473285117. *Bloomberg* suggested that "the fallout of

Hanjin Shipping is like Lehman Brothers to the financial markets. . . . It's a huge, huge nuclear bomb. It shakes up the supply chain, the cornerstone of globalization." See Heejin Kim, "Hanjin Brings One of World's Busiest Shipping Terminals Close to Standstill," Sept. 14, 2016, www.bloomberg.com/news/articles/2016-09-13/last-holdout-in-korean-war -sees-once-busy-docks-idled-by-hanjin; and Rishaad Salamat and Kyunghee Park, "Hanjin Fall Is Lehman Moment for Shipping, Seaspan CEO Says," www.bloomberg.com/news /articles/2016-09-13/hanjin-s-fall-is-lehman-moment-for-shipping-seaspan-ceo-says.

63. Their ghostly drifting signifies a logistics breakdown in what is a massive global operation that generally escaped significant public notice until Hanjin's collapse, except perhaps in the kind of informatic glimpses provided by online trackers like shipmap.org, which offers glimpses of the sublime entirety of global cargo shipping in real time, or important critical interventions like the work of Allan Sekula or Keller Easterling. The Hanjin bankruptcy story is similar to those other contexts, real or narrated, in which cargo shipping captures the public imagination: pirating and natural disaster. It may be, in fact, that container ship logistics are only appreciable at their limits, as in films like *Captain Phillips* (2013), *A Hijacking* (2012), *Haendae* (2009), or *2012* (2009). See Allan Sekula, *Fish Story* (Düsseldorf: Richter, 1995); Allan Sekula, dir., *The Forgotten Space* (Vienna: Wildart Film, 2010); and Keller Easterling, *Enduring Innocence: Global Architecture and Its Political Masquerades* (Cambridge, MA: MIT Press, 2005).

64. See Joshua Keating, "The Shipping Noose," slate.com Sept. 8, 2016, www.slate .com/articles/business/moneybox/2016/09/hanjin_s_bankruptcy_has_its_cargo_ships _unable_to_dock_is_global_shipping.html.

65. Sergio Bologna, "The Perfect Storm of Logistics," *Il Manifesto*, Sept. 20, 2016, repr. Oct. 3, 2016, at The Bullet, https://socialistproject.ca/2016/10/b1310/.

66. See Jillian Ambrose, "That Sinking Feeling for Hanjin as Falling Freight Rates Fuel a Global Shipping Crisis," *The Telegraph*, Sept. 17, 2016, www.telegraph.co.uk /business/2016/09/17/that-sinking-feeling-for-hanjin-as-falling-freight-rates-fuel-a/.

67. This vexed feeling of intimacy might also be described as what Youngmin Choe has called a "transitional emotion," which, as she describes, offers "insight not so much into the emotional states of these individual characters, but rather, into the geographic circula-tion of emotion in neoliberal Korea." Youngmin Choe, "Transitional Emotions: Boredom and Distraction in Hong Sang-su's Travel Films," *Korean Studies* 33 (2009): 1–28, 3.

68. See Joshua Clover, *Riot. Strike. Riot: The New Era of Uprisings* (London: Verso, 2016):

> The extraordinary development of transport, one of the hallmarks of our time, would seem at first to fit the bill, circulating products toward realizing as profit the surplus value valorized elsewhere. The change of location, some argue contrarily, increases the value of a commod-ity. In its most restricted sense, "pure circulation costs" might be limited to activities that make nothing but exchange itself. . . . But this can only affirm the proposition that the current phase in our cycle of accumulation is defined by the collapse of value production at the core of the world-system; it is for this reason that capital's center of gravity shifts toward circu-lation, borne by the troika of Toyotaization, information technology, and finance. (22–23)

69. See Roland Barthes, *Camera Lucida: Reflections on Photography*, trans. Richard Howard (New York: Hill and Wang, 1981), 27.

70. Goble, "Obsolescence," 186.

Chapter 5. Math Monsters

1. Edward LiPuma and Benjamin Lee, *Financial Derivatives and the Globalization of Risk* (Durham, NC: Duke University Press, 2004), 47. For a compelling account of derivatives logics in contemporary media production see Michael Szalay, "HBO's Flexible Gold," *Representations* 126, no. 1 (2014): 112–34.

2. Edward LiPuma and Benjamin Lee, "A Social Approach to the Financial Derivatives Market," *South Atlantic Quarterly* 111, no. 2 (2012): 289–320, 290.

3. Ibid., 289.

4. LiPuma and Lee, *Financial Derivatives*, 107–8.

5. Giovanni Arrighi, *The Long Twentieth Century: Money, Power, and the Origins of Our Times*, 2nd ed. (London: Verso, 2010), 31.

6. Ranajit Guha, *Dominance Without Hegemony: History and Power in Colonial India* (Cambridge, MA: Harvard University Press, 1998).

7. Lev Manovich, *The Language of New Media* (Cambridge, MA: MIT Press, 2001), 117; Wendy Hui Kyong Chun, "On Software, or the Persistence of Visual Knowledge," *Grey Room* 18, no. 4 (2004): 26–51, 44.

8. Jean-Louis Baudry, "Ideological Effects of the Basic Cinematographic Apparatus," trans. Alan Williams, *Film Quarterly* 28, no. 2 (1974–75): 39–47, 41.

9. D. N. Rodowick, *The Virtual Life of Film* (Cambridge, MA: Harvard University Press, 2007), 125.

10. LiPuma and Lee, *Financial Derivatives*, 26–28.

11. Ibid., 28.

12. See David Harvey, *The New Imperialism* (New York: Oxford University Press, 2010), 53, 62–74; and Michael Ignatieff, *Empire Lite: Nation-Building in Bosnia, Kosovo, and Afghanistan* (New York: Random House, 2003). See also Joseph Jonghyun Jeon, "Neoliberal Forms: CGI, Algorithm, and Hegemony in Korea's IMF Cinema," *Representations* 126, no. 1 (2014): 85–111. Readers of that earlier version of this chapter will note that I have greatly diminished the centrality of *neoliberalism* as an operative term. I continue to think it useful for periodizing Korean political economy beginning in the early 1990s, but I find its epistemological usage in contemporary criticism less productive. Cf. Sarah Brouillette, "Neoliberalism and the Demise of the Literary," in *Neoliberalism and Contemporary Literary Culture*, ed. Mitchum Huehls and Rachel Greenwald Smith (Baltimore: Johns Hopkins University Press, 2017), 280.

13. Fredric Jameson, "Culture and Finance Capital," in *The Cultural Turn: Selected Writings on the Postmodern, 1983–1998* (New York: Verso, 1998), 142.

14. Bruce Cumings, "The Korean Crisis and the End of 'Late' Development," *New Left Review* 231 (1998): 43–72, 51; and Bruce Cumings, *Dominion from Sea to Sea:*

Pacific Ascendancy and American Power (New Haven, CT: Yale University Press, 2009), 394.

15. Chalmers Johnson, *Sorrows of Empire: Militarism, Secrecy, and the End of the Republic* (New York: Metropolitan, 2004), 188. See also Cumings, *Dominion from Sea to Sea*, 388–423.

16. See Jang-Sup Shin and Ha-Joon Chang, *Restructuring Korea Inc.* (London: RoutledgeCurzon, 2003), 66–76. Although the policies of financial liberalization began as early as the 1980s under the Chun Doo-hwan regime, these were limited in scope. They were accelerated in the early 1990s. See David Harvey, *A Brief history of Neoliberalism* (New York: Oxford University Press, 2005): "The Wall Street-Treasury-IMF alliance had, in effect, done to South Korea what the investment bankers had done in the mid-1970s to New York City" (111). See also Cumings, "The Korean Crisis": "A mark of Washington's unipolar pre-eminence and the potency of its foreign economic policy under Clinton is that even mainstream pundits found the International Monetary Fund to be the mere creature of Treasury Secretary Robert Rubin and Deputy Lawrence H. Summers" (52).

17. Paul de Man, "The Rhetoric of Temporality," in *Blindness and Insight: Essays in the Rhetoric of Contemporary Criticism*, 2nd ed. (Minneapolis: University of Minnesota Press, 1983), 187–228, 222.

18. See Annie McClanahan, "Dead Pledges: Debt, Horror, and the Credit Crisis," May 7, 2012, "Peer Reviewed," *Post45*, http://post45.research.yale.edu/2012/05/dead-pledges -debt-horror-and-the-credit-crisis/; and Jim Hansen, "Formalism and Its Malcontents: Benjamin and de Man on the Function of Allegory," *New Literary History* 35, no. 4 (2004): 663–83, 671.

19. Paul Virilio, *War and Cinema: The Logistics of Perception*, trans. Patrick Camiller (London: Verso, 1989), 1.

20. Ibid., 3.

21. Ibid., 92.

22. Ibid., 20, 109–11.

23. Paul Virilio, *Desert Screen: War at the Speed of Light*, trans. Michael Degener (London: Continuum, 2002), 91, 93.

24. Tom Sito, *Moving Innovation: A History of Computer Animation* (Cambridge, MA: MIT Press, 2013), 37, 52.

25. Timothy Lenoir and Henry Lowood, "Theaters of War: The Military Entertainment Complex," in *Collection, Laboratory, Theater: Scenes of Knowledge in the 17th Century*, ed. Helmar Schramm, Ludger Schwarte, and Jan Lazardzig (Berlin: Walter de Gruyter, 2005), 453.

26. See Christina Klein, "Why American Studies Needs to Think About Korean Cinema," *American Quarterly* 60, no. 4 (2008): 871–98.

27. See Jin-Kyung Lee, *Service Economies: Militarism, Sex Work, and Migrant Labor in South Korea* (Minneapolis: University of Minnesota Press, 2010), 37–77; and Viet Thanh

Nguyen, *Nothing Ever Dies: Vietnam and the Memory of War* (Cambridge, MA: Harvard University Press, 2016), 129–55.

28. See Hye Jean Chung, "*The Host* and *D-War*: Complex Intersections of National Imaginings and Transnational Aspirations," *Spectator* 29, no. 2 (2009): 48–56. Chung reads the monster's hybridity in relation to its transnational mode of production.

29. For discussion of *The Host* as outbreak narrative see Hsuan L. Hsu, "The Dangers of Biosecurity: *The Host* and the Geopolitics of Outbreak," *Jump Cut: A Review of Contemporary Media* 51 (2009): www.ejumpcut.org/archive/jc51.2009/Host/.

30. See Chung, "*The Host* and *D-War*," 51. Chung points out that special effects constituted 40 percent of the film's overall budget.

31. See Nathan K. Hensley, "Allegories of the Contemporary," *Novel: A Forum on Fiction* 45, no. 2 (2012): 276–300, 288.

32. The United States, for example, dropped "the largest conventional bomb ever deployed" in 2017, which cost upwards of $300 million, in order to destroy an underground fortress in Afghanistan that the CIA had financed just a few decades earlier. See Ricky Twisdale, "Ed Snowden: Afghan Bunker 'Moab' Bomb Destroyed Was Built by CIA," *The Duran*, April 15, 2017, http://theduran.com/snowden-afghan-bunker-moab-bomb/. See also Mary Anne Weaver, "Lost at Tora Bora," *New York Times Magazine*, Sept. 11, 2005, www.nytimes.com/2005/09/11/magazine/lost-at-tora-bora.html.

33. Hsu, "The Dangers of Biosecurity."

34. Ibid.

35. See Shin and Chang, *Restructuring Korea Inc.*, 34–82; Cumings, "The Korean Crisis," 44–45; Kang-Kook Lee, "Neoliberalism, the Financial Crisis, and Economic Restructuring in Korea," in *New Millennium South Korea: Neoliberal Capitalism and Transnational Movements*, ed. Jesook Song (New York: Routledge, 2011), 29–45, 31–32; and Kwang-Yeong Shin, "Globalization and Social Inequality in South Korea," in *New Millennium South Korea: Neoliberal Capitalism and Transnational Movements*, ed. Jesook Song (New York: Routledge, 2011), 11–28, 16–17. Laura Hyun Yi Kang, "The Uses of Asianization: Figuring Crises, 1997–98 and 2007–?" *American Quarterly* 64, no. 3 (2012): 411–36, 411.

36. Harvey, *A Brief History of Neoliberalism*, 111–12. See also Lee, "Neoliberalism, the Financial Crisis, and Economic Restructuring in Korea," 31–32; Shin, "Globalization and Social Inequality in South Korea," 16–17. Both Lee and Shin state that neoliberal reform had been under way in Korea at least since the early 1990s as concessions for entrance into the Organization for Economic Co-operation and Development (OECD).

37. Hensley, "Allegories of the Contemporary," 278; see also Naomi Klein, *The Shock Doctrine: The Rise of Disaster Capitalism* (New York: Metropolitan, 2007), 14–17.

38. Rodowick, *The Virtual Life of Film*, 104.

39. See Christopher Nealon, "Value, Theory, Crisis," *PMLA* 127, no. 1 (2012): 101–6.

40. Roger Eckhardt, "Stan Ulam, Jon von Neumann, and the Monte Carlo Method,"

in *From Cardinals to Chaos: Reflections on the Life and Legacy of Stanislaw Ulam*, ed. Necia Grant Cooper et al. (New York: Cambridge University Press, 1989), 131.

41. See Robert L. Cook et al., "Stochastic Simplification of Aggregate Detail," Pixar Technical Memo #06-05a, May 2007, http://graphics.pixar.com/library/StochasticSimplification/paper.pdf.

42. Alexander R. Galloway, *The Interface Effect* (Malden, MA: Polity, 2012), 54, 76.

43. Ibid., 52, 9.

44. De Man, "The Rhetoric of Temporality," 207.

45. Galloway, *The Interface Effect*, 54.

46. Ibid., 72. *Allegorithm* is Galloway's term (which he later dismisses) describing how a gamer interprets the game's algorithm in order to win. See Alexander R. Galloway, "Playing the Code: Allegories of Control in Civilization," *Radical Philosophy* 128 (2004): 33–40, 35.

47. See Patrick Jagoda, *Network Aesthetics* (Chicago: University of Chicago Press, 2016).

48. Galloway, *The Interface Effect*, 117.

49. Aaron Kunin, "Character's Lounge," *Modern Language Quarterly* 70, no. 3 (2009): 291–317, 291.

50. See Katharine H. S. Moon, *Sex Among Allies: Military Prostitution in U.S.-Korea Relations* (New York: Columbia University Press, 1997); Lee, *Service Economies*, 125–83; and Na Young Lee, "The Construction of Military Prostitution in South Korea During the U.S. Military Rule, 1945–1948," *Feminist Studies* 33, no. 3 (2007): 453–81.

51. See Lee, *Service Economies*, 134.

52. Lauren Berlant, *Cruel Optimism* (Durham, NC: Duke University Press, 2011), 192–93.

53. Jane Tompkins, *West of Everything: The Inner Life of Westerns* (New York: Oxford University Press, 1992), 76.

54. See Joon Oh Jang, Kyungseok Choo, and Kyung-shik Choi, *Human Trafficking and Smuggling of Korean Women for Sexual Exploitation to the United States: A Critical Analysis of Transnational Displacement and Anti-trafficking Measures* (Seoul: Korean Institute of Criminology, 2009), 52, 71; Jesook Song, *South Koreans in the Debt Crisis: The Creation of a Neoliberal Welfare Society* (Durham, NC: Duke University Press, 2009), xv–xx; and Youngbee Dale, "South Korea: The Stimulus Plan, Sexism, and Sex Trafficking," *Washington Times*, Sept. 26, 2011.

55. Jin-Ho Jang, "Neoliberalism in South Korea: The Dynamics of Financialization," in *New Millennium South Korea: Neoliberal Capitalism and Transnational Movements*, ed. Jesook Song (New York: Routledge, 2011), 46–60, 48.

56. LiPuma and Lee, *Financial Derivatives*, 134.

57. Ibid., 167.

58. Myung-koo Kang, "Addiction to Uncertainty: Regulatory Rush and the Exponential Growth of Financial Derivatives Markets in South Korea," working paper, East Asia Institute, June 2013, 2.

59. See Yoolim Lee, "Korean Corporations Court Bankruptcy with Suicidal KIKO Options," *Bloomberg*, March 24, 2009, www.bloomberg.com/news/articles/2009-03-24 /korean-corporations-court-bankruptcy-with-suicidal-kiko-options.

60. J. A. Kregel, "Derivatives and Global Capital Flows: Applications to Asia," *Cambridge Journal of Economics* 22, no. 6 (1998): 677–92, 677–78, 686.

61. Jacques Derrida, *Edmund Husserl's "Origin of Geometry": An Introduction*, trans. John P. Leavey Jr. (Lincoln: University of Nebraska Press, 1978), 117.

62. Derrida, *Edmund Husserl's "Origin of Geometry,"* 161–63.

63. See Seung-Ook Lee, Sook-Jon Kim, and Joel Wainwright, "Mad Cow Militancy: Neoliberal Hegemony and Social Resistance in South Korea," *Political Geography* 29, no. 7 (2010): 359–69, 360.

64. Alexander R. Galloway, "The Poverty of Philosophy: Realism and Post-Fordism," *Critical Inquiry* 39, no. 2 (2013): 347–66, 347, 358, 362.

65. Ibid., 360 (Galloway's emphasis).

66. Niklas Luhmann, "The Autopoiesis of Social System," *Essays on Self-Reference* (New York: Columbia University Press, 1990), 1–20, 3, 13.

Chapter 6. Wire Aesthetics

1. Wendy Hui Kyong Chun, *Control and Freedom: Power and Paranoia in the Age of Fiber Optics* (Cambridge, MA: MIT Press, 2006), 250.

2. Ibid., 249.

3. See ibid.: "Early on, cyberspace's supposed openness and endlessness were key to imagining electronic networks as a terrestrial version of outer space" (51).

4. See Lynne Kirby, *Parallel Tracks: The Railroad and Silent Cinema* (Durham, NC: Duke University Press, 1997), 8.

5. Anne Friedberg, *Window Shopping: Cinema and the Postmodern* (Berkeley: University of California Press, 1993), 20. If the flâneur is the perfect spectator that can see while not being seen, as Chun writes, then on "the so-called information superhighway, flâneurs . . . would be roadkill . . . , for the internet makes it impossible to be at 'the center of the world' yet remain hidden." Wendy Hui Kyong Chun, *Control and Freedom*, 61.

6. See Enda Duffy, *The Speed Handbook: Velocity, Pleasure, Modernism* (Durham, NC: Duke University Press, 2009), 3–9.

7. See Tom Standage, *The Victorian Internet: The Remarkable Story of the Telegraph and the Nineteenth Century's On-line Pioneers* (New York: Bloomsbury, 1998), 67.

8. See ibid., 94–98.

9. Don DeLillo, *Americana* (1971; New York: Penguin, 1989), 95–96.

10. Tao Lin, *Taipei* (New York: Vintage, 2013), 25.

11. See Nicole Starosielski, *The Undersea Network* (Durham, NC: Duke University Press, 2015), 88.

12. This distinction is, of course, a messy one, since a good deal of network

infrastructure—including DSL, ADSL, SDSL, and CATV—still uses copper wiring to some degree.

13. See Dan Schiller, *Digital Capitalism: Networking the Global Market System* (Cambridge, MA: MIT Press, 1999), 82. Schiller makes the case that telecommunications was an explicit target of US financial expansion, including ownership of foreign telecommunications infrastructures.

14. Quoted in K. K. Ruthven, *A Guide to Ezra Pound's "Personae" (1926)* (Berkeley: University of California Press, 1969), 153.

15. Hugh Kenner famously calls the poem a "simile with the 'like' suppressed," in *The Pound Era* (Berkeley: University of California Press, 1971), 185.

16. Another modernist example might be Jean Toomer's "Her Lips Are Copper Wire."

17. Jonathan Sterne, "Compression: A Loose History," in *Signal Traffic: Critical Studies in Media Infrastructure*, ed. Lisa Parks and Nicole Starosielski (Urbana: University of Illinois Press, 2015), 39.

18. Ibid., 34.

19. See Mark Goble's capacious account of modernism in *Beautiful Circuits: Modernism and the Mediated Life* (New York: Columbia University Press, 2010): "This book is about how modernism itself desired communication and the many forms it took, not just as a response to the power of media technologies in the twentieth century but as a way of insisting that this power was already modernism's own" (3).

20. Cf. Joshua Clover's description of the film as "a historic advance in digital entertainment that is unpacifiably anxious about the dangers of digitality" and as "a critique of spectacles that is itself a spectacle." Joshua Clover, *The Matrix* (London: British Film Institute, 2004), 15.

21. Tung-Hui Hu, *A Prehistory of the Cloud* (Cambridge, MA: MIT Press, 2015), 1–11.

22. Standage, *The Victorian Internet*, 67–68.

23. N. Katherine Hayles, "Cognition Everywhere: The Rise of Cognitive Nonconscious and the Costs of Consciousness," *New Literary History* 45, no. 2 (2014): 199–220, 205.

24. Scott Patterson, *Dark Pools: The Rise of the Machine Traders and the Rigging of the U.S. Stock Market* (New York: Crown Business, 2012), 8.

25. Ibid., 46.

26. Ibid., 287–88.

27. See Scott W. Fitzgerald, *Corporations and Cultural Industries: Time Warner, Bertelsmann, and News Corporation* (London: Lexington Books, 2012), 209–18.

28. See Starosielski, *The Undersea Network*.

29. See Wendy Hui Kyong Chun, *Control and Freedom*, 24–25.

30. See, e.g., Geert Lovink, *Dark Fiber: Tracking Critical Internet Culture* (Cambridge, MA: MIT Press, 2002), 88–89. One possible version of this argument would involve consideration of US domination of internet protocols, both in selection of TCP/IP as

a global standard in 1983 over a competing protocol, OSI (Open Systems Interconnection), developed, primarily in Europe, and in the establishment of ICANN (the Internet Corporation for Assigned Names and Numbers), a US-based nonprofit under contract with the US Department of Commerce that managed internet address protocols for the global internet from 1998 to 2016. Uneasiness over this arrangement came to a head with the leak of documents by Edward Snowden in 2013 that disclosed the wide-ranging surveillance activities of the US National Security Agency, which itself also provides compelling evidence for this line of argument. See also Schiller, *Digital Capitalism*: "The open Internet remained largely a U.S. system. Some 60 percent of the Internet's host computers in early 1997 were located in the United States; the Net relies on English as its lingua franca; and its very architecture still forced *intra*-Asian traffic to transit to network exchange locations in the United States before being routed back to Asian destinations" (35).

31. See also Chun, *Control and Freedom*, 52.

32. Alexander R. Galloway and Eugene Thacker, *The Exploit: A Theory of Networks* (Minneapolis: University of Minnesota Press, 2007), 21.

33. Alexander R. Galloway, *Protocol: How Control Exists After Decentralization* (Cambridge, MA: MIT Press, 2004), 74–75.

34. Galloway and Thacker, *The Exploit*, 29.

35. Armand Mattelart, *Networking the World, 1794–2000*, trans. by Liz Carey-Libbrecht (Minneapolis: University of Minnesota Press, 2000), 11.

36. See, e.g., Galloway and Thacker, *The Exploit*; Galloway, *Protocol*; Alexander R. Galloway, *The Interface Effect* (Malden, MA: Polity, 2012); and Alexander R. Galloway, *Laruelle: Against the Digital* (Minneapolis: University of Minnesota Press, 2014).

37. Chun, *Control and Freedom*, 9.

38. Hu, *A Prehistory of the Cloud*, 7, xiii, xvi, 146.

39. Galloway and Thacker, *The Exploit*, 21.

40. Siegfried Zielinski, *Deep Time of the Media: Toward an Archaeology of Hearing and Seeing by Technical Means* (Cambridge, MA: MIT Press, 2008), 1–12.

41. Hu, *A Prehistory of the Cloud*, 10.

42. Chun, *Control and Freedom*, 130.

43. Ibid., 38.

44. Geert Lovink, *Dark Fiber: Tracking Critical Internet Culture* (Cambridge, MA: MIT Press, 2002), 184, 236.

45. Ibid., 331–32.

46. Quoted in Mattelart, *Networking the World, 1794–2000*, 86–87.

47. Robert Wade and Frank Veneroso, "The Asian Crisis: The High Debt Model Versus the Wall Street-Treasury-IMF Complex," *New Left Review* I/228 (1998): 3–23, 20. See also Schiller, *Digital Capitalism*: "U.S. acquisitions of Asian business properties

reached a value of $8 billion in the first half of 1998, double that of the previous year, with European buyouts at $4 billion, also at record levels" (39).

48. Schiller, *Digital Capitalism*, 63–66.

49. Google and the Fundamentals of Internet Business, https://sites.google.com/site/net205apples/network-economy.

50. Giovanni Arrighi, *The Long Twentieth Century: Money, Power, and the Origins of Our Times*, 2nd ed. (London: Verso, 2010), 248.

51. See Andrew Blum, *Tubes: A Journey to the Center of the Internet* (New York: Harper Collins, 2012), 95–99.

52. Ibid., 98.

53. Ibid., 164.

54. Mattelart, *Networking the World, 1794–2000*, 120.

55. See Mark James Russell, *Pop Goes Korea: Behind the Revolution in Movies, Music, and Internet Culture* (Berkeley, CA: Stone Bridge Press, 2008), 50.

56. Ibid., 38–48.

57. The company did have some hits, most notably *The Way Home* (2002), but the flops were highly visible in the Korean mass media.

58. Jinhee Choi, *The South Korean Film Renaissance: Local Hitmakers, Global Provocateurs* (Middletown, CT: Wesleyan University Press, 2010), 24, 32.

59. Kyung Hyun Kim, *The Remasculinization of Korean Cinema* (Durham, NC: Duke University Press, 2004), 133.

60. Galloway and Thacker, *The Exploit*, 19–20.

61. Steven Shaviro, *Post-Cinematic Affect* (Winchester, UK: Zero Books, 2010), 127.

62. J. D. Connor, *The Studios After the Studios: Neoclassical Hollywood (1970–2010)* (Stanford: Stanford University Press, 2015), 15.

63. See Darcy Paquet, review of *Resurrection of the Little Match Girl*, koreanfilm.org, http://koreanfilm.org/kfilm02.html#sungso.

64. I mean that the drama of class is more explicitly portrayed as such, whereas in *The Matrix*, class conflict becomes sublimated as a conflict between humans and their mechanic overlords. See Clover, *The Matrix*: "The ruling class's basic logistical issue: how to convince the underclass to offer up said energy, while at the same time keeping them alive but unresistant" (57).

65. *Resurrection of the Little Match Girl* (*Songnyangp'ali sonyoui chaerim*), dir. Jang Sun-woo (Seoul: Kijoek Sidae, 2002), DVD.

66. Shaviro, *Post-Cinematic Affect*, 136. While he doubts accelerationism as a politics, he claims value for aesthetic attempts "to explore the dangers of futurity" and to map these dangers "as thoroughly and intensively as possible" (139).

67. Shortly after the period discussed in the chapter, Korea Telecom and SK Telecom entered the film industry, both acquiring companies that would help them provide new (and old) media content. See Brian Yecies and Aegyung Shim, *The Changing Face of Korean Cinema, 1960–2015* (London: Routledge, 2016), 174.

68. See, e.g., Jennifer Jihye Chun, "Contesting Legal Liminality: The Gendered Labor Politics of Irregular Workers in South Korea," in *New Millennium South Korea: Neoliberal Capitalism and Transnational Movements*, ed. Jesook Song (London: Routledge, 2011), 63–83, esp. 63–65.

69. See D. Y. Jin, "Political and Economic Processes in the Privatization of the Korea Telecommunications Industry: A Case Study of Korea Telecom, 1987–2003," *Telecommunications Policy* 30, no. 1 (2006): 3–13, 8; Don Kirk, "World Business Briefing: Asia: South Korea: Share Limits Raised," *New York Times*, August 9, 2002, www.nytimes.com/2002/08/09/business/world-business-briefing-asia-south-korea-share-limit-raised.html?ref=topics; "Korea Telecom Approves Higher Foreign Ownership," *Telecompaper*, March 27, 2000, www.telecompaper.com/news/korea-telecom-approves-higher-foreign-ownership—243940.

70. Schiller, *Digital Capitalism*, 40.

71. Yecies and Shim, *The Changing Face of Korean Cinema*, 174.

72. Luc Boltanski and Ève Chiapello, *The New Spirit of Capitalism*, trans. Gregory Elliott (London: Verso, 2005), 155.

73. *Tube* (*T'yubŭ*), dir. Beak Woon-hak (2003; Culver City, CA: Sony Pictures Home Entertainment, 2004), DVD

74. Wade and Veneroso, "The Asian Crisis," 21.

75. Anwar M. Shaikh, "Explaining Inflation and Unemployment: An Alternative to Neoliberal Economic Theory," in *Contemporary Economic Theory: Radical Critiques of Neoliberalism*, ed. Adriana Vlachou (London: Palgrave Macmillan, 1999), 89–112, 93–96.

76. See also Dean Baker, "The NAIRU: Is It a Real Constraint?" in *Globalization and Progressive Economic Policy*, ed. Dean Baker, Gerald Epstein, and Robert Pollin (Cambridge: Cambridge University Press, 1998), 369–87; and Servaas Storm and C. W. M. Naastepad, *Macroeconomics Beyond the NAIRU* (Cambridge, MA: Harvard University Press, 2012), 1.

77. Bill Dunn, *The Political Economy of Global Capitalism and Crisis* (London: Routledge, 2014), 116.

78. Engelbert Stockhammer, "Is the NAIRU Theory a Monetarist, New Keynesian, Post Keynesian or a Marxist Theory?" *Macroeconomics* 59, no. 2 (2008): 479–510, 487.

79. William Mitchell and Joan Muysken, *Full Employment Abandoned: Shifting Sands and Policy Failures* (Northampton, MA: Edward Elgar, 2008), 116. Mitchell and Muysken offer the 1994 OECD Jobs Study Report as evidence for "a general trend among international financial organizations such as the OECD and the International Monetary Fund (IMF) to broaden their original role and to become fierce and influential public advocates for the emerging NAIRU ideology" (129).

80. Demophanes Papadatos, "Central Banking in Contemporary Capitalism: Inflation-Targeting and Financial Crisis," in *Financialisation in Crisis*, ed. Costas Lapavitsas (Leiden: Brill, 2012), 126–39.

81. Wade and Veneroso, "The Asian Crisis," 13–14.

82. Alan Liu and Scott Pound, "The Amoderns: Reengaging the Humanities: A Feature Interview with Alan Liu," *Amodern* 2 (2013): http://amodern.net/article /the-amoderns-reengaging-the-humanities/.

Coda

1. See Perry Anderson, *The H-Word: The Peripeteia of Hegemony* (London: Verso, 2017); Ernesto Laclau and Chantal Mouffe, *Hegemony and Socialist Strategy: Towards a Radical Democratic Politics*, 2nd ed. (London: Verso, 2001); and Antonio Gramsci, *The Antonio Gramsci Reader: Selected Writings, 1916–1935*, ed. David Forgacs (New York: New York University Press, 2000), 189–221.

2. Karl Marx, *Capital*, vol. 3, trans. David Fernbach (New York: Penguin, 1981), 368.

3. Quoted in Steven Borowiec, "IMF 20 Years On: S. Korea's Never-Ending Crisis," *Korea Exposé*, Dec. 29, 2017, www.koreaexpose.com/imf-economy-south-korea -asian-financial-crisis/.

4. See Bert Hofman, "China's One Belt One Road Initiative: What We Know Thus Far," *World Bank*, Dec. 4, 2015, http://blogs.worldbank.org/eastasiapacific /china-one-belt-one-road-initiative-what-we-know-thus-far.

5. Bruce Cumings, "The Abortive *Abertura*: South Korea in Light of the Latin American Experience," *New Left Review* 173 (1989): 5–32, 8.

6. See James Boyle, *The Public Domain: Enclosing the Commons of the Mind* (New Haven, CT: Yale University Press, 2008), 45–46.

7. Joseph R. Slaughter, "World Literature as Property," *Alif* 34 (2014): 39–73, 41.

8. Kim Nam-il, "'Snowpiercer' Labelled as Anti-market Economy, Encouraging Social Resistance by NIS," *The Hankyoreh*, Oct. 31, 2017, http://english.hani.co.kr/arti /english_edition/e_entertainment/816858.html.

9. Nellie Andreeva, "'Snowpiercer': Jennifer Connelly to Star in TNT Pilot Based on Movie," *Deadline Hollywood*, June 7, 2017, http://deadline.com/2017/06 /snowpiercer-jennifer-connelly-star-tnt-pilot-based-on-movie-1202109045/.

10. Ellen Brown, "Monsanto, the TPP, and Global Food Dominance," *Global Research*, May 23, 2016, www.globalresearch.ca/monsanto-the-tpp-and-global-food -dominance/5359491.

11. *Sympathy for Mr. Vengeance* (*Poksunŭn Naŭi Kŏt*), dir. Park Chan-wook (2002; Los Angeles: Tartan Video USA, 2005), DVD.

12. Lisa Lowe, *The Intimacies of Four Continents* (Durham, NC: Duke University Press, 2015), 110.

Index

Lytle Shaw, *Narrowcast: Poetry and Audio Research*

Stephen Schryer, *Maximum Feasible Participation: American Literature and the War on Poverty*

Margaret Ronda, *Remainders: American Poetry at Nature's End*

Jasper Bernes, *The Work of Art in the Age of Deindustrialization*

Annie McClanahan, *Dead Pledges: Debt, Crisis, and Twenty-First-Century Culture*

Amy Hungerford, *Making Literature Now*

J. D. Connor, *The Studios After the Studios: Neoclassical Hollywood (1970–2010)*

Michael Trask, *Camp Sites: Sex, Politics, and Academic Style in Postwar America*

Loren Glass, *Counterculture Colophon: Grove Press, the* Evergreen Review, *and the Incorporation of the Avant-Garde*

Michael Szalay, *Hip Figures: A Literary History of the Democratic Party*

Jared Gardner, *Projections: Comics and the History of Twenty-First-Century Storytelling*

Jerome Christensen, *America's Corporate Art: The Studio Authorship of Hollywood Motion Pictures*